Elgar Research Agendas outline the future of research in a given area. Leading scholars are given the space to explore their subject in provocative ways and map out the potential directions of travel. They are relevant but also visionary.

Forward-looking and innovative, Elgar Research Agendas are an essential resource for PhD students, scholars and anybody who wants to be at the forefront of research.

Titles in the series include:

A Research Agenda for Human Resource Management
Edited by Paul Sparrow and Cary L. Cooper, CBE

A Research Agenda for Shrinking Cities
Justin B. Hollander

A Research Agenda for Women and Entrepreneurship
Edited by Patricia G. Greene and Candida G. Brush

A Research Agenda for Entrepreneurial Cognition and Intention
Edited by Malin Brännback and Alan L. Carsrud

A Research Agenda for Entrepreneurship Education
Edited by Alain Fayolle

A Research Agenda for Service Innovation
Edited by Faïz Gallouj and Faridah Djellal

A Research Agenda for Global Environmental Politics
Edited by Peter Dauvergne and Justin Alger

A Research Agenda for New Institutional Economics
Edited by Claude Ménard and Mary M. Shirley

A Research Agenda for Regeneration Economies
Reading City-Regions
Edited by John R. Bryson, Lauren Andres and Rachel Mulhall

A Research Agenda for Cultural Economics
Edited by Samuel Cameron

A Research Agenda for Environmental Management
Edited by Kathleen E. Halvorsen, Chelsea Schelly, Robert M. Handler, Erin C. Pischke and Jessie L. Knowlton

A Research Agenda for Creative Tourism
Edited by Nancy Duxbury and Greg Richards

A Research Agenda for Public Administration
Edited by Andrew Massey

A Research Agenda for Tourism Geographies
Edited by Dieter K. Müller

A Research Agenda for Economic Psychology
Edited by Katharina Gangl and Erich Kirchler

A Research Agenda for Entrepreneurship and Innovation
Edited by David B. Audretsch, Erik E. Lehmann and Albert N. Link

A Research Agenda for Entrepreneurship and Innovation

Edited by

DAVID B. AUDRETSCH

Distinguished Professor and Ameritech Chair of Economic Development, Indiana University, Bloomington, USA

ERIK E. LEHMANN

Professor of Management and Organization, University of Augsburg, Germany

ALBERT N. LINK

Virginia Batte Phillips Distinguished Professor of Economics, University of North Carolina, Greensboro, USA

Elgar Research Agendas

Cheltenham, UK • Northampton, MA, USA

Published by
Edward Elgar Publishing Limited
The Lypiatts
15 Lansdown Road
Cheltenham
Glos GL50 2JA
UK

Edward Elgar Publishing, Inc.
William Pratt House
9 Dewey Court
Northampton
Massachusetts 01060
USA

A catalogue record for this book
is available from the British Library

Library of Congress Control Number: 2019930618

This book is available electronically in the **Elgar**online
Business subject collection
DOI 10.4337/9781788116015

ISBN 978 1 78811 600 8 (cased)
ISBN 978 1 78811 601 5 (eBook)

Typeset by Servis Filmsetting Ltd, Stockport, Cheshire
Printed and bound in Great Britain by TJ International Ltd, Padstow, Cornwall

Contents

List of contributors   vii

1   Introduction to *A Research Agenda for Entrepreneurship and Innovation*   1
    David B. Audretsch, Erik E. Lehmann, and Albert N. Link

2   Schumpeterian growth regimes   4
    Cristiano Antonelli

3   Measuring entrepreneurial impact through alumni impact surveys   30
    Shiri Breznitz, Brendan Hills, and Qiantao Zhang

4   Academic entrepreneurship: between myth and reality   40
    Alice Civera, Michele Meoli, and Silvio Vismara

5   Principal investigators and boundary spanning entrepreneurial
    opportunity recognition: a conceptual framework   55
    James A. Cunningham

6   The regional emergence of innovative start-ups: a research agenda   74
    Michael Fritsch

7   Public and policy entrepreneurship research: a synthesis of the
    literature and future perspectives   91
    Heike M. Grimm

8   A research agenda for entrepreneurship and innovation: the role of
    entrepreneurial universities   107
    Maribel Guerrero and David Urbano

9   Corporate governance and innovation   134
    Hezun Li, Timurs Uman, and Siri Terjesen

10 Research opportunities considering student entrepreneurship in
    university ecosystems   155
    Simon Mosey and Paul Kirkham

11 Entrepreneurial leadership in the academic community: a suggested
    research agenda   168
    Rati Ram, Devrim Göktepe-Hultén, and Rajeev K. Goel

12 The power of words and images: towards talking about and seeing
     entrepreneurship and innovation differently   179
     Friederike Welter

13 Artificial intelligence and entrepreneurship: some thoughts for
     entrepreneurship researchers   197
     Sameeksha Desai

14 Entrepreneurship studies: the case for radical change   208
     Mark Casson

Index   219

Contributors

Cristiano Antonelli Università di Torino and Collegio Carlo Alberto

David B. Audretsch Indiana University

Shiri Breznitz University of Toronto

Mark Casson University of Reading

Alice Civera University of Bergamo and University of Pavia

James A. Cunningham Northumbria University

Sameeksha Desai Indiana University

Michael Fritsch Friedrich Schiller University

Rajeev K. Goel Illinois State University and Kiel Institute for the World Economy

Devrim Göktepe-Hultén Lund University

Heike M. Grimm University of Erfurt

Maribel Guerrero School of Business and Economics at Universidad del Desarrollo, Chile and Newcastle Business School at Northumbria University

Brendan Hills University of Toronto

Paul Kirkham University of Nottingham

Erik E. Lehmann University of Augsburg

Hezun Li Central University of Finance and Economics and American University

Albert N. Link University of North Carolina at Greensboro

Michele Meoli University of Bergamo and University of Augsburg

Simon Mosey University of Nottingham

Rati Ram Illinois State University

Siri Terjesen American University and Norwegian School of Economics

Timurs Uman Jönköping International Business School

David Urbano Universitat Autònoma de Barcelona

Silvio Vismara University of Bergamo and University of Augsburg

Friederike Welter Institut für Mittelstandsforschung and University of Siegen

Qiantao Zhang University of Toronto

1 Introduction to *A Research Agenda for Entrepreneurship and Innovation*

David B. Audretsch, Erik E. Lehmann, and Albert N. Link

Within the span of a generation, innovation and entrepreneurship have emerged as two of the most vital forces in the economy and, even more broadly, in society (Link, 2017). It was not always that way. During the second industrial paradigm, or the era of mass production, particularly following World War II, innovation was barely on the radar screen of economics, management, and other social sciences.

Rather, what mattered for economic performance was articulated concisely by the management scholar, Alfred Chandler (1990), in the title of his seminal analysis of firm competitiveness and productivity – *Scale and Scope*. Economic success lies in large-scale production, which enabled companies to attain the highest levels of efficiency and productivity while reducing average cost to a minimum. The primacy of physical capital as the driving force underlying economic performance was mirrored at the macroeconomic level through the Solow (1956) model. Economic policy reflected the capital-driven economy with its focus on instruments to stimulate investment in physical capital. Innovation played at best a marginal role, which was considerably more than could be said for entrepreneurship. In an economy where scale and scope dictated competitiveness and efficiency, new and small firms were typically viewed as a burden on the economy, and they were characterized as constituting "sub-optimal capacity," meaning that they lacked sufficient scale to be efficient.

All of this changed as the managed economy of mass production eclipsed into decline and something new began to emerge, the third industrial paradigm or the computer era. At the heart of the third industrial paradigm was innovation, where change is the constant. Even as companies, industries, and regions predicated on the factor of production that had driven economic performance in the era of mass production struggled to maintain a positive economic performance, a new factor of production emerged for economic success – knowledge and ideas. As the models of endogenous growth highlighted, not only did knowledge and ideas generate innovative activity, but that knowledge was replete with externalities providing third-party firms with the opportunity to leverage new ideas that they did not have to pay for and create themselves. Thus, with the shift from the mass-production economy to the knowledge economy came a commensurate shift away from physical capital towards innovation.

Spurring innovative activity meant investing in key sources of knowledge and ideas, such as research and development (R&D) and human capital. However, leaders in business and policy discovered that investments in new knowledge alone did not guarantee the coveted innovative activity. In contrast to the assumption inherent in the models of endogenous growth (Romer, 1986), investment to create new knowledge and ideas was not tantamount to innovation. Rather, a clear gap or hurdle stood between knowledge and innovation. This gap became characterized in the scholarly literature as the knowledge filter, which is defined as barriers impeding the spillover and commercialization of knowledge and ideas preventing them from resulting in innovative activity.

Entrepreneurship emerged as an important remedy to the knowledge filter. By leveraging ideas that otherwise might have remained unutilized and dormant in the incumbent organization that had actually invested in and created that knowledge, entrepreneurship provides the conduit for the spillover of knowledge from the organization creating the knowledge to the new entrepreneurial startup actually commercializing it through innovative activity. Thus, entrepreneurship was found to provide the missing link between investments in new knowledge and the desired but elusive innovations.

The purpose of this book is to highlight new insights and new approaches that might serve to guide research in innovation in entrepreneurship. To accomplish that goal, we have assembled a broad group of accomplished scholars spanning a broad spectrum of research fields and academic disciplines, spanning economics, management, public policy, and finance. The style and focus of each of the chapters reflect the expertise and research field underlying the individual author or team of authors.

The book begins in the following chapter with a seminal contribution by Cristiano Antonelli that has its roots in the fundamental thinking about entrepreneurship and innovation, "Schumpeterian Growth Regimes." From this theoretical basis, Chapter 3 provides a more pragmatic but essential examination of "Measuring Entrepreneurial Impact through Alumni Impact Surveys," by Shiri Breznitz, Brendan Hills, and Qiantao Zhang.

In Chapter 4, Alice Civera, Michele Meoli, and Silvio Vismara consider, "Academic Entrepreneurship: Between Myth and Reality." In Chapter 5, James Cunningham analyzes the entrepreneurial context of scientific research in "Principal Investigators and Boundary Spanning Entrepreneurial Opportunity Recognition: A Conceptual Framework." The spatial dimension of innovation and entrepreneurship is the focal point for Michael Fritsch in Chapter 6, "The Regional Emergence of Innovative Start-ups: A Research Agenda." A research agenda for a very different context, public policy, is posited by Heike Grimm in Chapter 7, "Public and Policy Entrepreneurship Research: A Synthesis of the Literature and Future Perspectives."

The role of the university in entrepreneurship is the focus of Maribel Guerrero and David Urbano in Chapter 8, "A Research Agenda for Entrepreneurship and Innovation: The Role of Entrepreneurial Universities." A different perspective, corporate entrepreneurship, is provided in Chapter 9, "Corporate Governance and Innovation," by Hezun Li, Timurs Umans, and Siri Terjesen. In Chapter 10, Simon Mosey and Paul Kirkham provide an analysis of "Research Opportunities Considering Student Entrepreneurship in University Eco-systems." And Rati Ram, Devrim Göktepe-Hultén, and Rajeev Goel, in Chapter 11, propose a research agenda in "Entrepreneurial Leadership in the Academic Community: A Suggested Research Agenda."

The volume concludes with three provocative essays that reflect the undertones of the previous chapters. In Chapter 12, Friederike Welter offers a thoughtful analysis, "The Power of Words and Images – Towards Talking About and Seeing Entrepreneurship and Innovation Differently." In Chapter 13, "Artificial Intelligence and Entrepreneurship: Some Thoughts for Entrepreneurship Researchers," Sameeksha Desai discusses the nexus between artificial intelligence and entrepreneurship/innovation. Finally, an appropriate conclusion to this volume comes in Chapter 14, by Mark Casson, "Entrepreneurship Studies: The Case for Radical Change," in which he calls for radical changes in how entrepreneurship is studied.

Entrepreneurship and innovation have attracted considerable attention from both the research community as well as thought leaders in public policy and business. The contents contained in the subsequent chapters of this book promise a rich and fertile research field with diverse perspectives building upon multiple academic fields and disciplines. We look forward to seeing how these promises of research are actualized in the coming years.

References

Chandler, Alfred, 1990, *Scale and Scope: The Dynamics of Industrial Capitalism.* Cambridge: Harvard University Press.

Link, Albert N., 2017, "Ideation, Entrepreneurship and Innovation," *Small Business Economics: An Entrepreneurship Journal*, **48** (2), 279–85.

Romer, Paul, 1986, "Increasing Returns and Long-Run Growth," *Journal of Political Economy*, **94** (5), 1002–37.

Solow, Robert, 1956, "A Contribution to the Theory of Economic Growth," *Quarterly Journal of Economics*, **39**, 312–20.

2　Schumpeterian growth regimes

Cristiano Antonelli

1.　Introduction

The contributions of Joseph Schumpeter provide the basic reference to a variety of efforts made by the literature to elaborate a systemic interpretation of the general set of interdependent and structured interactions, coordination and institutional mechanisms that qualify the conditions of the economic systems into which the generation, exploitation and accumulation of technological knowledge, the introduction of technological and structural change, and long-term economic growth take place. Schumpeter was in fact, at the same time, well aware of the systemic quality of the Walrasian approach and yet convinced of the need to go beyond its static limitations.

The notion of Schumpeterian growth regimes builds upon his attempts to elaborate a systemic and yet dynamic account of the forces at work in economic growth. Schumpeter repeatedly attempted to implement a systemic frame of analysis that could account for economic growth in the early decades of the 20th century in Europe and eventually in the United States.

Careful reading of *The Theory of Economic Development* and *Capitalism, Socialism and Democracy* together with *Business Cycles* and the 1947 essay "The creative response in economic history" provides the tools to elaborate a "histoire raisonnèe" of the structural changes in the organization of the generation and exploitation of technological knowledge and the introduction of technological change that parallel the shift across different ideal types of growth regimes, based upon the analysis of the changing mechanisms of governance of the limited appropriability and exhaustibility of knowledge as the engine of economic growth (Antonelli and Link, 2015).

The notion of Schumpeterian growth regimes enables us to understand the endogeneity of growth and change. It shows how the organization of the system shapes the governance of the generation, exploitation and accumulation of technological knowledge, and hence the stochastic determinants of the creative reaction that leads to the introduction of innovations. Schumpeterian growth regimes focus the analysis on the mechanisms by means of which the generation, exploitation and accumulation of knowledge take place and shape the creative reaction that changes firms, product and factor markets, the structural characteristics of the system and its mesoeconomic and macroeconomic dynamics (Antonelli, 2011, 2017).

All changes in the structure, organization, technology and knowledge governance are intertwined not only at the firm level but also, and primarily, at the system level and reshape the entire architecture of interactions and transactions with major effects on both upward and downward complementarities (Perez, 2010; Dopfer, Potts and Pyka, 2015).

As Freeman and Louçã noted: "The structural transformation arising from (these) new industries, services, products and technologies is inevitably associated with the combination of organizational innovations needed to design, use, produce, and distribute them" (Freeman and Louçã, 2001: 147).

2.   The antecedents

Preliminary attempts to implement the Schumpeterian legacy on growth regimes have been made with the notions of "Technological Regimes," "National Systems of Innovation," "Accumulation Regimes" and "Varieties of Capitalism." They share the basic intuition that the generation of technological knowledge and the consequent introduction of innovations are determined by the systemic characteristics into which firms are embedded. Let us recall them briefly in turn.

The notion of "Technological Regimes" was first introduced by Nelson and Winter (1982) and enriched by the literature that builds upon the founding contributions by Winter (1984), and Malerba and Orsenigo (1997) (Breschi, Malerba and Orsenigo, 2000). Castellacci and Zheng (2010) provide an excellent synthesis of this literature. According to Castellacci and Zheng (2010) "Technological Regimes" are defined exclusively by the industry-specific characteristics of the technological environment in which innovative activities take place, such as: i) the cumulativeness conditions, the extent to which technological activities and performances build upon the accumulated stock of knowledge of each firm; ii) the levels of technological opportunities defined as the likelihood that R&D activities may yield an innovative output; iii) external sources of opportunities defined as the amount of knowledge externalities upon which firms may access; iv) appropriability conditions. As Castellacci and Zheng state: "In a nutshell, the main insight of this approach is that the innovative strategies and activities of enterprises vary greatly across sectors because industries differ fundamentally in terms of the properties of their technological regimes" (Castellacci and Zheng, 2010: 1835).

As it seems clear, the notion of "Technological Regimes" explores the determinants of the variance of the rates of innovative activity at the industrial levels with special attention to the differences in the rates of introduction of innovations across industrial sectors. The conditions of knowledge generation and appropriation are regarded as the main determinants of the interindustrial variance of innovative levels. The "Technological Regime" approach makes an important contribution to the neo-Schumpeterian literature that had primarily focused on the types and intensity of competition and specifically the size of firms and the levels of concentration to account for the variance of innovative activity. The "Technological Regime" approach, in fact, calls attention on the role of the characteristics of knowledge as the determinants of the rates of innovation. It is worth noting that the "Technological Regime" approach is fully silent about the systemic determinants of the direction of technological change.

The "National Systems of Innovation" approach elaborated by Lundvall (1992) and Nelson (1993) extends the scope of analysis of the "Technological Regime" approach with a systemic analysis of the mechanisms put in place at the national level to support the generation of knowledge including the role of service industries and especially of the public research system. The role of the university as the prime supplier of basic knowledge is emphasized. The interaction between research activities funded and performed by the private sector and the research activities carried out by the public research system is analyzed as a major factor in the generation of new knowledge. The complementarity between the different layers of research activities whether basic, applied or development is analyzed in depth together with the division of labor between the public and the private sector in their implementation (Fagerberg and Sapprasert, 2011).

The "National Systems of Innovation" approach has stirred much research on the mechanisms and channels of knowledge interactions not only between firms and research centers but also among firms. The analyses of the effects of knowledge spillovers has enabled appreciation of the distinction between horizontal imitation within the same industry and vertical user-producer interactions within value chains (Von Hippel, 1988, 1994, 1998) and to identify the significance of institutional, organizational, technological and, most importantly, geographic proximity in supporting the access and use of external knowledge as an input in the generation of new knowledge (Boschma, 2005). The "National Systems of Innovation" approach enables application of the mechanisms of the knowledge governance approach (Ostrom, 2010; Antonelli and Link, 2015).

The "National Systems of Innovation" approach complements the "Technological Regimes" focusing the analysis on the role of the systemic interactions in the generation of knowledge and in the introduction of innovations at the national and regional level. Both make an important contribution in calling attention to the role of the systemic conditions that now include a broad array of institutions and procedures, to shaping the generation of knowledge and hence defining the rates of innovation activity. Both approaches, however, do not take into account the crucial role of the relationship between finance and innovation and of industrial relations and corporate governance. As a matter of fact, both the notion of "Technological Regimes" and the notion of "Systems of Innovation" share the focus on the determinants of the rates of introduction of innovations and do not explore the determinants of the direction of technological change. Neither one has the ambition to explore the systemic conditions of the relationship between the conditions of knowledge funding, generation and exploitation and the macroeconomic performances of the system into which firms are embedded. The "Accumulation Regime" and the "Varieties of Capitalism" approaches contribute to explore these latter aspects.

The notions of "Regulation Mode" and "Accumulation Regimes" have been introduced and implemented by the "École de la régulation." According to Aglietta:

> For the study of a mode of production will seek to isolate the determinant relationships that are reproduced in and through the social transformation, the changing forms in which they are reproduced, and the reasons why this reproduction is accompanied by ruptures at different points of the social system. To speak of a mode of production is to try to formulate in general laws the ways in which the determinant structure of a society is reproduced. (Aglietta, 1976/2000: 12–13)

This approach has been implemented systematically to distinguish between Pre-Fordist, Fordist and Post-Fordist "Accumulation Regimes." "Accumulation Regimes" are identified by six key features: i) monetary and credit relationships; ii) the wage-labor nexus; iii) the type of competition; iv) the relationship between wages and productivity; v) the mode of adhesion to the international regime; vi) the types and tools of economic policy.

The notion of "Accumulation Regimes" is far richer and more inclusive than the "Technological Regimes" and the "National Systems of Innovation" approaches. It pays attention to the role of the financial system and generally to the different mechanisms of providing financial resources to innovation activities as well as to the levels of openness of economic systems to international trade and international financial markets. The core of the analysis is provided by the analysis of the macroeconomic coherence between production and distribution processes. The analysis of the relationship between capital and labor, as well as between management and employees plays a central role in the identification of different "Accumulation Regimes." The notion of "Accumulation Regimes" pays much attention to the wage-labor nexus and to the relationship between wage and productivity. According to Boyer (1988a: 72, 73):

> the wage-labour nexus is defined by a coherent system encompassing the following five components: the types of means of production and control over workers; the technical and social division of labour and its implications for skilling/deskilling; the degree of stability of the employment relation, measured, for example, by the speed of employment duration adjustments; the determinants of direct and social wages in relation to the functioning of labour markets and state welfare services; the standard of living of wage-earners in terms of the volume and the origin of the commodities they consume.

Boyer (1988a, 1988b) makes clear that cumulative growth is possible when real wage income increases with productivity. The actual development of the Fordist

"Regime of Accumulation" took place only when real wage income could increase so as to make possible the actual exploitation of the economies of density stemming from the extensibility of knowledge. The distinction between price competition and oligopolistic competition is the third pillar. Price competition among small firms characterized the Pre-Fordist "Accumulation Regime" while the Fordist and the Post-Fordist "Accumulation Regimes" were characterized by oligopolistic competition, based upon product differentiation where prices are derived from a mark-up applied to average costs, among corporations.

In the analysis of the "École de la régulation" the nexus between production and distribution plays a central role also with respect to the analysis of the introduction of new technologies. The introduction of new technologies is associated to investments following the Kaldorian tradition of the demand-pull account of technological change. New vintages of capital embody – necessarily – new technologies. The rate of investment is the key determinant of the rate of innovation.

The poor analysis of the role of technological knowledge and of the innovation process is the main limit of the notion of "Accumulation Regimes." New technologies seem to be "on the shelf" *readily available* and at the same time *necessarily* embodied in investments. This analysis may apply to understanding the diffusion of innovations but fails to identify the actual determinants of the generation of new technologies and of the introduction of new technologies.

The strength of the "Accumulation Regimes" approach on the other hand consists in the clear articulation of the relationship between given rates of generation of technological knowledge and introduction of innovations and the actual rates of economic growth. The main contribution of the "Accumulation Regimes" approach rests on the wage-labor nexus. The analysis of the determinants of investments in fact enables the avoidance of the dangers of technological determinism. The very same wage-labor nexus led to both the stagnation of the third decade of the 20th century and the "trente glorieuses." The radical difference in terms of growth of output and productivity is found in the shift from profit-led investment to demand-led-investment. The quest for profits led to shrinking wages and consequently aggregate demand with the depressive consequences experienced in the third decade. The increase of wages experienced after WWII supported the rapid growth of aggregate demand that, via the accelerator dynamics, stirred additional investment that could embody new technologies with consistent and self-supporting productivity growth that in turn enabled further the increase in levels of aggregated demand.

The literature on the "Accumulation Regimes" has neglected to stress the strict complementarity with the demand-pull approach to explaining the rate of innovation. The increase of the demand is expected to augment the extent of the market, hence the division of labor and the levels of specialization that in turn make the accumulation of knowledge and the introduction of innovations not only possible but also more and more convenient.

However, the "Accumulation Regimes" approach is not able to account for the high levels of variance across regions, countries, industries, nor the historic speed of the rates of generation of new technological knowledge and the rates and direction of technological change that are the ultimate determinants of the growth of output and productivity. This approach contributes to understanding the macroeconomic context into which growth may take place but fails to articulate the analysis of its causes.

Recent advances in this line of analysis, however, enabled us to elaborate on the "Cognitive Capitalism" approach according to the which advanced economies are centered upon knowledge as the key component of the process of accumulation and valorization of capital (Vercellone, 2003, 2006).

The "Cognitive Capitalism" approach calls attention on the role of learning by doing and learning by using in the generation of knowledge nested into the capitalization of knowledge as a financial asset, and provides a relevant contribution to articulating an analytical apparatus that allows us to include in the analysis the characteristics of the social organization of the knowledge economy (Petit, 1986; Vercellone, 2003; Boyer, 2004; Coriat, Petit and Schmeder, 2006).

The "Cognitive Capitalism" approach enables us to grasp the overlapping of knowledge and capital: knowledge becomes capital by means of the interface between knowledge generation as a specialized activity intertwined with the working of financial markets that play the indispensable role of mechanisms of knowledge exploitation and valorization (Petit, 1986; Boyer and Schmeder, 1990; Jin and Stough, 1998).

The "Varieties of Capitalism" approach stresses the role of the institutional coherence of socio-economic systems in accounting for their economic performances (Hall and Soskice, 2001; Amable, 2003). Different types of capitalism can be identified according to their coordination mechanisms. Two coordination mechanisms are identified: market-coordination mechanisms and institutional mechanisms. Four main economic spheres are investigated: i) industrial relations; ii) vocational training and education; iii) corporate governance; iv) inter-firms relations along value chains.

Industrial relations play a central role in the analysis. They include the variety of bargaining relations over wages and working conditions, the definition of incentives and the participation of workers to the definition of the procedures and goals of the firms. Two alternative types of capitalism are identified: coordinated market economies and liberal market economies. The former rely more on institutional coordination mechanisms, the latter use the market place as the primary mechanism to coordinate the system.

Hall and Gingerich (2009) and Kenworthy (2005: 73) have elaborated a measure of the levels of institutional coherence based upon the following indicators that focus on corporate governance and industrial relations:

(1)   share of corporations based upon the separation between management and control, measured by the role of managers coupled with dispersed shareholders with respect to dominant shareholders;

(2)   relative size of the stock market, measured by the ratio of the value of public corporations on gross domestic product of a country;

(3)   wage coordination, measured by the level at which unions normally coordinate wage claims and the degree to which wage bargaining is (strategically) coordinated by unions;

(4)   labor turnover, measured by the share of employees who had held their jobs for less than one year.

The levels of institutional coherence of a system are determined by the levels of institutional complementarity: "two institutions can be said to be complementary if the presence (or efficiency) of one increases the returns from (or efficiency of) the other" (Hall and Soskice, 2001: 17).

The "Varieties of Capitalism" approach contends that the level of performances of an economic system is a function of its institutional coherence: "When firms coordinate successfully, their performances will be better, and the result will be better overall economic performances" (Hall and Soskice, 2001: 45).

The institutional coherence of a system influences its performances not only in terms of levels and quality of the coordination procedures that reduce risks, uncertainty and transaction costs, but also in terms of innovative capabilities.

Coordinated market economies are better able to generate and exploit incremental technological changes while liberal market economies are better able to generate and exploit radical innovations. Corporations managed by controlling shareholders that rely on skilled workers and managerial regimes that provide enough worker autonomy and secure employment can take advantage of learning processes on the shop floor and capitalize on the tacit knowledge accumulated and introduce incremental innovations. Corporations with dispersed shareholders active in labor markets with high rates of turnover coupled with extensive equity markets are not only better able to hire talent with high levels of human capital, but also to take advantage of the flows of new high-tech firms generated by venture capitalism, to acquire by means of take-overs in equity markets and to introduce radical innovations. It is worth noting that also the "Varieties of Capitalism" approach falls short of exploring and assessing the systemic determinants of the direction of technological change.

3.   Schumpeterian growth regimes at work

The grafting of the recent advances of the economics of knowledge upon the Schumpeterian legacy and the early attempts to articulate a systemic analysis of the changing organization of innovation systems enables us to elaborate a framework that is able to highlight the central role of the systemic characteristics that make possible the generation and exploitation of technological knowledge as the fundamental condition for the introduction of innovations as a creative response.

Schumpeterian growth regimes define the alternative sets of systemic conditions that shape the mechanisms of governance of the generation, appropriation, exploitation and accumulation of knowledge as the engine of growth that supports the creative reaction and the consequent introduction of innovations that change firms, products and factor markets, the structure of the system and its aggregate dynamics.

The notion of Schumpeterian growth regimes integrates in the Schumpeterian framework the achievements of the "Technological Regimes," the "National Systems of Innovation," the "Accumulation Regimes," and the "Varieties of Capitalism" approaches and augments them with the advances of the economics of knowledge that enable the appreciation of the systemic processes that qualify the funding, generation, appropriation, accumulation and exploitation of knowledge with a new crucial layer of analysis. In so doing it frames the systemic and institutional conditions that enable us to take advantage of the potential capabilities of knowledge to make the reaction of firms creative, and hence to introduce innovations and to increase the levels of total factor productivity at the system level. Schumpeterian growth regimes define the set of conducive conditions that make the creative response possible and elaborate their implications both at the firm and the system levels.

The economics of knowledge since its inception, and even more since its recent advances, provide the tools to grasp the dynamics of the mechanisms put in place to organize the generation and exploitation of knowledge as the "special" good that is at the origin of economic growth (Hayek, 1945; Arrow, 1962, 1969).

The special properties of knowledge – i.e. its limited appropriability and exhaustibility, and its multiple role as both a key input and the output of the upstream knowledge generation function and an input of the downstream technology production function – because of the pecuniary knowledge externalities stemming from the size and composition of the stock of quasi-public knowledge and appropriate knowledge governance mechanisms – trigger out-of-equilibrium conditions that consist in the augmented likelihood of the creative response of firms facing the mismatch between expected and actual product and factor market conditions and an increase in the levels of total factor productivity at the system level. The likelihood of the creative, as opposed to passive, response and of the increase of the total factor productivity are in fact greater the larger the gap between the equilibrium cost of knowledge and its actual costs. This dynamics may be recursive if and when the augmented flows of knowledge generated at each point in time accumulate in the stock of quasi-public knowledge that can be accessed and used at decreasing costs and increasing levels of pecuniary knowledge externalities (Antonelli, 2017, 2018, 2019).

The economic implications of the analysis of the knowledge generation and valorization processes are most important, not only at the microeconomic level but also at the macroeconomic level. The characteristics of the knowledge generation process that are relevant at the aggregate level are: i) knowledge is at the same time the output of the knowledge generation activities that are at the core of the new knowledge economy; and ii) knowledge is an essential input into the production function of all the other goods. The appreciation of the dual nature of knowledge is indispensable to grasp its macroeconomic implications; iii) knowledge generation is a labor-intensive process where labor is characterized by highly specific skills and intrinsic idiosyncratic features. Creative labor is not abundant and is itself the result of tough selection and training processes. The income of creative workers is high as the participation to the rents associated to the capitalization of knowledge complements the low wages; iv) the generation of knowledge requires sophisticated routines both at the firm level and at the system level; v) the stock of existing knowledge – capitalized as an asset – is a central input that receives a large share of the revenue; vi) the quasi-markets for knowledge exhibit the typical traits of monopolistic competition; vii) the definition of the price of knowledge includes substantial rents (Antonelli, 2017, 2018, 2019).

Let us analyze in detail the wheels of the mechanisms by means of which the limited appropriability and exhaustibility of knowledge, and its dual role as both an input and an output, may trigger dynamic increasing returns.

The larger is the knowledge output at each point in time and the larger – because of its limited exhaustibility and appropriability – is the stock of quasi-public knowledge at time t+1. The larger the stock of quasi-public knowledge, the lower is the cost of knowledge – with appropriate knowledge governance conditions in the system that reduce absorption costs and enable effective access to it – both in the knowledge generation function and in the technology production function at time t+1.

The recombinant generation of technological knowledge relies on the access and use of existing knowledge. Knowledge shares all the intrinsic characteristics of an essential facility as its use as an input is indispensable not only for the production of all the other goods – in the technology production function – but also in the generation of knowledge. The variety of the stock of quasi-public knowledge matters as much as its size: the larger the variety of knowledge each agent can access and use, the larger is the knowledge output. Specifically, knowledge output increases at a more than proportionate rate with respect to the increase in the size and variety of knowledge inputs.

According to the Schumpeterian framework of analysis of the creative response, the access to knowledge at costs below equilibrium enables firms to try and cope with emerging mismatches between expected and actual factor and product market conditions (Schumpeter, 1947) with a creative response. Technological knowledge is the key factor of the innovative activity of an economic system.

The rate of introduction of innovations depends upon the levels of pecuniary knowledge externalities, i.e. upon the conditions at which firms can access and use technological knowledge in order to cope with the necessary mismatches between expected and actual product and factor market conditions. When the structural and institutional conditions of the system make the generation of new knowledge too expensive, firms can only implement adaptive responses and move on the map of existing isoquants. When, instead, the structural and institutional conditions, of the economic system including its mechanisms of knowledge governance, enable the access and use of the stock of existing knowledge at low costs and, consequently, pecuniary knowledge externalities are large, firms are able to generate new knowledge and implement a creative reaction and introduce innovations.

The stock of knowledge plays a critical role in the dynamics of the system. The access to stock of quasi-public knowledge is an indispensable input both upstream in the recombinant knowledge generation function and downstream in the technology production function of all the other goods. The larger is the stock of quasi-public knowledge available in the system and the lower its costs. The levels of pecuniary knowledge externalities in the system stem directly from the size and the composition of the stock of quasi-public knowledge. In turn the likelihood of the creative response and the eventual introduction of productivity enhancing innovations is strictly associated to the levels of pecuniary knowledge externalities and ultimately to the size and composition of the stock of knowledge available in the system. Productivity growth and hence economic growth is possible only when and if the potentialities for dynamic increasing returns – intrinsic to the idiosyncratic characteristics of knowledge and especially its limited exhaustibility, cumulability and extensibility – can actually be exploited.

The exploitation and generation of knowledge are the cause and the consequence of conditions that are far from equilibrium. This dynamic is further reinforced by the forces that shape the endogenous direction of technological change and the search for technological congruence. At each point in time the availability of a larger stock of knowledge that can be accessed at lower costs induces the introduction of biased technological change directed at increasing the output elasticity of knowledge and its intensity of use.

The augmented levels of technological congruence provided by better matching between the availability of the cheaper input knowledge and its increased output elasticity in the technology production function, have the multiple effects of: i) increasing the demand for knowledge, hence its eventual generation with additional expansion of the knowledge stock, ii) enhancing the levels of total factor productivity; and iii) strengthening its appropriability in the global product markets as rivals localized in less knowledge-abundant countries can imitate but bear larger operating costs.

This dynamic process exhibits the evident characters of dynamic increasing returns well beyond the boundaries of equilibrium. The systemic conditions that enable the generation, appropriation, accumulation and exploitation of knowledge are crucial to enable the dynamic increasing returns to take place. The notion of Schumpeterian growth regimes provides the tool for the investigation of the different mix of knowledge governance mechanisms that have been elaborated to try and take advantage of the scope for such increasing returns and their implications for the types of aggregate dynamics at work within economic systems.

Building upon the Schumpeterian legacy, three growth regimes can be identified: i) the entrepreneurial growth regime; ii) the corporate growth regime; iii) the knowledge growth regime (see Table 2.1). Let us analyze them in detail.

3.1   The entrepreneurial growth regime

Schumpeter's *The Theory of Economic Development* provides the basic tools to identify the entrepreneurial growth regime at work in Europe since the end of the 18th century.

The generation of new knowledge is the outcome of a bottom-up process of accumulation of competence and tacit knowledge that relies on learning by doing and learning by using. The bottom-up generation of new knowledge relies heavily on the access to the stock of quasi-public knowledge made possible by proximity within industrial districts. Technological knowledge is a collective good and its accumulation takes place primarily within the web of interactions that take place in industrial districts that are the depositary of technological knowledge.

In the entrepreneurial growth regime there is a continuous flow of entry of new entrepreneurs. The life cycle of firms is short. Like the Marshallian forest trees, the survival of firms is rare and the decline and exit of firms are rapid. Entrepreneurs acquire their competence on the job and are often former employees of incumbents. The short life cycle of firms reduces the accumulation of the stock of knowledge within firms.

Industrial relations are characterized by low levels of turnover of highly-skilled manpower with distinctive craft competences that retains the full control of its competences and is actively involved in the accumulation of tacit knowledge and its eventual exploitation.

The innovation process rests heavily upon the laws of accumulation of tacit knowledge and competence and is directed primarily upstream towards the introduction of new capital and intermediary goods that lengthen the value chain and increase the levels of specialization and division of labor. The rates of imitation and introduction of incremental innovation are fostered by the low levels of knowledge appropriability that is based upon the relevance of tacit knowledge. The dissemination of technological knowledge is possible only by means of personal interactions within industrial districts.

Table 2.1   Types and features of the Schumpeterian growth regimes

	Entrepreneurial growth regime	Corporate growth regime	Knowledge growth regime
Knowledge cumulability	High within industrial districts	High within corporate borders	Very high at the system level
Knowledge extensibility	Low	High	High
Knowledge appropriability	Low, based upon tacit knowledge	Medium, based upon barriers to entry and imitation	High, based upon intellectual property rights
Primary sources of knowledge	Learning by doing, by using and by interacting	Internal R&D	Science
External knowledge	Most relevant as a source of imitation externalities within Marshallian districts	Spillovers from competitors in product markets: imitation externalities	Most relevant as a source of knowledge externalities in the recombinant generation of knowledge within scientific clusters
Typical job profile	Skilled craftworkers with low turnover	De-skilled mass workers in assembly lines	Scientific manpower with high turnover
Direction of technological change	Strongly labor saving and capital intensive	Neutral	Knowledge intensive: fixed capital and standard labor saving
Types of innovation	Process innovations embodied in new capital goods	Product innovations	Process innovations
Mechanism of knowledge exploitation	As an input for the introduction of innovations that command short-lived extraprofits	As an input for the introduction of innovations that command persistent extraprofits	Capitalization of knowledge as a financial asset
Income distribution	High wage and rent inequalities triggered by high wages of industrial workers, low wages for standard labor and high profits	Low wage and rent inequalities with high efficiency wages	High levels of wage and rent inequalities triggered by knowledge capitalization
Size of firms	Small	Large	Small
Source of finance	Debt capital provided by banks	Retained extraprofits	Venture capitalism

Table 2.1   (continued)

	Entrepreneurial growth regime	Corporate growth regime	Knowledge growth regime
Types of competition	Marshallian competition in intermediary and capital goods markets	Oligopolistic rivalry in product markets	Monopolistic competition in knowledge markets
Engines of growth	Profit-led investment embodying technological change in intermediary and capital goods	High-wage, demand-led investment in final product markets	Intangible investment global financial markets

The entrepreneurial growth regime exhibits the typical traits of a profit-led mechanism of accumulation: the introduction of innovations is driven by the high levels of transient profitability (Lavoie, 2017). Investments in upstream activities in turn are driven by the rates of introduction of innovations and support their diffusion. At the system level the accelerator dynamics contribute to the increase of the aggregate demand. The direction of technological change is strongly capital intensive for two broad sets of reasons: i) the introduction of capital-intensive technological change is induced by the strong trend of increased wages of workers more and more able to organize themselves by means of trade unions and acts as a form of meta-substitution of labor; ii) the capital-intensive direction of technological change is consistent and complementary with the introduction of process innovations that increase the levels of roundaboutness of the production process.

The distribution of income is highly skewed with high levels of both wage and rent inequalities. Successful entrepreneurs cash the short-lived extraprofits and the levels of retention are very low. Entrepreneurial families grasp a large part of national income and systematically increase their wealth. Industrial wages are far above the average in agriculture and traditional service activities.

The innovative banker is the primary source of the financial resources for new undertakings and plays a key role in the selection of and support to the introduction of innovations. The innovative banker relies on a web of professional competences to sort the projects that are more likely to be successful and pay back the credits provided by the bank. The errors of exclusion are limited by the quality of the portfolio of professional competences that the innovative banker uses to sort the projects. The innovative banker suffers the intrinsic asymmetry: he or she cannot participate in the profits of successful ventures but is fully exposed to the negative effects of the failures in terms of non-performing loans.

3.2   The corporate growth regime

Schumpeter's 1942 contribution, *Capitalism, Socialism and Democracy*, provides the basic tools to identify the corporate growth regime. The introduction of radical innovations in the organization of firms, the separation between ownership and control, and the creation of the corporation are the key characteristics of the "American capitalism" identified by Schumpeter as the major institutional and organizational innovation that gave the United States international leadership in innovation and economic growth since the early 20th century. The generation of technological knowledge takes place primarily within the corporation where specific activities, eventually named Research and Development (R&D), guided by corporate scientists are dedicated to the introduction of innovations. External knowledge is relevant but to a lesser extent with respect to the entrepreneurial regime (Chandler, 1962, 1977; Lazonick, 2010).

The corporate growth regime is characterized by large firms, ruled by managers, and engaged in oligopolistic rivalry based upon systematic product differentiation of final goods in consumer markets. Industrial relations are characterized by mass production based upon assembly chains that engage workers with low levels of skills, competence and human capital, and participation in the accumulation of tacit knowledge. Within the corporation, a core of highly skilled workers with managerial functions takes responsibility for the accumulation of knowledge and its exploitation for the introduction of innovations within the context of long-term corporate strategies.

The direction of technological change in the corporate growth regime is basically neutral. However, this neutrality is the result of two contrasting forces. The innovative process is mostly directed towards the introduction of product innovations that require higher levels of labor intensity. At the same, however, the efforts to reap all the benefits of knowledge extensibility push towards the introduction of mass production that requires high levels of capital intensity.

In corporations, wages are above short-term productivity levels pushed by the strong bargaining power of a highly unionized labor force that enables workers to share the large mark-up (Farber et al., 2018). Corporate high wages, however, are efficiency wages as they enhance the participation of workers to the accumulation of competence by means of learning processes that enable the generation of technological knowledge at costs below equilibrium and support the creative response (Stiglitz, 1974).

The dynamic of wages is strongly associated to the rates of introduction of innovations and the increase in productivity levels, not only by means of the accumulation of tacit knowledge but also by the effects on the aggregate demand: the demand pull comes into play. The high-wage strategy supports the multiplier-accelerator dynamics within the loop aggregate demand-investment-demand-pulled innovations that feeds the introduction of product and process innovations. Increasing wages support the aggregate demand that in turn pulls the introduction of further innovations and their diffusion embodied in the new vintages of capital goods brought into the system by the accelerator dynamics of investment.

The wage-productivity nexus has positive effects not only on the persistence of the rates of growth of output and productivity, but also on income distribution. Rent inequality declines from the high levels that characterized the entrepreneurial regime.

The levels of knowledge appropriability are increased not only by more stringent intellectual property rights regimes but also and primarily by substantial barriers to entry and mobility – based upon cost advantages stemming from the extensibility of knowledge, prime-mover advantages and economies of scale and scope – that reduce the risk of imitative entry. Incumbents are able to stretch the duration of transient monopolistic rents stemming from the introduction of innovation. The extended duration of the exclusive command of technological knowledge favors the internal accumulation of technological knowledge and its systematic use to feed the persistent introduction of additional innovations. The separation between ownership and control enables managers to retain a large share of extraprofits and use them internally to fund the innovation process.

Competent teams of managers elaborate long-term planning devices to focus the internal generation of knowledge, to sort the array of possible innovations generated by internal R&D laboratories and to implement consistent innovative strategies. The errors of inclusion of bad projects are reduced by the quality of the internal teams highly competent in their fields of expertise and practice.

For this very same reason, however, the corporate growth regime suffers dramatically from the errors of exclusion. Internal selection procedures are unable to identify radical innovations that impinge upon technological knowledge(s) that are far away from the current core competence of the managerial teams.

The twin globalization of product and financial markets undermined the viability and economic sustainability of the corporate growth regime. The competition in global product markets of the output manufactured in low-wage countries often by global corporations could not be resisted by the manufacturing industry of advanced countries. At the same time, the globalization of financial markets favored the reduction of the levels of international spread and the access of industrializing countries to credit provided by global financial institutions. The creative response of advanced countries could not be based upon the introduction of biased technological change directed to increased levels of output elasticity of fixed capital: the difference in the cost of capital was not sufficient to secure an effective division of labor.

The relative abundance of the stock of quasi-public knowledge embedded in the economic systems of advanced countries and the high quality of their knowledge governance mechanisms pushed the introduction of knowledge-intensive technologies able to increase the technological congruence and provided the opportunity to implement a new specialization based upon the generation and exploitation of knowledge as a financial asset.

3.3   The knowledge growth regime

In advanced countries, the knowledge growth regime has been substituting the corporate growth regime since the end of the 20th century. The knowledge growth regime is characterized by the vertical disintegration of the generation and exploitation of knowledge that leaves the corporation and becomes the core activity of a specialized knowledge industry.

Forced by the globalization of product and capital markets, advanced countries have specialized in the upstream and downstream rings of the value chains, focusing on: i) upstream in the generation of the technological know-how necessary for the design and engineering of products and processes; ii) financing the generation of knowledge as well as the production cycle; and iii) downstream in the process of enhancing tangible goods – physically produced in industrialized countries – controlling the wide range of activities ranging from logistics, distribution, marketing and advertising that can be defined as commercial knowledge.

The organization of the production process is fully redesigned: advanced countries retain the knowledge-intensive phases both upstream and downstream in the manufacturing process. Upstream activities such as the generation of new knowledge, its transformation into prototypes and advanced production, as well as downstream activities and the financial process take place in advanced countries. The manufacturing process itself is redesigned with the identification of knowledge-poor activities that are assigned to plants located in industrial countries, and knowledge-intensive activities with higher requirements in terms of skills and greater opportunities in terms of learning processes are kept in knowledge-abundant countries.

The decomposition of value chains in the global economy and the redefinition of the international division of labor see emerging countries take on the role of industrial economies specializing in manufacturing products and advanced countries in the role of producers of inputs of knowledge, not only technological but also organizational and commercial, in the form of intermediate goods and especially intangible capital assets and knowledge-intensive business services (KIBS).

The specialization in knowledge-intensive activities is the result of a dual process of vertical disintegration of the chain value at the firm level and the international division of labor where industrializing countries specialize in the manufacturing industries and advanced countries specialize in KIBS. The generation and exploitation of knowledge, as a capital asset and a service, becomes the core of separated activities performed by specialized firms. Venture capitalism provides the supporting institutional and organizational infrastructure.

The extensive literature that explores the digital economy since the introduction of the new information and communication technologies complements the advances of the economics of knowledge as it has enabled us to grasp the radical changes in the generation and use of knowledge. Digital technologies, in fact, provide the basic infrastructure that enables us to collect, retrieve and store the knowledge items dispersed in the system and to manage the recombination process. In so doing the digital infrastructure is the basic infrastructure of the knowledge economy (Frøslev Jens and Maskell, 2003; Johansson, Karlsson and Stough, 2006; Greenstein, Goldfarb and Tucker, 2013; Goldfarb, Greenstein and Tucker, 2015).

The new organization of the generation of knowledge parallels significant changes in its exploitation and valorization. The effects of the limited appropriability and exhaustibility of knowledge are most relevant not only in its generation, but also in its exploitation and valorization as they engender radical information asymmetries between vendors and customers. The working of the "quasi-markets" for knowledge acquire the typical traits of monopolistic competition. Each bit of knowledge is a unique product that commands quasi-rents. The exploitation and valorization of knowledge take place in a context characterized by a web of knowledge interactions and transactions where the price is contextual.

Venture capitalism supports the embodiment of new knowledge in new firms assisting their birth and selective growth through the process that leads to their eventual entry in the stock markets and the final acquisition by corporations. Financial markets enable the systematic exploration of the knowledge landscape embodied by new firms based upon scientific entrepreneurship, and become the new mechanism to coordinate the generation and the exploitation of knowledge capital.

Venture capital companies perform the crucial selective provision of: i) the necessary financial resources with the direct participation into the equity of new firms; and ii) management able to support scientific entrepreneurs in the engineering process that leads to the production of prototypes and their marketing test. Venture capital companies rely on qualified polyarchies to identify the promising ventures, and are able to minimize both errors of exclusion and inclusion. Market trials enable the test of the transformation of scientific knowledge into technological knowledge and its actual scope of application to the downstream economic activities run by corporations. Successful startups eventually enter the financial markets. The funders can cash the significant capital gains that compensate for the losses stemming from the large share of failures; capital gains are especially large when corporations acquire the new high-tech public companies by means of take-overs and integrate them into their production process. The acquisition of the new public companies complements if not substitutes the internal performance of R&D activities. Financial investments provide the demand for the output of the new knowledge industry (Lazonick, 2007).

KIBS are able to trade knowledge as a service. The stock of proprietary knowledge is the principal input. Its application enables providers to satisfy the specific and highly idiosyncratic needs of customers. Intensive learning processes, articulated in learning-by-doing, learning-by-using and learning-by-interacting within user-producer relations, enable knowledge producers to supply knowledge as a dedicated service applied to the specific needs of customers and at the same time to implement their stock of proprietary knowledge and to access relevant knowledge externalities.

Scientific entrepreneurship is an indispensable mechanism for the effective use of the opportunities provided by the limited appropriability of knowledge generated by scientific institutions. Scientific entrepreneurship is a distinctive and effective mechanism for the generation of new knowledge by means of the recombination of scientific knowledge spilling from academic institutions and the necessary variety of other knowledge types and sources including commercial and technological knowledge. Spillover entrepreneurship has been able to guide the creative destruction that has characterized the shake-up of traditional corporate sectors such as hardware electronics and big pharma with the introduction of digital and bio technologies that were far away from the core competence of incumbent corporations.

Scientific entrepreneurs try and apply the results of basic scientific research achieved in academic and public research centers with the creation of startups. Industrial relations within startups are based on high levels of turnover and direct participation of selected and highly skilled personnel to the generation of new knowledge and its transformation into prototypes.

Employees participate directly not only in the generation of knowledge but also in its exploitation: their payment consists mainly if not exclusively in shares of the new venture distributed by means of stock options that associate directly the amount of wealth – as distinct from income – distributed to workers with the actual levels of capitalization of the knowledge assets that have been produced and exploited by means of knowledge and financial markets. The governance of startups is shaped by the increasing levels of separation between the original ownership of scientific entrepreneurs and the increasing role of competent managers seconded by venture capital firms.

The knowledge spillover theory of entrepreneurship identifies the new channel by means of which knowledge spillover is actually useful. So far, the literature had focused primarily on the knowledge interactions that take place among incumbents, paying little attention to the role of newcomers as users of knowledge spillovers both to introduce innovations and to generate new technological knowledge. The extensive literature based upon the knowledge spillover theory of entrepreneurship systematically explores how and why knowledge spillovers provide entrepreneurs with the opportunity to create a new firm (Audretsch and Keilbach, 2007, 2008). The rich and systematic evidence collected and analyzed shows clearly how the rates of creation of new firms and the flows of entrepreneurship are associated with the opportunities provided by the regional concentration of innovative activities, and take place in science-based fields in which the advances of knowledge have been more rapid (Audretsch and Link, 2018).

The knowledge spillover theory of entrepreneurship enables us to grasp the central role of startups as the new strategic interface between the generation of scientific knowledge, again centered in the public research system – as in the entrepreneurial growth regime – and the corporation. Startups fill the gap between science and technology, between pure research and applied research and development. The process of trial and error is now fully performed by the startups supported by venture capitalism. Eventual successes will become public companies and later on will be acquired by and integrated into corporations that retain the control of global value chains, marketing and distribution in the markets of advanced countries (Audretsch, Keilbach and Lehmann, 2006).

The valorization of knowledge capital shifts upstream. The change is quite radical. Downstream corporations acquire knowledge assets that already incorporate a large chunk of the knowledge value that used to be valorized in product markets.

The likelihood of the creative reaction in the knowledge growth regime depends on the evolution of the upstream knowledge industry driven by scientific entrepreneurship and venture capitalism. Downstream firms can react creatively and introduce innovations only if the upstream firms specializing in the generation of knowledge provide the system with a flow of knowledge inputs that allow the introduction of innovations. The conditions in which upstream knowledge firms make available their knowledge output to the rest of the system become crucial to assess the rate of innovation at the system level. At the same time the user-producer relations between upstream knowledge producers and downstream knowledge users are crucial to assess the distribution of wealth and income along the new extended value chain.

The production and sale of any tangible (final and capital) good engender proceeds that are recorded as revenue and, after paying intermediary inputs, contribute to the production of value added. The valorization of knowledge not embodied in tangible goods or services increasingly takes place by means of the creation and subsequent sale of knowledge-intensive assets (Antonelli and Teubal, 2010). The sale of assets and equity that incorporate knowledge is not recorded as revenue and does not contribute to the definition of value added.

The specificity of the incorporation of knowledge into financial capital calls into question not only the prevailing theoretical apparatus but also the statistical methods that define the gross domestic product. The traditional scheme assumes that the production activity is responsible for the production of a revenue that is distributed to the productive factors and can be accumulated – through savings – in wealth.

In the case of the knowledge growth regime, however, the exploitation of knowledge directly produces wealth, which is distributed without taking the form of income.

The traditional laws of income distribution do not apply to the wealth created and its distribution to the production factors does not follow any clear (economic) rule (Stiglitz and Greenwald, 2014).

The inclusion of the wealth triggered by the generation and exploitation of new knowledge as a financial asset is necessary to appreciate at the aggregate level the role of knowledge as an explicit output of economic activity. The total output of an economic system should include the knowledge that has been generated explicitly as the result of a dedicated activity, and implicitly as the outcome of a learning process (Stiglitz, 1987). So far, this inclusion takes place in a cursory way.

The central relationship between the rates of increased labor productivity and the rates of growth of output centered upon the manufacturing industry that shaped the Fordist age is now being questioned (Boyer, 2004). The distribution of wealth and income stemming from the generation and exploitation of knowledge exhibits a significant shift. A large part of the wealth is retained upstream by the producers of knowledge and the financial system that makes its exploitation possible. The knowledge and the financial industries are characterized by high wages and especially by the direct participation to the stream of wealth by means of stock options. The share of appropriation of the stream of income generated by knowledge concentrates upstream. Downstream customers appropriate declining shares and consequently squeeze the remuneration of production factors and especially labor engaged in downstream activities.

The new specialization in the generation and exploitation of knowledge triggers the segmentation of the labor markets into two sections: the market for creative labor and the market for standard labor. The markets for standard labor are fully exposed to the dynamics of factor costs equalization triggered by the globalization of product markets: the demand exhibits a clear decline and leads to increased levels of unemployment. Workers excluded from the manufacturing industry are not able to meet the high requirements of the knowledge industries in terms of human capital and skills. The markets for creative labor, conversely, are protected by international competition due to the relative scarcity and higher costs of knowledge in the new industrial countries and, on the demand side, the knowledge-intensive direction of technological change exerts powerful effects supporting wage levels. Increasing wage inequalities add to the wealth and rent inequalities triggered by the new mechanisms of knowledge exploitation based upon the capitalization of knowledge and contribute to increasing the levels of income inequality (Atkinson, 2015).

4. Conclusions

The Schumpeterian notion of growth regimes becomes necessary to understand the structural transformation of advanced economies. The discontinuity experienced by advanced economies since the last decade of the twentieth century can be fruitfully analyzed as the consequence of the shift from a mode of organizing the generation, exploitation and accumulation of knowledge centered upon the industrial corporation to a new mode based upon a specialized knowledge industry.

Schumpeterian growth regimes define the alternative sets of systemic conditions at the microeconomic, mesoeconomic, macroeconomic and institutional levels that shape both the out-of-equilibrium conditions that stir the reaction of firms and the mechanisms of knowledge governance that support the generation, exploitation and accumulation of knowledge and the generation of the endogenous knowledge externalities upon which the creative reaction and the consequent introduction of innovation are contingent.

The knowledge governance mechanisms that enable the generation and exploitation of knowledge are crucial to maintaining the dynamics of increasing returns associated to knowledge at work and to making it effective.

In the entrepreneurial growth regime knowledge was generated mainly within small firms, taking advantage of tacit knowledge accumulated by means of learning processes and shared within industrial districts, funded by innovative bankers, and exploited by means of the introduction of innovations that generated transient monopolistic rents. In the corporate growth regime knowledge was generated by structured research activities funded internally by retained extraprofits and exploited by means of the advantages triggered by its extensibility coupled with the persistent introduction of innovations in product markets based upon its accumulation in internal stocks of knowledge. The knowledge growth regime that is substituting the corporate growth regime can be regarded as the new institutional and organizational set-up implemented in advanced countries to structure the generation and exploitation of knowledge around a specialized knowledge industry based upon the accumulation of scientific knowledge and scientific entrepreneurship that provides the rest of the system with new knowledge capitalized as a financial asset.

The emergence of the knowledge industry parallels the demise of the corporation as the locus of generation and exploitation of knowledge and the shift of the locus of appropriation of knowledge rents. The vertical disintegration of the knowledge generation activities – traditionally performed by the corporation – and the stretching of the chain of value parallels the shifts of the locus of exploitation and valorization of knowledge as an asset.

Firms specializing in knowledge generation activities exploit their output with two mechanisms: i) they sell knowledge directly as a service in the quasi-markets for knowledge; and ii) they transform knowledge into knowledge-intensive equity that can be sold in financial markets with venture capitalism.

The shift from a Schumpeterian growth regime to another takes place when the mechanisms of knowledge generation and exploitation in place reveal their limits and are no longer compatible with the structure of the system and when relevant organization innovations at the system level provide new opportunities. The entrepreneurial growth regime was limited by the contradictions of the credit system as the prime provider of finance for innovation and by the small size of firms that could not reap the benefits of the extensibility of knowledge in terms of its repeated use for large-scale production. The corporate growth regime had been able to combine equity finance with its exploitation of knowledge cumulability and extensibility. The corporate growth regime failed because of its limits in funding radical technological breakthroughs. The new knowledge growth regime is based upon the combination of scientific entrepreneurship with equity finance organized by venture capitalism and financial markets that enable the exploitation of knowledge as a capital asset. The vertical disintegration between the generation of knowledge and its repeated use as an input into the production of other goods made possible the combination of the benefits of small size in its generation with large size in its use.

The knowledge growth regime has its own limits and weaknesses. The capitalization of knowledge undermines the distribution of the income generated by the exploitation of knowledge. The limited access to the existing stock of technological change raised by the current intellectual property rights regime impedes the full exploitation of the benefits of the limited exhaustibility of knowledge (Stiglitz and Greenwald, 2014).

The solution of the appropriability trade-off is at the heart of the long-term viability of the knowledge growth regime. On the one hand, it is in fact clear that patents are indispensable to increase the appropriability of knowledge; on the other hand, however, patents reduce the pace of the recombinant generation of new knowledge as they limit the access to indispensable inputs. All changes in the intellectual property rights regime modify the effects of the appropriability trade-off. The augmented levels of knowledge appropriability provided by the strengthening of the intellectual property rights implemented since the last decade of the twentieth century play a central role in the exploitation and valorization of knowledge as capital (Orsi and Coriat, 2006).

Patents and trademarks enable knowledge holders to reduce the risks stemming from the limited appropriability of knowledge. Patents and trademarks provide the foundations for the monopolistic exploitation of technological and commercial knowledge. Patents and trademarks provide the institutional foundations for the working of knowledge quasi-markets. Without patents and trademarks, knowledge trade would be impeded by the uncontrolled leakage of knowledge. Patents and trademarks enable the valorization of knowledge not only by means of knowledge transactions, but also by means of the embodiment of intellectual property rights in capital by means of the creation of knowledge equity. Patents are indispensable not only to increase the appropriability of knowledge and its exploitability, but also to favor the dissemination of knowledge. Patents avoid or reduce the systematic use of secrecy that would become the unique tool of knowledge holders to increase the chances to retain the flows of rents stemming from knowledge. Moreover, patents are a powerful mechanism that makes the advances of the knowledge frontier publicly known: patents provide information to the system.

At the same time, however, patents limit the access to existing knowledge as an indispensable input in the recombinant generation of new knowledge. It is clear that a tight intellectual property rights regime based upon the strong exclusivity of property rights undermines the opportunities provided by the limited exhaustibility of knowledge in terms of cumulability. The implications of the new understanding of the crucial role of the recombinant generation of knowledge and its effects – in terms of increasing returns based upon its limited exhaustibility for the analysis of the working of the knowledge economy – are far reaching. The knowledge growth regime suffers the intrinsic contradiction between the conditions of the generation of technological knowledge and the conditions of its exploitation (Boldrin and Levine, 2002, 2013).

The analysis of the appropriability trade-off should take into account the pervasive role of the limited exhaustibility of knowledge, and acknowledge its implications for rebalancing the properties of the intellectual property rights regime with the introduction of patents with a limited exclusivity.

The over-privatization of knowledge, in fact, curbs the rates of generation of new knowledge. The levels of exclusivity granted to proprietary knowledge need to be reconsidered. The application of the liability rule to intellectual property rights with the introduction of patents characterized by limited exclusivity, especially when proprietary knowledge is not used in the same product markets but as an input in the generation of new knowledge relevant for other product markets, can help to solve the intrinsic contradiction of knowledge appropriability that limits the viability of the knowledge growth regime.

References

Aglietta, M. (1976). *Régulation et crises du capitalism*, Calman-Levy, Paris. (The quotes are drawn from the English translation: Aglietta, M. (2000). *A Theory of Capitalist Regulation. The US Experience*, Verso, New York.)

Amable, B. (2003). *The Diversity of Modern Capitalism*, Oxford University Press, Oxford.

Antonelli, C. (ed.) (2011). *Handbook on the Economic Complexity of Technological Change*, Edward Elgar, Cheltenham, UK and Northampton, MA, USA.

Antonelli, C. (2017). *Endogenous Innovation: The Economics of an Emergent System Property*, Edward Elgar, Cheltenham, UK and Northampton, MA, USA.

Antonelli, C. (2018), Knowledge exhaustibility and Schumpeterian growth, *Journal of Technology Transfer*, **43** (3), 779–91.

Antonelli, C. (2019), Knowledge as an economic good: Exhaustibility versus appropriability? *Journal of Technology Transfer*, **44**, Forthcoming.

Antonelli, C. and Link, A. (eds.) (2015). *Handbook on the Economics of Knowledge*, Routledge, London.

Antonelli, C. and Teubal, M. (2010). Venture capital as a mechanism for knowledge governance, in

Viale, R. and Etzkowitz, H. (eds.), *The Capitalization of Knowledge*, Edward Elgar, Cheltenham, UK and Northampton, MA, USA, pp. 98–120.

Arrow, K. J. (1962). Economic welfare and the allocation of resources for invention, in Nelson, R. R. (ed.), *The Rate and Direction of Inventive Activity: Economic and Social Factors*, Princeton University Press for NBER, Princeton, pp. 609–25.

Arrow, K. J. (1969). Classificatory notes on the production and transmission of technical knowledge, *American Economic Review*, **59**, 29–35.

Atkinson, A. B. (2015). *Inequality. What Can be Done?* Harvard University Press, Cambridge, MA.

Audretsch, D. B. and Keilbach, M. (2007). The theory of knowledge spillover entrepreneurship, *Journal of Management Studies*, **44**, 1242–54.

Audretsch, D. B. and Keilbach, M. (2008). Resolving the knowledge paradox: Knowledge-spillover entrepreneurship and economic growth, *Research Policy*, **37**, 1697–705.

Audretsch, D. B. and Link, A. (2018), *Sources of Knowledge and Entrepreneurial Behavior*, Toronto University Press, Toronto.

Audretsch, D. B., Keilbach, M. and Lehmann, E. E. (2006). *Entrepreneurship and Economic Growth*, Oxford University Press, Oxford.

Boldrin, M. and Levine, D. K. (2002). The case against intellectual property rights, *American Economic Review*, **92**, 209–12.

Boldrin, M. and Levine, D. K. (2013). The case against patents, *Journal of Economic Perspectives*, **27**, 1–22.

Boschma, R. A. (2005). Proximity and innovation: A critical assessment, *Regional Studies*, **39**, 61–74.

Boyer, R. (1988a). Technical change and the theory of 'regulation', in Dosi, G., Freeman, C., Nelson, R. R., Silverberg, G. and Soete, L. (eds.), *Technical Change and Economic Theory*, Pinter Publishers, London and New York, pp. 67–94.

Boyer, R. (1988b). Formalizing growth regimes, in Dosi, G., Freeman, C., Nelson, R. R., Silverberg, G. and Soete, L. (eds.), *Technical Change and Economic Theory*, Pinter Publishers, London and New York, pp. 608–30.

Boyer, R. (2004). *Théorie de la régulation*, Éditions la Découverte, Paris.

Boyer, R. and Schmeder, G. (1990). Un retour à Adam Smith, *Revue Française d'Économie*, **5**, 125–59.

Breschi, S., Malerba, F. and Orsenigo, L. (2000). Technological regimes and Schumpeterian patterns of innovation, *Economic Journal*, **110**, 388–410.

Castellacci, F. and Zheng, J. (2010). Technological regimes. Schumpeterian patterns of innovation and firm-level productivity growth, *Industrial and Corporate Change*, **19** (6), 1829–65.

Chandler, A. D. Jr. (1962). *Strategy and Structure: Chapters in the History of the American Industrial Enterprise*, MIT Press, Cambridge, MA.

Chandler, A. D. Jr. (1977). *The Visible Hand: The Managerial Revolution in American Business*, The Belknap Press of Harvard University Press, Cambridge, MA.

Coriat, B., Petit, P. and Schmeder, J. (eds.) (2006). *The Hardship of Nations. Exploring the Paths of Modern Capitalism*, Edward Elgar, Cheltenham, UK and Northampton, MA, USA.

Dopfer, K., Potts, J. and Pyka, A. (2015). Upward and downward complementarity: The meso core of evolutionary growth theory, *Journal of Evolutionary Economics*, **26**, 753–63.

Fagerberg, J. and Sapprasert, K. (2011). National innovation systems: The emergence of a new approach, *Science and Public Policy*, **38** (9), 669–79.

Farber, H. S., Herbst, D., Kuziemko, I. and Suresh, N. (2018). Unions and inequality over the twentieth century: New evidence from survey data, NBER Working Paper 24587.

Freeman, C. and Louçã, F. (2001). *As Time Goes By. From the Industrial Revolution to the Information Revolution*, Oxford University Press, Oxford.

Frøslev Jens, C. and Maskell, P. (2003). *The Industrial Dynamics of the New Digital Economy*, Edward Elgar, Cheltenham, UK and Northampton, MA, USA.

Goldfarb, A., Greenstein, S. and Tucker, C. (2015), *Economic Analysis of the Digital Economy*, University of Chicago Press, Chicago.

Greenstein, S., Goldfarb, A. and Tucker, C. (2013). *Economics of Digitization*. Edward Elgar Publishing, International Library of Critical Writings in Economics series, #280, Cheltenham, UK and Northampton, MA, USA.

Hall, P. A. and Gingerich, D. W. (2009). Varieties of capitalism and institutional complementarities in the political economy, *British Journal of Political Science*, **39** (3), 449–82.

Hall, P. A. and Soskice, D. (2001). *Varieties of Capitalism: The Institutional Foundations of Comparative Advantage*, Oxford University Press, Oxford.

Hayek, F. A. (1945). The use of knowledge in society, *American Economic Review*, **35** (4), 519–30.

Jin, D. J. and Stough, R. R. (1998). Learning and learning capability in the Fordist and Post-Fordist age: An integrative framework, *Environment and Planning A*, **30**, 1255–78.

Johansson, B., Karlsson, C. and Stough, R. (2006). *The Emerging Digital Economy: Entrepreneurship, Clusters, and Policy*, Springer, Berlin.

Kenworthy, L. (2005). Institutional coherence and macroeconomic performance, *Socio-Economic Review*, **4**, 69–91.

Lavoie, M. (2017). The origins and evolution of the debate on wage-led and profit-led regimes, *European Journal of Economics and Economic Policies*, **14** (2), 200–221.

Lazonick, W. (2007), The US stock market and the governance of innovative enterprise. *Industrial and Corporate Change*, **16** (6): 983–1035.

Lazonick, W. (2010), The Chandlerian corporation and the theory of innovative enterprise, *Industrial and Corporate Change*, **19** (2), 317–49.

Lundvall, B. (ed.) (1992). *National Systems of Innovation: Toward a Theory of Innovation and Interactive Learning*, Pinter Publishers, London.

Malerba, F. and Orsenigo, L. (1997). Technological regimes and sectoral patterns of innovative activities, *Industrial and Corporate Change*, **6** (1), 83–117.

Nelson, R. R. (ed.) (1993). *National Innovation System: A Comparative Analysis*, Oxford University Press, Oxford.

Nelson, R. R. and Winter, S. G. (1982). *An Evolutionary Theory of Economic Change*, The Belknap Press of Harvard University Press, Cambridge, MA.

Orsi, F. and Coriat, B. (2006). The new role and status of intellectual property rights in contemporary capitalism, *Competition and Change*, **10** (2), 162–79.

Ostrom, E. (2010). Beyond markets and states: Polycentric governance of complex economic systems, *American Economic Review*, **100** (3), 641–72.

Perez, C. (2010). Technological revolutions and techno-economic paradigms, *Cambridge Journal of Economics*, **34**, 185–202.

Petit, P. (1986). *Slow Growth and the Service Economy*, Frances Pinter, London.

Schumpeter, J. A. (1942). *Capitalism, Socialism and Democracy*, Harper and Brothers, New York.

Schumpeter, J. A. (1947). The creative response in economic history, *Journal of Economic History*, **7**, 149–59.

Stiglitz, J. E. (1974), Alternative theories of wage determination and unemployment in LDCs: The labor turnover model, *Quarterly Journal of Economics*, **88** (2), 194–227.

Stiglitz, J. E. (1987). Learning to learn, localized learning and technological progress, in Dasgupta, P. and Stoneman, P. (eds.), *Economic Policy and Industrial Performance*, Cambridge University Press, Cambridge.

Stiglitz, J. E., Greenwald, B. C. (2014), *Creating a Learning Society. A New Approach to Growth, Development, and Social Progress*, Columbia University Press, New York.

Vercellone, C. (ed.) (2003). *Sommes-nous sorti du capitalism industriel?* La Dispute, Paris.

Vercellone, C. (ed.) (2006). *Capitalismo cognitivo. Conoscenza e finanza nell'epoca postfordista*, Manifestolibri, Roma.

Von Hippel, E. (1988). *The Sources of Innovation*, Oxford University Press, Oxford.

Von Hippel, E. (1994). Sticky information and the locus of problem-solving: Implications for innovation, *Management Science*, **40**, 429–39.

Von Hippel, E. (1998). Economics of product development by users: The impact of sticky local information, *Management Science*, **44**, 629–44.

Winter, S. G. (1984). Schumpeterian competition in alternative technological regimes, *Journal of Economic Behavior and Organization*, **5**, 137–58.

3 Measuring entrepreneurial impact through alumni impact surveys

Shiri Breznitz, Brendan Hills, and Qiantao Zhang

Introduction

Universities are an essential part of the entrepreneurship and innovation system on both the local and global scale. As such, understanding the impact of university alumni is important. Historically, the great majority of alumni studies have focused on measuring engagement and competencies, and on alumni giving (Cabrera et al. 2005). This chapter highlights the distinctly new phenomenon of alumni impact surveys, which are a relatively new tool used mostly by universities to address policy makers and future students. Much focus has been given in these studies to entrepreneurship, but it has not been well connected to the wider role of universities, or the social impact of alumni. At this moment, only seven universities have conducted alumni impact surveys. All but one are North American institutions. The execution of such large-scale surveys is expensive and time consuming. Moreover, there are many issues involving both the use of the data and its analysis in academic papers. Of the seven surveys, three have been used in five academic publications. Only one has provided a cross-university analysis. This chapter begins with a recount of the origin of alumni impact surveys, it continues with a review of the reasons for and the process of survey implementations; section four highlights the results from the surveys as they were published in university reports; section five reviews the published academic papers. The chapter concludes with a discussion on the state of alumni impact surveys.

From outcomes to impacts: the historical development of alumni surveys

Alumni surveys have been used by American universities and colleges to quantify alumni outcomes since as early as the 1930s (Cabrera et al. 2005). There is an established body of literature which has examined the kinds of information alumni surveys have collected (e.g., Pace 1979; Delaney 2004; Borden 2005; Cabrera et al. 2005; Volkwein 2010), but there is a much smaller body of literature on the development of survey methods over time. Of the literature that does exist, Cabrera et al. (2005) provide one of the most comprehensive overviews of the historical evolution of alumni surveys, while also identifying three distinct historical approaches.[1] Alumni surveys have sought to collect information on alumni post-graduation job choices, job satisfaction, the extent to which graduates utilized knowledge acquired from their major field of study, other skills acquired during respondents' time in school, as well as the extent to which alumni plan on donating, or already have donated, funds to their alma mater (Volkwein 2010). In their chapter, entitled "Making an Impact with Alumni Surveys," Cabrera et al. identify three approaches to alumni surveys: an *alumni outcome* approach, an *engagement and competencies* approach, and an *alumni giving* approach (Cabrera et al. 2005).

The *"alumni outcome"* approach was most prominent from the 1930s through the 1970s. In practice, the alumni outcome approach seeks to gather information on three broad categories related to the respondent's post-graduation professional life: alumni job satisfaction, the applicability of college major to profession, and the process of alumni transition into the workforce (Pace 1979). This approach has often been used because of its easily defined metrics for success; using the alumni outcome approach, universities and institutions of higher learning can gather information on the post-graduation professional success of their alumni, which can then be used as a proxy for quality of education received while attending college. Information returned from these surveys can be utilized to both (a) further cater educational instruction, and curriculum development to the needs of employers, as well as (b) attract prospective students, through the use of alumni data as a recruitment tool (Pace 1979). This approach has received criticism, however, as some authors have found that current career accomplishments of alumni can affect how collegiate experiences are viewed; survey responses may not, in this instance, be accurate then, as alumni may place disproportionate importance on their educational experience in times of success, and disproportionate blame on their educational experience in times of failure (Pike 1994).

Since the 1980s, alumni surveys have begun to include questions which seek to identify the competencies and skills acquired by alumni during their time spent attending university. Peter Ewell (2005) attributes this shift in methodology to a more general shift towards "accountability for results" within the American higher education system. In an effort to more accurately capture the totality of benefits acquired from university attendance, the *"engagement and competencies"* approach seeks to capture both the practical knowledge and skills acquired by alumni during their time of study, as well as the extent to which alumni participated in, and benefitted from, engagement with university faculty, staff and peers (Cabrera et al. 2005). Further, this approach also seeks to gather information on the effectiveness of different teaching methods, involvement and rigor required for coursework, as well as different levels of competencies acquired based on the intensity of student

---

1 It is worth noting that the three approaches identified by Cabrera et al. (2005) are nearly identical to approaches identified in other works (e.g., Volkwein 2010), but for the sake of consistency, this chapter will borrow terminology from Cabrera et al. (2005).

Table 3.1 Four categories of alumni surveys

Approach	Purpose
Alumni outcome approach	Measure what alumni have accomplished since graduation.
Engagement and competencies approach	Measure particular skillset(s) acquired during school, and engagement with program, faculty, extracurricular groups, etc.
Alumni giving approach	Measure willingness and capacity of alumni to donate to institution.
Alumni impact approach	Measure entrepreneurship and innovation activities of alumni.

involvement. However, it is difficult to gauge the extent to which the college or university afforded alumni a particular skillset or set of competencies; while the alumni themselves might point to the university as the source of a particular competency, the extent to which this is true cannot be tested or confirmed.

The third approach has been termed by Cabrera et al. (2005) the "alumni giving" approach. This approach seeks to capture information on the extent to which alumni give back to their alma mater in the form of charitable donations in the years following graduation. The rise in popularity of this survey method coincides with the decline in state support for institutions of higher learning since the end of the 1980s, which has forced many universities in subsequent years to turn to alternative sources of funding. Cabrera et al. (2005) use the state of Wisconsin as an empirical example of this phenomenon; during fiscal year 1973–1974, alumni gifts, grants and trust funds supplied 35% of total funding for the state university system, with state support making up 52%. Twenty-five years later, alumni gifts made up 50% of the funding for the state university system, while state support made up only 33% (Cabrera et al. 2005). Further, alumni tendency to donate to their alma mater has been found to be partially determined by graduates' perception of institutional quality and positive collegiate experience (e.g., Brittingham and Pezzullo 1990; Taylor and Martin 1995; Brodigan and Dehne 1997), which can be further supported and demonstrated to be true by the inclusion of the engagement and competencies approach. Cabrera et al. (2005) point to the "alumni giving" approach's usefulness as a tool for campus foundation officers, deans, presidents and other administration officials looking to identify key alumni partners.

Each of the methods discussed above is concerned with the benefits individual alumni obtained through their time spent at university, but they do not measure the social and economic contribution of alumni. A distinctly new approach related to the *impact* of a university's alumni on their local, regional and national economies post-graduation started in the early 2000s. The first user of this method was the Massachusetts Institute of Technology (MIT), which in their 2001 "alumni outcome" survey added a question about firm foundation.[2] Using the information, in 2003 the institution, led by professor Edward Roberts, followed up with an entrepreneurship focused survey of firm founders, who represented about 18% of all MIT alums. This survey was followed up in 2009 by an MIT all living alumni survey. Since its first alumni impact survey, MIT conducted a similar survey again in 2014 (Roberts et al. 2015), while a number of other institutions have conducted alumni impact surveys of their own, including: Tsinghua University (2007); Stanford University (2011); the University of Alberta (2012); University of Virginia (2013); Harvard University (2015); and, most recently, the University of Toronto (2017). The following section reviews the similarities and differences between these surveys.

Trends in alumni impact survey conduction[3]

The history of the alumni impact survey begins at MIT with the lead faculty on the survey, Edward Roberts. Roberts himself, as well as post-doctorate and PhD students who worked with him on the MIT survey, were either the initiators of, or involved with, the Tsinghua, Stanford, Alberta and Virginia surveys. Thus, it is not surprising that the majority of surveys were initiated and led by a business school faculty. Only Stanford and the University of Toronto surveys received leadership from other areas of the university. In the case of Stanford, the survey initiated through the engineering school, while the administration led the drafting of the survey at the University of Toronto. The universities had several reasons to participate in the survey: (1) marketing – to alumni as well as potential students; (2) feedback – in order to improve programming; (3) as an input for government to indicate the important contribution of the university to the local and national economy. Several universities emphasized the importance of "telling a story" to university stakeholders, the public and the government. Some universities noted the benefit this data might have for prospective students; in collecting and publishing findings on the degree to which the university produces entrepreneurs, more students may be attracted to attend the institution. Most of the surveys focused on entrepreneurship while a few added a social and cultural focus.

Logistically, of the seven surveys, two were funded privately by an alumni donor while the others were funded jointly by alumni offices and individual schools within the university. The databases used to contact the alumni were mostly drawn from the central alumni office, but two universities received data directly from the schools/department that participated in the survey. Most contacted all living alums, with one exception that used a representative sample. All but one university verified the data returned using external databases such as Dun & Bradstreet.

---

2 Faculty-lead Edward Roberts built on the traditional survey by incorporating an additional question: "Have you ever participated in forming an enterprise?"

3 This section is based on interviews with all but one university. Interviews were conducted with both principle investigators and administrators.

Similarly, each university established an advisory committee made up of faculty members to advise the university on survey methods, research, questions, etc. In addition, the principle investigators (PIs), along with input from administrators, were responsible for survey question formulation. Interestingly, four of the seven surveys were implemented by the PIs, whereas the other three hired an external consulting or market research firm to conduct the survey. Most of the surveys were done online with some following up by mail or telephone. Finally, and perhaps most relevant to the aims of this chapter, all of the surveys went through a university ethics review.

Survey results vary. Response rates range from as high as 19.5% to as low as 8.1%. Interestingly, Harvard allowed for survey-takers to populate their personal work history – and other career-related data – directly from LinkedIn, which improved the accuracy and overall amount of data collected. The analysis was done mostly by PIs, with some of the consulting firms providing initial analysis. The survey results were reported in several ways. Most universities had press releases and articles in local newspapers and universities' magazines.[4] Results have also been published in survey outcome reports, mostly used for either internal purposes or marketing, dedicated webpages, and some in academic publications. However, despite the clear *intentions* by the faculty involved to have the survey data utilized in academic publications, only four academic publications based on the MIT, Stanford and Tsinghua data have been published, with Charles Eesley acting as co-author for each (Hsu et al. 2007; Eesley 2016; Eesley et al. 2016a; Eesley et al. 2016b; Lee and Eesley 2018).

Survey reports

In all but the case of Tsinghua University,[5] a survey outcome report has been published by the institution detailing the results.[6] While each of the reports provides a snapshot of their institution's impact, the way that the data and analysis is presented varies. Some reports (e.g., Stanford and the University of Alberta) provide in-depth analysis of both the state of entrepreneurship and innovation at their institution, trends and analysis of the data, as well as detailed overviews of the innovation and entrepreneurship resources available on campus (Eesley and Miller 2012; Briggs and Jennings 2013). By contrast, others (e.g., Harvard and the University of Virginia) only provide snapshots of notable data trends and concise analysis (Lenox et al. 2014; Harvard University 2015).

---

4 Stanford: https://news.stanford.edu/news/2012/october/innovation-economic-impact-102412.html; Alberta: https://www.ualberta.ca/newtrail/winter2013/features/alumni-impact-report; MIT: http://news.mit.edu/2015/report-entrepreneurial-impact-1209; UVA: https://www.darden.virginia.edu/news/2014/Survey-Shows-UVA-Entrepreneurs-Significant-Impact-on-Economy/; UofT: https://alumni.utoronto.ca/news-and-stories/news-and-articles/measuring-our-impact

5 A report was generated for internal use, but no publicly-available report exists for Tsinghua.

6 Such a report is forthcoming in the case of the University of Toronto.

Each of the reports examined within this section were accompanied by an official press release from their respective university. Reports received public attention through official press releases, as well as through newspaper and online media publications.[7] Despite some minor external media coverage, Stanford's report has largely remained an internal resource; while the authors of the report have presented its findings at academic conferences, the dedicated AIS website which existed at the time of the survey's conduction has since been taken down, and the results have not been used by the university as a marketing or branding resource. The Harvard and University of Virginia reports on the other hand were clearly designed with an external audience in mind. The University of Virginia report was accompanied by a dedicated website for the report and its findings, which remains online today; hosted by and accessible via the Batten Institute at UVA's Darden School of Business, the website provides a concise overview of the report's findings, along with a link to an audio podcast which details the research process and findings.[8] Select findings from the report have also been incorporated into the university's dedicated economic impact webpage and continue to be used directly in branding material by the central university administration.[9] Similarly, the Harvard report was accompanied by an initial press release from the central administration in December 2015,[10] and a second press release from Harvard Business School in March 2016.[11] Harvard's dedicated alumni impact study webpage continues to operate today, providing interactive infographics that highlight some of the most notable findings from the report. From the outset, the Harvard report was intended for the survey data to be utilized as a marketing tool; in particular, the university hoped to use the survey report data to highlight Harvard's local, regional and national impact through its entrepreneurial alumni. The Alberta report has been used as a tool to highlight the school's central economic role to the provincial and national government.

The detail of the analysis in each report varies according to the intended audience. All of the reports provide an overview of the economic impact of alumni-founded firms, including, but not limited to, information on: the raw number of alumni-founded firms; collective amount of annual revenue received; collective employment; and geographic distribution of alumni-founded ventures. In addition, each of the reports provides information related to personal characteristics of alumni entrepreneurs, including: mean and/or median age of alumni at first venture-founding; gender distribution of entrepreneurs; domestic vs. international student entrepreneurs; and alumni entrepreneur breakdown by degree received. Finally, all of the reports, save for MIT's, provide information on the *social* impact of their alumni through either an examination of the number of non-profit ventures

---

7   The Stanford report was covered by both Bloomberg and Forbes; while the University of Alberta report was covered by Canadian media outlet, Global News.

8   UVA, Batten Institute: https://web3.darden.virginia.edu/uva-alumni/

9   UVA: http://illimitable.virginia.edu/economicimpact/

10   Harvard: https://news.harvard.edu/gazette/story/2015/12/harvards-alumni-impact/

11   HBS: https://www.alumni.hbs.edu/stories/Pages/story-bulletin.aspx?num=5166

founded by alumni, or the number of alumni who have participated in some form of non-profit activity.

Three reports (Alberta, MIT and Stanford) provide information on university entrepreneurship and innovation support and the degree to which alumni participated in those activities. Further, these reports also address alumni innovation on campus, examining the number of alumni who hold, or who have applied for, patents, and which of them did so through a firm. Finally, the Stanford and MIT reports also provide case studies of specific individual entrepreneurs, or firms which have been founded by alumni, and to what extent those firms/entrepreneurs were influenced by their time spent at the university. For example, the Stanford report provides a historical recount of Google's growth from startup to success, and at what points in the company's history the university influenced its development.

Academic papers

Only three universities have utilized their survey data in one or more academic publications (see Table 3.2). This is despite the fact that all of the surveys have gone through an ethics review in order for their data to be utilized in academic publications. The five publications which have utilized AIS data have all contributed to the extensive body of literature on entrepreneurship. However, within the broad topic of entrepreneurship, the five papers examined here tend to focus on one of two questions: (1) what is the effect of either reforming, or implementing, new entrepreneurship-focused institutions on the rate of entrepreneurship (Eesley 2016; Eesley et al. 2016a)? (2) what kinds of alumni are most likely to become entrepreneurs, and how, if at all, has this changed overtime (Hsu et al. 2007; Eesley et al. 2016b; Lee and Eesley 2018)?

Eesley (2016) and Eesley et al. (2016a) both exclusively utilize data from the 2007 Tsinghua University alumni impact survey in combination with policy changes to evaluate policy impact on entrepreneurship. In the first of these two papers, Eesley

Table 3.2 Surveys and their publications

Survey	Year of survey	Publications
MIT	2003 and 2014	Hsu et al. 2007; Eesley et al. 2016b.
Tsinghua University	2007	Eesley 2016; Eesley et al. 2016a; Eesley et al. 2016b.
Stanford University	2011	Lee and Eesley 2018.
University of Alberta	2012	None.
University of Virginia	2013	None.
Harvard University	2015	None.
University of Toronto	2017	None.

(2016), examines changes in the rate of entrepreneurship after policy attempts to lower barriers to growth in China in 1988 and 1999. The author is able to demonstrate that sufficiently lowering barriers to growth not only leads to *more* entrepreneurship, but to *better* entrepreneurship in terms of the level of human capital. Similarly, Eesley et al. (2016a) examine Chinese entrepreneurs seeking to identify whether Project 985 – a Chinese government initiative which provided funding for higher education institutions across the country to build new research centers which would emphasize university entrepreneurship – altered student/ alumni beliefs and behaviors towards entrepreneurship. Using data from the Tsinghua alumni impact survey, the authors are able to demonstrate that alumni who attended universities which were part of Project 985 expressed greater beliefs in innovation and entrepreneurship, and subsequently founded more high-tech ventures (Eesley et al. 2016a). These two papers add to the body of literature on institutional barriers to growth (e.g., Xin and Pearce 1996; Peng and Luo 2000; Li and Zhang 2007) and seek to examine how and which kinds of institutions, or institutional barriers, impact rates of entrepreneurship.

Hsu et al. (2007) is the earliest example of the use of alumni impact data in an academic publication. The authors utilize the data from the MIT alumni impact survey to identify common characteristics of entrepreneurial alumni, tracking the growth of entrepreneurial activity over time and finding that the rate of firm founding by alumni has increased dramatically since the earliest data available in the 1950s (Hsu et al. 2007). The authors also find that the median age of first-time entrepreneurs has declined from forty during the 1950s, to thirty during the 1990s; women alumnae lag behind their male counterparts in propensity to pursue entrepreneurship; and non-U.S. citizen alumni tend to enter entrepreneurship at higher rates than citizens. Lee and Eesley (2018) also utilize alumni impact survey data, this time from Stanford University, to highlight the propensity for entrepreneurship within particular ethnic groups. The authors find that Asian Americans have the highest rate of entrepreneurship of any one ethnic group, but that non-American Asians have a much lower rate of entrepreneurship than their American counterparts.

Importantly, Eesley et al. (2016b) ask a similar question to that of Lee and Eesley (2018) and Hsu et al. (2007), but also consider performance outcomes through an added element of comparison across two institutions: Tsinghua University and MIT. The authors find a number of similarities between the two universities, namely levels of alumni entrepreneurship (as a proportion of total graduates), as well as the types of students (by major field of study) who pursue entrepreneurship. Major differences appear however, when the *performance*, as opposed to simply the rate, of entrepreneurship is considered: firms founded by Tsinghua University alumni, on average, attracted far lower amounts of capital, resulting in more firm closures and inability to scale. Further, the average age of founder alumni from Tsinghua was much lower (with most founders having graduated in the 1990s or 2000s), than their MIT counterparts (with the majority of founders having graduated in the 1960s–1980s). The authors speculate that institutional barriers to growth in China which favor state-owned and foreign-invested firms may explain some of the performance gaps. These papers add to an extensive body of literature which assesses common characteristics of entrepreneurs (e.g., Baum and Locke 2004; Benedict et al. 2012; Densberger 2014; Blume-Kohout 2016) and can provide better insight into the kinds of people who become entrepreneurs, how this has changed over time, and how this impacts entrepreneurial performance outcomes.

Conclusion

The above review of existing alumni impact surveys raises a few questions regarding the future of research in this field. In particular, the academic value of the studies themselves as well as their comparability. Conducting a singular study allowed the PIs to publish papers related to subgroups within the university, mostly entrepreneurs vs. non-entrepreneurs, and local vs. international students. Even within these subgroups, there are difficulties with data corroboration. Survey data on its own is hard to verify. For that, access to individual-level information is required. Being able to supplement the data with location-specific information, patents and firm foundation would allow researchers to conduct quantitative analysis and infer economic outcomes.

However, the greater value for the academic community at large is a cross-university comparative study. For that, one must ensure that the same survey instrument has been used, something that is very difficult to do when studying different institutions, in different countries/regions, and with different economic and social backgrounds. However, access to this plethora of information can provide much needed information on the local and international impact of universities in general, and on their entrepreneurship education and innovation-related activities in particular.

Bibliography

Baum, J.R., and Locke, E.A. (2004). The relationship of entrepreneurial traits, skill, and motivation to new venture growth. *Journal of Applied Psychology*, **89** (4): 587–98.

Benedict, M.E., McClough, D., and Hoag, J. (2012). STEM: a path to self-employment and jobs? *Journal of Entrepreneurship Education*, **15**: 99–122.

Blume-Kohout, M.E. (2016). *Imported Entrepreneurs: Foreign-Born Scientists and Engineers in U.S. STEM Fields Entrepreneurship*. Washington, DC: Office of Advocacy, U.S. Small Business Administration.

Borden, V.M. (2005). Using alumni research to align program improvement with institutional accountability. *New Directions for Institutional Research*, **2005**: 61–72.

Briggs, A., and Jennings, J. (2013). *Uplifting the Whole People: The Impact of University of Alberta Alumni through Innovation and Entrepreneurship*. Alberta: University of Alberta.

Brittingham, B.E., and Pezzullo, T.R. (1990). *The Campus Green: Fund Raising in Higher Education*. Washington, DC: ERIC Clearinghouse on Higher Education.

Brodigan, D.L., and Dehne, G.C. (1997). Data for effective marketing in an uncertain future. *Journal of College Admission*, **155**: 16–21.

Cabrera, A.F., Weerts, D.J., and Zulick, B.J. (2005). Making an impact with alumni surveys. In *Enhancing Alumni Research: European and American Perspectives*, edited by David J. Weerts and Javier Vidal. San Francisco, CA: Jossey-Bass, 126.

Delaney, A.M. (2004). Ideas to enhance higher education's impact on graduates' lives: alumni recommendations. *Tertiary Education and Management*, **10** (2): 89–105.

Densberger, K. (2014). The self-efficacy and risk-propensity of entrepreneurs. *Journal of Enterprising Culture*, **22** (4): 437–62.

Eesley, C. (2016). Institutional barriers to growth: entrepreneurship, human capital and institutional change. *Organization Science*, **27** (5): 1290–306.

Eesley, C.E., and Miller, W.F. (2012). Impact: Stanford University's economic impact via innovation and entrepreneurship. Available at SSRN: https://ssrn.com/abstract=2227460

Eesley, C.E., Li, J.B., and Yang, D. (2016a). Does institutional change in universities influence high-tech entrepreneurship? Evidence from China's Project 985. *Organization Science*, **27** (2): 446–61.

Eesley, C.E., Yang, D., Roberts, E.B., and Li, T. (2016b). Understanding entrepreneurial process and performance: a cross-national comparison of alumni entrepreneurship between MIT and Tsinghua University. *Asian Journal of Innovation and Policy*, **5**: 146–84.

Ewell, P.T. (2005). Alumni studies as instruments of public policy: the U.S. experience. *New Directions for Institutional Research*, **Special Issue** (126): 19–29.

Harvard University. (2015). *Global Economic and Social Impact of Harvard Alumni*. Cambridge, MA: Harvard University Press.

Hsu, D.H., Roberts, E.B., and Eesley, C.E. (2007). Entrepreneurs from technology-based universities: evidence from MIT. *Research Policy*, **36**: 768–88.

Lee, Y.S., and Eesley, C.E. (2018). The persistence of entrepreneurship and innovative immigrants. *Research Policy*. **47** (6): 1032–1044.

Lenox, M., King, A., Eesley, C., and Mehedi, A. (2014). *The Economic Impact of Entrepreneurial Alumni: A Case Study of the University of Virginia*. Charlottesville, VA: Batten Institute, Darden School of Business, University of Virginia.

Li, H., and Zhang, Y. (2007). The role of managers' political networking and functional experience in new venture performance: evidence from China's transition economy. *Journal of Strategic Management*. **28** (8): 791–804.

Pace, C.R. (1979). *Measuring Outcomes of College: Fifty Years of Findings and Recommendations for the Future*. San Francisco, CA: Jossey-Bass.

Peng, M.W., and Luo, Y. (2000). Managerial ties and firm performance in a transition economy: the nature of a micro-macro link. *Academy of Management Journal*, **43** (3): 486–501.

Pike, G.R. (1994). The Relationship between alumni satisfaction and work experiences. *Research in Higher Education*, **35** (1): 105–23.

Roberts, E.B., Murray, F., and Kim, J.D. (2015). Entrepreneurship and innovation at MIT: continuing global growth and impact. Available at SSRN: https://ssrn.com/abstract=2772695

Taylor, A.L., and Martin, J.C. (1995). Characteristics of alumni donors and non-donors at a Research 1, Public University. *Research in Higher Education*, **36** (3): 283–302.

Volkwein, F.J. (2010). Assessing alumni outcomes. *New Directions for Institutional Research* (S1): 125–39.

Xin, K.K., and Pearce, J.L. (1996). Guanxi: connections as substitute for formal institutional support. *Journal of Academy Management*, **39** (6), 1641–58.

4 Academic entrepreneurship: between myth and reality

Alice Civera, Michele Meoli, and Silvio Vismara

1. Introduction

Academic entrepreneurship encompasses the set of activities with the aim of transferring knowledge as well as commercializing the innovations and the technology developed by academics within universities. Academic entrepreneurial activity makes use of both formal and informal intellectual property (IP) mechanisms. The former includes university patents, licensing and spin-offs, while the latter refers to the collaborative research, contract research and consulting, as well as ad hoc advice and networking with practitioners (Grimaldi et al., 2011).

In the last three decades, we attended to the emergence of university spin-offs as the most studied instrument to diffuse and commercialize knowledge. Academic spin-offs have irrefutably attracted a lot of attention from academics (see Perkmann et al., 2013), as shown by several bibliographical reviews found in the literature on the subject. Among others, we identified those by O'Shea et al. (2004), Mustar et al. (2006), Rothaermel et al. (2007), Djokovic and Souitaris (2008), Mars and Rios-Aguilar (2010), Yusof and Jain (2010) and the very recent Miranda et al. (2017). Reviews on academic spin-offs are encouraged insofar as they contribute to the research area concerning the role of entrepreneurial universities, entrepreneurship, and innovation and they are beneficial for practitioners.

Policymakers are interested in this phenomenon as well (Audretsch et al., 2015). The European Commission recommends incentivizing researchers taking part in knowledge transfer activities. Coherently, several governments in several states created regulation to foster, among others, technology transfer mechanisms, such as academic spin-off activity. University spin-offs are indeed expected to play a crucial role for economic and societal development (Griliches, 1992), both directly by starting new businesses and creating job places, and indirectly by contributing to technology-using sectors (Bathelt et al., 2011; Ljungberg and McKelvey, 2012).

The object of this chapter is not to comprehensively review the burgeoning literature on academic entrepreneurship, as comprehensive reviews have been already published with this aim (e.g., Rothaermel et al., 2007; Wright et al., 2007; Siegel and Wright, 2015b). Rather, it is in understanding the shifts in practice to provide the basis for new directions in theorizing and empirical analysis regarding academic entrepreneurship. The interest in academic entrepreneurship has not been exhausted yet as this process is indeed complex and dynamic enough to require a future research agenda for the topic. The entrepreneurial ecosystems surrounding the universities are filling up with several new actors, such as property-based institutions (i.e., incubators/accelerators and science/technology/research parks), entrepreneurship centers, and "surrogate" entrepreneurs on campus (Siegel and Wright, 2015a). Beyond new actors, they are enriched with entrepreneurship courses and programs on campus, as well as alumni support including alumni commercialization funds and student business plan competitions.

The increasing university commitment to academic entrepreneurship is due to several rationales. As public funding for higher education declines in both the U.S. and Europe, universities are forced to draw upon alternative sources of financing. In America, public and private research university donations from alumni are rapidly gaining ground. Accordingly, universities increasingly rely on funding from federal agencies to support academic entrepreneurship such as the U.S. government's Small Business Innovation Research and Small Business Technology Transfer programs. Moreover, entrepreneurial outcomes have become a matter of competition among universities. In this regard, the Association of University Technology Managers in the U.S. and Canada has recently spurred benchmarking of academic entrepreneurship based on metrics such as patenting, licensing, and start-up activity (see AUTM, 2013). Concurrently, we have observed an increasing interest in academic entrepreneurship from different fields of studies, ranging from social sciences (e.g., economics, sociology, psychology, and political science), to business administration and management (see the literature reviewed in Rothaermel et al., 2007; Siegel and Wright, 2015b). In order to improve the rigor and relevance of research on this topic, an increasingly multidisciplinary approach should be taken into account.

In the following sections, we will outline our main contribution to the academic entrepreneurship literature and then we will propose future lines of research. We will then finish with some concluding remarks.

2.   What we know about academic spin-offs

Quantitative studies about academic spin-offs can be classified in two different categories according to the dimension of analysis: (1) papers on the establishment of academic spin-offs; (2) studies on the performance of academic spin-offs in terms of exiting strategies such as initial public offerings (IPOs) and mergers and acquisitions (M&As), in terms of growth and in terms of internationalization (Colombo et al., 2019).

2.1   The establishment of academic spin-offs

The success in the establishment of academic spin-offs can be attributed to several factors, summarized in three categories: individual motivations, affiliation with parent universities, and supportive external environment (see Civera et al., 2017 for a detailed review of the antecedents for the establishment of academic spin-offs). Concerning the first stream of literature, among others, a contribution from Horta et al. (2016) sheds new insights on the "push" and "pull" factors that influence individuals' propensity to create firms (Thurik et al., 2008). They analyzed the key role of regional unemployment, by distinguishing between skilled and non-skilled unemployment. Whereas the authors showed that the rate of academic spin-off creation is positively associated with the skilled unemployment rate, they found that non-skilled unemployment reduced the probability of academic spin-off establishment, yet up to a threshold, beyond which the effect reversed.

Referring to the role of parent universities in the establishment of their affiliated firms, we focused on specific institutional aspects, such as the university governance and leadership as well as the university administrative support. Meoli et al. (2019), for the first time, related the governance structure of universities to their capacity to foster the establishment of academic spin-offs. They found that variance in the university's board of directors is a stimulus for the establishment of academic spin-offs. In particular, the presence of appointed entrepreneurs fosters the creation of technology spin-offs while local stakeholders are crucial to promote the service-oriented university spin-offs. The rationale behind this study is the regulatory change that imposes on Italian state universities the enrolment of lay members in their own governance and management structures. Similarly, the recent institutional governance reform (Law 240/2010), which strengthened the role of the rector in the Italian state universities, is at the heart of a recent paper by Civera et al. (2019). They focused exclusively on the role of university leadership, among the main triggers for stimulating entrepreneurship, showing that the role of senior academic authorities is pivotal. They found that the mobility of university leaders positively affects the rate of establishment of academic spin-offs, as rectors who experienced international mobility in their career develop networks and collaborations that facilitate the business involvement of their institutions. They are catalysts for entrepreneurship by mobilizing resources internal and external to their organizations. Indeed, these positive externalities are greater in internationalized universities as well as in international-oriented regions.

In another study, Meoli and Vismara (2016) scrutinized the role of administrative staff in a context such as Italy, where due to the highly-regulated state-funded higher education system (Donina et al., 2015) the vexing bureaucracy of universities may be among the motivations for becoming academic entrepreneurs (Fini et al., 2009). The effect of administrative support varies according to the level of technology of academic spin-offs: whereas a positive relationship exists in the case of technology firms, a U-shaped relationship exists in the case of non-technology affiliated companies. When the number of administrative staff is either lower or higher than the optimal level, scientists prefer to create their own business to be much freer to manage the resources and improve their cash-flow management.

Finally, in relation to the support of external context, Meoli et al. (2018) analysed the role played by public policies in fostering university spin-offs. They investigated whether and how the introduction of performance-based research funding systems, which use the number of academic spin-offs as a measure of the impact of the university third mission, affects the establishment of such firms. They found that often the proliferation of academic spin-offs is unrelated to the research profile of universities but is rather correlated to regional features such as the lack of job opportunities and the relative skilled unemployment. This is in accordance to the "entrepreneurship of need" literature (see e.g., Fritsch et al., 2015; and Wang, 2006 for the implications of the "recession-push" hypothesis toward academic entrepreneurship, which states a positive relationship between unemployment and self-employment). This paper then casts doubt on the appropriateness of the number of academic spin-offs as an indicator for the university societal engagement as well as of the implemented funding policies.

2.2   The performance of academic spin-offs

The ability to successfully exit from an investment is a univocal measure of firm performance. IPOs and acquisitions are considered the best exit outcomes, while firm owners prefer IPOs as an exit mechanism, since they may regain control of the firm, which is not guaranteed through an acquisition. Bonardo et al. (2011) investigated for the first time the ability of university-based companies to translate the potential benefits of academic affiliation into performance gains. The affiliation with a university enhances the valuation of academic spin-offs, in particular when academics are present in the top management team at the time of the initial public offering. Meoli et al. (2013) confirmed that affiliation with a university is recognized as beneficial by investors as such affiliation enhances the valuation of the firms and the probability of being targeted in subsequent mergers and acquisitions, particularly in cross-border deals. In particular, university prestige and internationalization affect the propensity of affiliated spin-offs to be targeted in cross-border M&As (Cattaneo et al., 2015). The affiliation with a prestigious university is expected to increase the technological capabilities and network opportunities of affiliated firms and to provide a more dynamic and mobile human capital (Wang and Shapira, 2012). Moreover, the reputation of the parent university helps in overcoming information asymmetry on the quality of the firm and its market value (Sine et al., 2003). The international orientation of the universities is instead highly valued by international acquirers as it provides affiliated firms with a more dynamic and mobile human capital (Edler et al., 2011) as well as foreign external networks.

However, not all academic spin-offs are involved in IPOs or M&As. Civera and Meoli (2018) focused on the initial growth as an alternative performance measure. They provide empirical evidence that prestigious universities foster spin-off companies with high-growth potential, as highly reputed universities are likely to provide crucial information, resources, and contacts to affiliated firms, enhancing their performances. Moreover, since university reputation is at stake, there is an incentive for prestigious institutions to scrutinize the quality of their spin-offs before allowing them to hit the market.

The studies listed in the previous section have the peculiarity of illustrating success-ful examples of university spin-offs. Most of the extant empirical evidence shows instead that academic spin-offs do not outperform other peer companies, except in very few cases (Wennberg et al., 2011). Nonetheless, paradoxically, academic spin-offs often seek to internationalize their activities at an early stage (Bjørnåli and Aspelund, 2012). The internationalization of university spin-offs has been studied in relation to their top management teams (Pettersen and Tobiassen, 2012; Franco-Leal et al., 2016) as well as to environmental support provided by universities, incubators, and science parks (e.g., Lawton-Smith et al., 2008; Styles and Genua, 2008). However, neither academic entrepreneurship studies nor the international entrepreneurship literature has quantitatively addressed whether academic spin-offs are more or less inclined to internationalize than other comparable firms. Civera et al. (2018) show that university spin-offs are more prone to internationalize than their non-academic counterparts do and that this is not only intrinsic to their affiliation with universities but is also related to the degree of internationalization of the parent university.

3.   Future research agenda

Some avenues for future research can be derived starting from our experience of research in the field. By maintaining the same division in subsections, we discuss potential future contributions below. A summary of our proposals is provided in Table 4.1.

3.1   The establishment of academic spin-offs

As mentioned above, the establishment of academic spin-offs can be analysed through three different levels: individual level, university level, and system level.

At the *individual level*, there are some individual behaviors not fully explored yet. Academic entrepreneurs tend to establish networks with partners from the indus-try, as they provide capabilities and resources that academics lack. At present, how-ever, we have very limited knowledge about how scholars successfully identify and establish such contacts (see, for example, Wright et al., 2004). Accordingly, gener-ally neglected aspects concern knowledge transfer through contract researches as well as through the mobility of academics between the university and industry. The most debated issue refers to the incentives that should be set for individual academics to undertake secondments to industry aligned with those of the univer-sity, for example in terms of fit with promotion criteria (see Grimaldi et al., 2011). Beyond the sectorial mobility, we have little systematic evidence relating to any aspect of mobility, including the international one (Wright, 2011; Krabel et al., 2012). Individual researchers, especially the star scientists, are more likely to move both between regions within a country and across countries and this has implica-

Table 4.1   Future research on academic spin-offs

	Establishment	Performance
Individual level	• Identification of industrial partners • Sectorial and international mobility • Incentive and promotion criteria	• Evolution of academic entrepreneurial teams into boards • Set of skills and networks enabling growth • Organizational justice theory
University level	• Procedures to recruit the appropriate TTO staff • Heterogeneity of incubators • New forms of academic entrepreneurship (business plan competition, entrepreneurial garage, alumni/student start-ups, business schools, peer academics mentorship) • The role of the department and academic disciplines	• Suitable and complete information • Longitudinal and comparable data • Measuring the impact, quality, and value of academic entrepreneurship • Organizational design, organizational culture, and organizational structure theories
System level	• Different "optimal" portfolios of academic entrepreneurship activities • Appropriate types of regional collaborations • Conflicts between national and sub-national system levels need to be reconciled	• Integration and effectiveness of accelerator programs • Measuring non-economic outcomes (e.g., health, happiness, life expectancy, and job satisfaction) • Ethics and social responsibility theory

tions for universities as well as for national economies. The international mobility of scientists is particularly relevant in an historical period like ours, characterised by Brexit and the presidency of Donald Trump.

At the *university level*, there is some heterogeneity in the skills required to pursue different modes of research commercialization. Universities may be able to adopt different structures according to their aims, namely to promote either global high-tech high-growing firms or traditional firms operating only in the local market (Clarysse et al., 2005). Traditionally, universities support academic entrepreneurship through dedicated Technology Transfer Offices (henceforth TTOs). Nonetheless, there have been critiques of the role and skills of TTOs (Lowe, 2006; Siegel et al., 2007) whose role in creating and developing start-ups especially appears to be limited. Further research should be devoted to university procedures to recruit the appropriate TTO staff.

Another traditional channel to promote academic entrepreneurship by targeting start-ups at the early stages (Mian, 1996; Rothaermel and Thursby, 2005) consists of university incubators. They provide several support services, including faculty consultants, student employees, enhancement of reputation, library services, and related R&D activities. Furthermore, by virtue of their physical proximity to the campus labs they offer to scientists the opportunity of developing their businesses in close proximity to the universities (Di Gregorio and Shane, 2003). However, future research should focus on identifying both internal and external university intermediaries to connect the academic and the commercial context (Wright et al., 2009). In addition, there is still room for improvement in terms of detecting the effect of heterogeneity in university configurations (Siegel et al., 2003; Barbero et al., 2014) as well as in the new ventures created (Mair et al., 2012).

Nevertheless, universities may also need to shift from their traditional trajectories to create new development paths (Ahuja and Katila, 2004; Rasmussen et al., 2011). A non-traditional relatively recent activity to foster entrepreneurship within universities is business plan competition (Barr et al., 2009). This evolved in response to similar international initiatives (e.g., the Rice Business Plan Competition, the European Business Plan of the Year Competition, the Research Councils UK Business Plan Competition). Although its effectiveness for early-stage businesses is under criticism (Honig and Karlsson, 2004), its training function is precious for a variety of aspects including the launch of a new business, cash awards, consultancy services, as well as in relation to potential networking with the industrial and financial communities.

An increasing number of institutions are instead investing in educational programs as entrepreneurship faculty in business schools can be active actors in creating university spin-offs (Wright et al., 2009). Indeed, business schools are involving students and faculty in the internal university processes for promoting academic entrepreneurship. The Johns Hopkins University is one of the institutions at the vanguard of this movement (Phan, 2014); students in the Carey Business School are required to conduct a market analysis and commercialization plan for a university-based innovation by collaborating with the Hopkins Technology Transfer Office. A long list of American universities offering similar curricular experiences includes Oregon State University, Rensselaer, the University of Montana, the University of Wisconsin-Madison, and the University at Albany. However, the involvement of students in advisory positions within companies may be critical especially if the business schools promoting the initiative are not high-quality institutions (Siegel and Wright, 2015a). Universities are then equally engaged in developing "entrepreneurial garages" providing space, resources, and mentoring to facilitate student and alumni start-ups (Siegel and Wright, 2015a). However, this innovative aspect is mostly neglected at present.

Other pioneering university experiments include the "Carolina Express Licensing Agreement" developed at the University of North Carolina at Chapel Hill (Kenney and Patton, 2005). This is an agreement valid for university faculty, students, or staff members wishing to establish a company to commercialize their inventions. To apply, a business plan must be approved by the TTO and by a faculty member from the business school. A similar case concerns the University of Missouri where in 2011 a regulation was set to entitle students to own any invention or plant variety made during enrolment as a student of the university, without requiring the student to assign his/her ownership to the university. It would be interesting to investigate if there are any other experiences in this sense outside the U.S. context or if this is purely an American peculiarity.

Albeit disregarded, peer academics who already have experienced the entrepreneurial process are suggested as a valuable source of expertise and advice (Grimaldi et al., 2011). These individuals can indeed act as mentors but can also act as intermediaries between the academic and industrial reality (Mosey and Wright, 2007). This topic should be explored in future research in addition to other support mechanisms such as industrial liaison offices or business relationship offices (Perkmann et al., 2013). Similarly, an almost ignored area of analysis is the role of the department from which potential academic entrepreneurship emerges, which has attracted far less attention (Murray, 2004; Bercovitz and Feldman, 2008). The local work environment may also influence entrepreneurial activity (Stuart and Ding, 2006) as certain departments may have a culture of supporting academic entrepreneurship, while others may be hostile; some departments may have extensive and deep linkages with industry while others may not. Further research would shed light on the contextual influence of whether scientists create ventures, and how they then develop them. In addition to the department, academic disciplines also play a role (Kenney and Goe, 2004; Mustar et al., 2006). The vast majority of studies are focused on the biomedical sciences, and to a lesser degree on engineering, mathematics and statistics, and the physical sciences. Yet, the digital technologies are transforming traditionally less technological fields and new firms are emerging from the humanities including music and the visual and creative arts. New insights should be derived from these kinds of business.

Finally, concerning future system-level research, universities should take into consideration the differences in the local and regional contexts in which they operate (Audretsch et al., 2016). Indeed, academic institutions in unsupportive environments need to be proactively involved in the screening of entrepreneurial activities (Clarysse et al., 2005; Wright et al., 2007, 2008), while in a conducive context the capacity of selecting the most promising start-up projects is likely to be present (Degroof and Roberts, 2004). This suggests that it is counterproductive to apply the same rigid, uniform, system-level rules to deeply different organizations because it risks leading to outcomes contrary to those desired by policymakers. Accordingly, universities operating in different contexts should adopt different strategies for academic entrepreneurship to be consistent with these environments (Fini et al., 2009). Likewise, the configuration of the university entrepreneurial ecosystems can vary according to the university's peculiarities (Autio et al., 2014). In reference to the university research strength, elite universities are different from their mid-range counterparts in terms of resources, capabilities, and configurations within the same region, as well as in the scope and quality of knowledge and technology generated (Wright et al., 2008), which raises potential issues about the complementarities and incompatibilities across these institutions. Likewise, universities which do not belong to the field of life sciences and physical sciences are less inclined to technology commercialization (Wright et al., 2004), as are universities without a critical mass of research excellence or sufficient TTO expertise. In these cases, the institutions may need to establish a regional collaboration even if there is a lack of systematic analysis of appropriate collaborations that can generate local knowledge spillover benefits (Zucker et al., 1998). It follows that different combinations of universities and local contexts require different "optimal" portfolios of academic entrepreneurship activities (Grimaldi et al., 2011).

3.2   The performance of academic spin-offs

Similar to their establishment, the performance of academic spin-offs is related to *individual dimensions*, such as, for instance, the founding team. However, whereas there is some investigation on the initial creation of such a team (Vanaelst et al., 2006), how it evolves into boards able to take the venture to IPO or to become an established private business is almost unexplored. Nonetheless, addressing this gap is fundamental to fully understand the set of networks and skills that determines business growth by providing a competitive advantage for the spin-off (Zahra et al., 2009; Bercovitz and Feldman, 2011).

At *university level*, future research should be devoted to some methodological issues. Data are mostly collected referring to the most successful universities or the most successful forms of technology and knowledge transfer, thereby the access to suitable and complete information is required in order to draw conclusions of entrepreneurial studies generalizable both academically and for policy. An effort in this direction was made by the U.S. Association of University Technology Managers by recording the number of IPOs and strategic sales involving university spin-offs. However, recent research increasingly indicates the need to move beyond count results of key outcome measures of academic entrepreneurship, in order to estimate the value and quality of that activity. It is undeniably difficult to evaluate the success of entrepreneurial initiatives due to the lack of general agreement on the appropriate standard (Thursby et al., 2009). Some scholars suggest addressing academic entrepreneurs directly through surveys in order to collect longitudinal and comparable data (Perkmann et al., 2013). Nonetheless, there is a call for measuring impacts and not only outcomes (see Bozeman et al., 2013) and for developing convincing measures beyond the well-established indicators for measuring the effectiveness of formal IP mechanisms in terms of patenting, licensing, and spin-off activity (for a review, see Siegel and Wright, 2015b). While formal mechanisms of academic entrepreneurship have received great attention, other not legally protectable knowledge is more important in terms of contributing to employment and regional economic development (Amoroso et al., 2018). Measuring the impact of informal university-industry exchanges such as collaborative research, contract research, and consulting should be at the center of future research (see Perkmann et al., 2013).

Determining the most adaptable set of indicators poses several challenges as a large number of actors are involved, ranging from academics, to policymakers and senior university management, each with different goals (Link, 2017). This opens up new possibilities for investigating the interactions between the actors involved in developing and implementing academic entrepreneurship (Battilana et al., 2009). Indeed, as academic entrepreneurship evolves university-based entrepreneurial ecosystems to facilitate academic entrepreneurship at *system level* need to evolve as well. A recent development of the ecosystem is the emergence of accelerator programs (Siegel and Wright, 2015a). Their main task is selecting promising entrepreneurial teams and providing them with pre-seed investment and time-limited support comprising programmed events, and intensive mentoring exclusively in the early phase of the life cycle of a new venture. Although interest from scholars is increasing, it still lacks an integration between academic entrepreneurs and these mechanisms, by distinguishing among the variety of accelerators and the nature and effectiveness of their links with universities. Likewise, it also lacks a systematic analysis of the effectiveness of accelerators involving scientists and students in the emergence and growth of start-ups (Smith and Hannigan, 2014).

As a generalization, measuring academic entrepreneurship effectively may require multiple variable approaches, as patents, publications, citations, and licenses granted are all suitable indicators (Nelson, 2009). Moreover, to have a complete overview it is recommended to extend the analysis of outcomes beyond economic statistics, analyzing the impact of entrepreneurship on other aspects of development such as welfare (e.g., health, happiness, life expectancy, and job satisfaction) and sustainability (Miranda et al., 2017). Beyond measurement issues, extant studies on academic entrepreneurship also present a methodological issue; namely, there is a call for tackling practical phenomenon-driven evidence with theoretical explanations (Djokovic and Souitaris, 2008). Along with the maturing of academic entrepreneurship, a variety of theories and concepts became salient, among which are organizational behavior, organizational theory, human resource management, and ethics and social responsibility (Siegel and Wright, 2015a). The macro perspective is most often adopted as reviews of the literature have shown (Rothaermel et al., 2007; Siegel and Wright, 2015a). There is a call for applying more micro theories and concepts to this phenomenon, including theories of organizational commitment, organizational culture, and organizational justice (Greenberg, 1987). In addition, ethics and social responsibility are becoming crucial. This applies for example to the concerns about commercialization and global public health. At the center of the debate is the concept that private-property rights should not be for profit maximization but should be for a public purpose, namely to ensure that the benefits of research are widely shared. The answers from universities were very diverse, and some of them developed socially responsible licensing programs, such as policies adopted by the University of California at Berkeley.

4.   Conclusions

Siegel and Wright (2015a) recommend a rethinking of academic entrepreneurship in light of its greater variety in extent and nature within the context of the changing role and purpose of universities. We identified different levels of analysis and relatively open questions related to the role of invention ownership and incentives, the nature of incubators, accelerators, and TTOs, and entrepreneurial mobility, among others. New areas of research are drawn in organizational behavior, organizational theory, human resource management, ethics and social responsibility, as well as social network theory applied to academic entrepreneurship. We also raised methodological issues and called for a greater comparability between studies across countries. Meta-analyses of existing studies may constitute a good starting point in order to detect similarities and dissimilarities in different contexts. Moreover, Miranda et al. (2017) suggest using a sophisticated combination of analytical techniques, as research incorporating both qualitative and quantitative approaches may offer complementary knowledge. In sum, there is still a need to develop policy, especially focused at the individual level to support university spin-offs.

References

Ahuja, G., and Katila, R. (2004). Where do resources come from? The role of idiosyncratic situations. *Strategic Management Journal*, **25** (8–9), 887–907.

Amoroso, S., Audretsch, D. B., and Link, A. N. (2018). Sources of knowledge used by entrepreneurial firms in the European high-tech sector. *Eurasian Business Review*, **8** (1), 55–70.

Association of University Technology Managers (AUTM) (2013). *The AUTM Licensing Survey, Fiscal Year 2012*. Norwalk, CT: AUTM, Inc.

Audretsch, D. B., Lehmann, E. E., and Paleari S. (2015). Academic policy and entrepreneurship: a European perspective. *Journal of Technology Transfer*, **40** (3), 363–8.

Audretsch, D. B., Lehmann, E. E., Meoli, M., and Vismara, S. (2016). *University Evolution, Entrepreneurial Activity and Regional Competitiveness*. Springer International Publishing.

Autio, E., Kenney, M., Mustar, P., Siegel, D., and Wright, M. (2014). Entrepreneurial innovation: the importance of context. *Research Policy*, **43** (7), 1097–108.

Barbero, J. L., Casillas, J. C., Wright, M., and Garcia, A. R. (2014). Do different types of incubators produce different types of innovations? *Journal of Technology Transfer*, **39** (2), 151–68.

Barr, S. H., Baker, T. E. D., Markham, S. K., and Kingon, A. I. (2009). Bridging the valley of death: lessons learned from 14 years of commercialization of technology education. *Academy of Management Learning & Education*, **8** (3), 370–88.

Bathelt, H., Kogler, D. F., and Munro, A. K. (2011). Social foundations of regional innovation and the role of university spin-offs: the case of Canada's Technology Triangle. *Industry and Innovation*, **18** (5), 461–86.

Battilana, J., Leca, B., and Boxenbaum, E. (2009). 2 How actors change institutions: towards a theory of institutional entrepreneurship. *Academy of Management Annals*, **3** (1), 65–107.

Bercovitz, J., and Feldman, M. (2008). Academic entrepreneurs: organizational change at the individual level. *Organization Science*, **19** (1), 69–89.

Bercovitz, J., and Feldman, M. (2011). The mechanisms of collaboration in inventive teams: composition, social networks, and geography. *Research Policy*, **40** (1), 81–93.

Bjørnåli, E. S., and Aspelund, A. (2012). The role of the entrepreneurial team and the board of directors in the internationalization of academic spin-offs. *Journal of International Entrepreneurship*, **10** (4), 350–77.

Bonardo, D., Paleari, S., and Vismara, S. (2011). Valuing university-based firms: the effects of academic affiliation on IPO performance. *Entrepreneurship Theory and Practice*, **35** (4), 755–76.

Bozeman, B., Fay, D., and Slade, C. P. (2013). Research collaboration in universities and academic entrepreneurship: the-state-of-the-art. *Journal of Technology Transfer*, **38** (1), 1–67.

Cattaneo, M., Meoli, M., and Vismara, S. (2015). Cross-border M&As of biotech firms affiliated with internationalized universities. *Journal of Technology Transfer*, **40** (3), 409–33.

Civera, A., & Meoli, M. (2018). Does university prestige foster the initial growth of academic spin-offs?. *Economia e Politica Industriale*, **45** (2), 111–42.

Civera, A., Meoli, M., and Vismara, S. (2017). Policies for the provision of finance to science-based entrepreneurship. *Annals of Science and Technology Policy*, **1** (4), 317–469.

Civera, A., Donina, D., Meoli, M., & Vismara, S. (2019), Fostering the creation of academic spinoffs: does the international mobility of the academic leader matter? *International Entrepreneurship and Management Journal*, 1–27. DOI: 10.1007/s11365-019-00559-8.

Civera, A., Meoli, M., and Vismara, S. (2018) Do academic spinoffs internationalize? *Journal of Technology Transfer*, 1–23.

Clarysse, B., Wright, M., Lockett, A., Van de Velde, E., and Vohora, A. (2005). Spinning out new ventures: a typology of incubation strategies from European research institutions. *Journal of Business Venturing*, **20** (2), 183–216.

Colombo, M. G., Meoli, M., and Vismara, S. (2019). Signalling in science-based IPOs: the combined effect of affiliation with prestigious universities, underwriters, and venture capitalists. *Journal of Business Venturing*, **34** (1), 141–77.

Degroof, J. J., and Roberts, E. B. (2004). Overcoming weak entrepreneurial infrastructures for academic spin-off ventures. *Journal of Technology Transfer*, **29** (3–4), 327–52.

Di Gregorio, D., and Shane, S. (2003). Why do some universities generate more start-ups than others? *Research Policy*, **32** (2), 209–27.

Djokovic, D., and Souitaris, V. (2008). Spinouts from academic institutions: a literature review with suggestions for further research. *Journal of Technology Transfer*, **33** (3), 225–47.

Donina, D., Meoli, M., and Paleari, S. (2015). Higher education reform in Italy: tightening regulation instead of steering at a distance. *Higher Education Policy*, **28**, 215–34.

Edler, J., Fier, H., and Grimpe, C. (2011). International scientist mobility and the locus of knowledge and technology transfer. *Research Policy*, **40** (6), 791–805.

Fini, R., Grimaldi, R., and Sobrero, M. (2009). Factors fostering academics to start up new ventures: an assessment of Italian founders' incentives. *Journal of Technology Transfer*, **34** (4), 380–402.

Franco-Leal, N., Soetanto, D., and Camelo-Ordaz, C. (2016). Do they matter? The role of non-academics in the internationalization of academic spin-offs. *Journal of International Entrepreneurship*, **14** (3), 410–40.

Fritsch, M., Kritikos, A., and Pijnenburg, K. (2015). Business cycles, unemployment and entrepreneurial entry – evidence from Germany. *International Entrepreneurship and Management Journal*, **11** (2), 267–86.

Greenberg, J. (1987). A taxonomy of organizational justice theories. *Academy of Management Review*, **12** (1), 9–22.

Griliches, Z. (1992). Introduction to "output measurement in the service sectors." In Z. Griliches (ed.), *Output Measurement in the Service Sectors* (pp. 1–22). Chicago, IL: University of Chicago Press.

Grimaldi, R., Kenney, M., Siegel, D. S., and Wright, M. (2011). 30 years after Bayh–Dole: reassessing academic entrepreneurship. *Research Policy*, **40** (8), 1045–57.

Honig, B., and Karlsson, T. (2004). Institutional forces and the written business plan. *Journal of Management*, **30** (1), 29–48.

Horta, H., Meoli, M., and Vismara, S. (2016). Skilled unemployment and the creation of academic spin-offs: a recession-push hypothesis. *Journal of Technology Transfer*, **41** (4), 798–817.

Kenney, M., and Goe, W. R. (2004). The role of social embeddedness in professorial entrepreneurship: a comparison of electrical engineering and computer science at UC Berkeley and Stanford. *Research Policy*, **33** (5), 691–707.

Kenney, M., and Patton, D. (2005). Entrepreneurial geographies: support networks in three high-technology industries. *Economic Geography*, **81** (2), 201–28.

Krabel, S., Siegel, D. S., and Slavtchev, V. (2012). The internationalization of science and its influence on academic entrepreneurship. *Journal of Technology Transfer*, **37** (2), 192–212.

Lawton-Smith, H., Romeo, S., and Bagchi-Senb, S. (2008). Oxfordshire biomedical university spinoffs: an evolving system. *Cambridge Journal of Regions, Economy and Society*, **1** (2), 303–19.

Link, A. N. (2017). Assessing technology and innovation policies: introduction to the special issue. *Economics of Innovation and New Technology*. DOI: 10.1080/10438599.2017.1374035.

Ljungberg, D., and McKelvey, M. (2012). What characterizes firms' academic patents? Academic involvement in industrial inventions in Sweden. *Industry and Innovation*, **19** (7), 585–606.

Lowe, R. A. (2006). Who develops a university invention? The impact of tacit knowledge and licensing policies. *Journal of Technology Transfer*, **31** (4), 415–29.

Mair, J., Battilana, J., and Cardenas, J. (2012). Organizing for society: a typology of social entrepreneuring models. *Journal of Business Ethics*, **111** (3), 353–73.

Mars, M. M., and Rios-Aguilar, C. (2010). Academic entrepreneurship (re)defined: significance and implications for the scholarship of higher education. *Higher Education*, **59** (4), 441–60.

Meoli, M., and Vismara, S. (2016). University support and the creation of technology and non-technology academic spin-offs. *Small Business Economics*, **47** (2), 345–62.

Meoli, M., Paleari, S., and Vismara, S. (2013). Completing the technology transfer process: M&As of science-based IPOs. *Small Business Economics*, **40** (2), 227–48.

Meoli, M., Pierucci, E., and Vismara, S. (2018). The effects of public policies in fostering university spin-offs in Italy. *Economics of Innovation and New Technology*, **27** (5–6), 479–92.

Meoli, M., Paleari, S., and Vismara, S. (2019, forthcoming). The governance of universities and the establishment of academic spin-offs. *Small Business Economics*.

Mian, S. A. (1996). Assessing value-added contributions of university technology business incubators to tenant firms. *Research Policy*, **25** (3), 325–35.

Miranda, F. J., Chamorro, A., and Rubio, S. (2017). Re-thinking university spin-off: a critical literature review and a research agenda. *Journal of Technology Transfer*, **43** (4), 1007–38.

Mosey, S., and Wright, M. (2007). From human capital to social capital: a longitudinal study of technology-based academic entrepreneurs. *Entrepreneurship Theory and Practice*, **31** (6), 909–35.

Murray, F. (2004). The role of academic inventors in entrepreneurial firms: sharing the laboratory life. *Research Policy*, **33** (4), 643–59.

Mustar, P., Renault, M., Colombo, M. G., Piva, E., Fontes, M., Lockett, A., . . . and Moray, N. (2006). Conceptualising the heterogeneity of research-based spin-offs: a multi-dimensional taxonomy. *Research Policy*, **35** (2), 289–308.

Nelson, A. J. (2009). Measuring knowledge spillovers: what patents, licenses and publications reveal about innovation diffusion. *Research Policy*, **38** (6), 994–1005.

O'Shea, R., Allen, T. J., O'Gorman, C., and Roche, F. (2004). Universities and technology transfer: a review of academic entrepreneurship literature. *Irish Journal of Management*, **25** (2), 11.

Perkmann, M., Tartari, V., McKelvey, M., Autio, E., Broström, A., D'Este, P., . . . and Krabel, S. (2013). Academic engagement and commercialisation: a review of the literature on university–industry relations. *Research Policy*, **42** (2), 423–42.

Pettersen, I. B., and Tobiassen, A. E. (2012). Are born globals really born globals? The case of academic spin-offs with long development periods. *Journal of International Entrepreneurship*, **10** (2), 117–41.

Phan, P. H. (2014). The business of translation: the Johns Hopkins University discovery to market program. *Journal of Technology Transfer*, **39** (5), 809–17.

Rasmussen, E., Mosey, S., and Wright, M. (2011). The evolution of entrepreneurial competencies: a longitudinal study of university spin-off venture emergence. *Journal of Management Studies*, **48** (6), 1314–45.

Rothaermel, F. T., and Thursby, M. (2005). University–incubator firm knowledge flows: assessing their impact on incubator firm performance. *Research Policy*, **34** (3), 305–20.

Rothaermel, F. T., Agung, S. D., and Jiang, L. (2007). University entrepreneurship: a taxonomy of the literature. *Industrial and Corporate Change*, **16** (4), 691–791.

Siegel, D. S., and Wright, M. (2015a). Academic entrepreneurship: time for a rethink? *British Journal of Management*, **26** (4), 582–95.

Siegel, D. S., and Wright, M. (2015b). University technology transfer offices, licensing, and start-ups. In Al Link, Donald S. Siegel, and Mike Wright (eds.), *Chicago Handbook of University Technology Transfer and Academic Entrepreneurship* (pp. 1–40). Chicago, IL: University of Chicago Press.

Siegel, D. S., Westhead, P., and Wright, M. (2003). Assessing the impact of science parks on the research productivity of firms: exploratory evidence from the United Kingdom. *International Journal of Industrial Organization*, **21** (9), 1357–69.

Siegel, D. S., Veugelers, R., and Wright, M. (2007). Technology transfer offices and commercialization of university intellectual property: performance and policy implications. *Oxford Review of Economic Policy*, **23** (4), 640–60.

Sine, W. D., Shane, S., and Di Gregorio, D. (2003). The halo effect and technology licensing: the influence of institutional prestige on the licensing of university inventions. *Management Science*, **49** (4), 478–96.

Smith, S. W., and Hannigan, T. J. (2014). Home run, strike out, or base hit: how do accelerators impact exit and VC financing in new firms? In *Academy of Management Proceedings* (vol. 2014, no. 1, p. 13811). Academy of Management.

Stuart, T. E., and Ding, W. W. (2006). When do scientists become entrepreneurs? The social structural antecedents of commercial activity in the academic life sciences. *American Journal of Sociology*, **112** (1), 97–144.

Styles, C., and Genua, T. (2008). The rapid internationalization of high technology firms created through the commercialization of academic research. *Journal of World Business*, **43** (2), 146–57.

Thurik, A. R., Carree, M. A., van Stel, A. J., and Audretsch, D. B. (2008). Does self-employment reduce unemployment? *Journal of Business Venturing*, **23** (6), 673–86.

Thursby, M. C., Fuller, A. W., and Thursby, J. (2009). An integrated approach to educating professionals for careers in innovation. *Academy of Management Learning & Education*, **8** (3), 389–405.

Vanaelst, I., Clarysse, B., Wright, M., Lockett, A., Moray, N., and S'Jegers, R. (2006). Entrepreneurial team development in academic spinouts: an examination of team heterogeneity. *Entrepreneurship Theory and Practice*, **30** (2), 249–71.

Wang, J., and Shapira, P. (2012). Partnering with universities: a good choice for nanotechnology start-up firms? *Small Business Economics*, **38** (2), 197–215.

Wang, S. (2006). Determinants of new firm formation in Taiwan. *Small Business Economics*, **27**, 313–21.

Wennberg, K., Wiklund, J., and Wright, M. (2011). The effectiveness of university knowledge spillovers: performance differences between university spinoffs and corporate spinoffs. *Research Policy*, **40** (8), 1128–43.

Wright, M. (2011). Entrepreneurial mobility. In D. D. Bergh and D. J. Ketchen (eds.), *Building Methodological Bridges* (pp. 137–59). Bingley, UK: Emerald Group Publishing Limited.

Wright, M., Birley, S., and Mosey, S. (2004). Entrepreneurship and university technology transfer. *Journal of Technology Transfer*, **29** (3–4), 235–46.

Wright, M., Clarysse, B., Mustar, P., and Lockett, A. (2007). *Academic Entrepreneurship in Europe*. Cheltenham, UK and Northampton, MA, USA: Edward Elgar Publishing.

Wright, M., Clarysse, B., Lockett, A., and Knockaert, M. (2008). Mid-range universities' linkages with industry: knowledge types and the role of intermediaries. *Research Policy*, **37** (8), 1205–23.

Wright, M., Piva, E., Mosey, S., and Lockett, A. (2009). Business schools and academic entrepreneurship. *Journal of Technology Transfer*, **34** (6), 560–87.

Yusof, M., and Jain, K. K. (2010). Categories of university-level entrepreneurship: a literature survey. *International Entrepreneurship and Management Journal*, **6** (1), 81–96.

Zahra, S. A., Filatotchev, I., and Wright, M. (2009). How do threshold firms sustain corporate entrepreneurship? The role of boards and absorptive capacity. *Journal of Business Venturing*, **24** (3), 248–60.

Zucker, L. G., Darby, M. R., and Brewer, M. B. (1998). Intellectual human capital and the birth of US biotechnology enterprises. *American Economics Review*, **88** (1), 290–306.

5 Principal investigators and boundary spanning entrepreneurial opportunity recognition: a conceptual framework

James A. Cunningham

1. Introduction

National governments through relevant funding agencies are investing significant levels of public finance to grow their scientific, economic and technological capacities and capabilities. Such funding typically supports basic and applied research in national laboratories and or in university research centres or groups. Some of this public funding is also used to support commercialisation and technology transfer to industry (Cunningham and Harney, 2006). This in turn has seen the evolution and growth of university-based technology transfer offices to support the commercialisation of publicly funded research (see Geoghegan et al., 2015). Universities now have become more formally organised to respond to industry needs through technology transfer offices and other organisational structural means (see Geoghegan and Pontikakis, 2008).

Such investment in publicly funded research leads to direct and spillover benefits to firms as well as to the wider economy and society. Benefits can include increase in the stock of useful knowledge, creation of new knowledge and methodologies, stimulation and creation of new networks as associated social interactions, new venture creation, localisation effects and enhancement of problem-solving capabilities (see Martin and Tang, 2007). To illustrate such positive benefits of publicly funded science in the pharmaceutical industry Cockburn and Henderson (2000) note that "public sector science creates new knowledge and new tools, and produces large numbers of highly trained research, all which are a direct and important input to private sector research". Firms benefit from close research and development (R&D) collaboration with universities (Cunningham and Link, 2015). These benefits include increased R&D productivity (Link and Rees, 1990), economics of technological scope (Leyden and Link, 2013), new discoveries (Lee, 2000), and shared R&D expenditure (Sheehan and Wyckoff, 2003). Such collaboration and exploitation of public research through appropriate technology transfer mechanisms can provide firms with a distinct marketplace competitive advantage, as well as supporting their innovation strategies and ambitions. Firms also use universities as a source of innovation (Laursen and Salter, 2004). In sum, the new paradigm of public funded science is that it delivers multiple and multiplier benefits to different stakeholders. This is reflected in funding agencies' research programme funding calls and how research proposals are evaluated. Creation of scientific knowledge is just one aspect of public science that principal investigators (PIs) need to focus on, as the role has a multidimensional focus, given the heightened and demanding expectations surrounding publicly funded research.

The scientist in the PI role for publicly funded research is the instigator and is at the centre of the creation of new scientific knowledge which Chiesa and Piccaluga (2000) suggest is "considered the most important raw material for economic growth". The primary role and function of a PI for a large-scale publicly funded research programme is to provide the scientific leadership to a research team that may be located in different universities, public research labs' institutions and with industry partners to deliver the envisaged scientific results. To be the instigator the PI has to be able to spot and anticipate and respond to new opportunities in different domains through their boundary spanning activities. The emerging and growing body of literature and empirical studies of PIs highlight that the role of the PI is more complex than just fulfilling a primary role of scientific leadership and delivery (see Kidwell, 2013; Mangematin et al., 2014; Cunningham et al., 2017a). The new paradigm for publicly funded science means that PIs need to have a capability and capacity through their scientific leadership to create beneficial outcomes and value for multiple stakeholders (Cunningham et al., 2018). Cunningham et al. (2016c) define PIs "as scientists who orchestrate new research projects, combine resources and competencies, deepen existing scientific trajectories or shape new ones that are transformative in intent, nature and outcome that can be exploited for commercial ends and or for societal common good".

The purpose of this chapter is to explore some of the key factors that influence the boundary spanning entrepreneurial opportunity recognition of PIs through a conceptual framework. The chapter is structured as follows. Our first section focuses on PIs and current themes emerging from the literature and empirical studies. Our next section focuses on the conceptual model of boundary spanning opportunity recognition of PIs. The chapter concludes with a discussion of some areas of future research and implications.

2.   Principal investigators

2.1   Expectations

Within the entrepreneurship, innovation and strategic management fields there is a growing body of literature and empirical studies that is seeking to better understand how scientists in the PI shape and influence public science. This individual actor can as Cunningham et al. (2016c) argue transform public sector entrepreneurship programmes and is described as a 'linchpin' by Mangematin et al. (2014). The challenge facing scientists is best summed up by Ambos et al. (2008), as they are "not simply required to switch from one (single-handed) activity to another, but to develop the simultaneous capacity for two activities (academic rigor and commercialization)". When scientists take on the PI role by successfully applying for public funding to support their research, additional expectations and tensions emerge. Simultaneously, PIs have to balance academic rigour and commercialisation. Increasingly, PIs also have to consider societal and broader welfare issues along with academic rigour and commercialisation. In taking on the role of PI there is a benign or a more explicit expectation that they will be involved in the supporting entrepreneurship and innovation through their leadership role as a PI. For some publicly funded science programmes at the application stage, PIs have to state very explicitly in their proposal how are they going to deliver on entrepreneurship and innovation that benefits industry and society. This might include forming a spin-out company based on scientific knowledge, licensing technology to an industry partner or supporting new product development with an industrial partner, or knowledge transfer between university research environment to industrial partners. PIs also can position their proposal to demonstrate how supporting their scientific trajectory through public funding can provide underpinning scientific support to the economic vibrancy, productivity and international competitiveness of a cluster of firms in a sector in their locale. In essence, to be an effective publicly funded PI, Cunningham et al. (2016c) argue that they are:

> required to have the ambidextrous qualities that enable them to lead highly complex and technically advanced research programmes while having the dexterity to simultaneously manage a set of relationships that extends to their institution, industry partners, research funders, government agencies, and research team members.

This also would suggest that to manage this complexity an ability of PIs is to identify potential boundary spanning opportunities that can create value for multiple stakeholders.

2.2 Tensions and governance

In taking on the role of PI for publicly funded science research programmes tensions do emerge that have implications for the exploitation of entrepreneurial opportunity recognition. Based on empirical studies of PIs to date, some key tensions have been identified by Cunningham et al. (2016c) and Mangematin et al. (2014) that focus on science versus other activities and impacts, governance, professional development and preparedness for the role. A core tension and challenge for the PI is how to appropriately balance focusing and delivering on the scientific research programme in a publicly funded programme against the economic and societal impacts that are expected. If a PI is not able to achieve this appropriate balance this means that the entrepreneurship- and innovation-related outcomes are not fully realised to end beneficiaries such as firms. If PIs can realise entrepreneurship- and innovation-related outcomes this can further enhance their individual reputation among funding agencies, their own institution and firms. Moreover, this in turn provides the PI with further tangible evidence of capability and competence with respect to innovation and entrepreneurship outcomes that can be used to support further public funding applications.

Being a PI comes with governance responsibilities that are usually set out by the funding agencies as well as complying with the governance arrangement in place in their own institution. These typically cover budgetary, employment, research ethics and control issues and set out how the PI governs and reports to the funding agency on the progress of the funded project against a detailed plan that has been peer evaluated and approved. Depending on the scale of the publicly funded research programme, the number of institutions and industry partners and their geographical spread, this adds even greater governance complexity. Previously publicly funded research was described as the "freest form of support" by Chubin and Hackett (1990) that supports research autonomy. However, the current public science research funding paradigm means that research programmes are aligned with national economic priorities and are designed to support industries and sectors of national economic competitive importance. This means that PIs have to contend with greater levels of administration that takes their main focus away from research leadership and orientates it towards research management (see Cunningham et al., 2014). Moreover, PIs have to manage multiple principal agent relationships with a variety of stakeholders while simultaneously creating value for each (Cunningham et al., 2017a). The project dynamics centred around governance tensions means that PIs can become more internally and narrowly focused on effectively managing the governance of the funded project. This can impede the realisation of stated and envisioned opportunities. This can result in the PI not identifying early enough or effectively entrepreneurial opportunities to dynamically exploit scientific knowledge for entrepreneurship and or innovation ends. Such an internally orientated focus can also mean that PIs could choose more expeditious approaches to exploiting the funded project for entrepreneurship and innovation ends to meet the short-term demands and expectations of funding agencies. This can be done at the expense of the overall long-term scientific and economic potential. Furthermore, such a narrow focus can inhibit PIs' ability to react effectively to recasting or shaping the envisaged opportunity, when industry partners' interest in publicly funded research project changes due to their business needs.

2.3   Role learning

Scientists in the PI role in essence learn on the job (Cunningham et al., 2014). The professional development they receive in their formative professional career prepares them to be effective researchers and scientists and provides very little formalised professional development for the managerial and leadership roles that are part of the PI role. However, their scientific and research training prepares them well for opportunity recognition in their scientific domain in terms of developing original knowledge. PIs may have little understanding or knowledge of entrepreneurship and innovation and how this relates to their scientific domains or how it works in practice. The deficit in professional development for the PI role means that they poorly understand the commercial potential of their scientific knowledge and discovery. Moreover, this deficit also means that PIs can be more reliant on their institution's support to help develop and support entrepreneurial opportunity recognition for the economic and societal arenas. This institutional support is also vital during the lifetime of publicly funded research projects for PIs with limited industry experience or professional support. However, as O'Kane et al. (2017) discovered, based on a study of New Zealand health scientists, PIs reported commercialisation training deficiencies. Similarly, Cunningham et al. (2014, 2015) also found a lack of professional development support and experiences among PIs in an Irish study centred on managerial, project management and human resource tasks. This lack of professional development support as well as institutional support can constrain the true benefits of publicly funded public science to key beneficiaries. This also limits the PIs' ability to realise the entrepreneurial opportunity recognition.

2.4   PI definitional challenges

In research and university environments there is a common and tactical understanding of who PIs are and what do they do among researchers and administrators. The emerging literature on PIs suggests that there are a variety of definitions of who PIs are and what do they do among funding agencies, national governments and universities (see Cunningham et al., 2014). O'Kane et al. (2017) describe PIs as "lead researchers on successful programme and project grants". What is evident is that PIs are research leaders, and taking on the role encompasses other activities and responsibilities. Casati and Genet (2014) argue that they take on more than scientific leadership in the role and that there is a dissonance between the descriptions of PIs and what they actually do in practice. Kidwell (2014) views PIs as being at "the forefront of new scientific knowledge" and Baglieri and Lorenzoni (2014) posit that PIs play a pivotal role in technology transfer on the user side. In discussing the findings of their study of PIs, Boehm and Hogan (2014) affirm the "entrepreneurial role of PIs in building and shaping networks", while Feeney and Welch (2014) emphasise the more prominent nature of the PI role. In practice and in the emerging literature on PIs there is some focus on the distinction made between the role of PI and co-PI. This distinction is put simply by Feeney and Welch (2014) as: "The primary responsibility for the conduct, completion and reporting on the research outlined in the proposal, while the co-PI has secondary responsibility. The PI has primary accountability to the grant agency, while the co-PI is primarily accountable to the PI." In essence, the co-PI provides a supporting role to the PI and this could be in respect to project management, people management, or leading a particular strand of research as part of the wider publicly funded research programme. While there are definitional challenges, what is clear is that becoming a PI as a scientist is based on a scientific competence and track record. This is an essential core requirement and can be demonstrated through traditional output means, such as journal publications, monographs, book chapters, journal editorial positions, etc. The extant literature on PIs and who they are suggests that scientists in the role are boundary spanners and have to be able to respond to opportunities with credible research programmes that meet multiple outcomes for different stakeholders. This would suggest that having entrepreneurial opportunity recognition beyond their scientific domain is essential.

2.5   Managerial responsibilities

In becoming a PI, the emerging empirical studies illustrate the nature of the responsibilities that are involved (Menter, 2016). In addition to scientific research tasks, an increased level of managerial responsibilities is required. Cunningham et al. (2015) found in a study of Irish PIs that they are: "heavily involved in the operational management of their projects and active in project compliance of their funding awards". These managerial responsibilities are usually outside the formation professionalisation experiences of PIs and it can be particularly challenging and complex dealing with the core managerial functions of a large-scale publicly funded project – planning, leading, organising and controlling. These managerial challenges for publicly funded research focus on project management, project adaptability and project network management (Cunningham et al., 2015). Moreover, in exploring gender differences Cunningham et al. (2017b) found that female PIs tend to be more internally project focused that male PIs. In essence, in order to effectively deliver large-scale public funding PIs need to be competent managers. This includes the research team, financial resources and stakeholders within and outside the institution.

2.6   Skills and capabilities

Leading publicly funded science in the PI role is demanding and challenging for scientists. Empirical studies to date on PIs, such as Cunningham et al. (2014), suggest that they learn on the job to become a PI and require multiple skills beyond being an excellent scientist. As Kidwell (2014) notes: "PIs must expand their roles and take on activities that are beyond the mere definition of a PI." This requires PIs to have or acquire skills and capabilities in order to lead effectively and to become a serial and high performing PI. Cunningham et al. (2017a) identify these skills and capabilities as researcher and scientific excellence; research leadership; managerial responsiveness; resource acquisition; envisioning, strategising and value creation, and posits that: "it is the PI's competency and experience that contributes to the efficient and effective value creation process". The ability to manage stakeholders in order to bridge, broker and navigate the divides between the research funding agencies, industry partners and end users is emerging from the literature as another key skill that PIs need to acquire (see Casati and Genet, 2014; Kidwell, 2014). Furthermore, the entrepreneurial skills and capabilities of individual PIs is evident, as Casati and Genet (2014) describe that it is the PIs that: "shape and 'enact' their environments by changing the boundaries of organizations and setting up new ones". Balgieri and Lorenzoni (2014) go even further by arguing that PIs with an end user focus: "exhibit superior capabilities in turning generic technology into several selected market application with no negative effective on their academic role". Both Casati and Genet (2014) and Mangematin et al. (2014) suggest that PIs act as scientific entrepreneurs, while Boehm and Hogan (2014) suggest that PIs are similar to entrepreneurs: "Not unlike the entrepreneurs, the PI has to be 'a jack of all trades', taking on the roles of project manager, negotiator, resource acquirer as well as the traditional academic role of Ph.D. supervision and mentoring." Each of these roles and activities requires distinct skills and capabilities. A clear finding from some empirical studies to date is that PIs need more enhanced dedicated institutional support and professional development in order to be effective in the PI role (see Cunningham et al., 2014).

2.7   PIs' entrepreneurial opportunity recognition

Within the entrepreneurship field, entrepreneurial opportunity and recognition has been the focus of much research interest (see Ardichvili and Cardozo, 2000; Singh 2001; Ardichvili et al., 2003; Baron, 2006). The innovation field also has focused on opportunity recognition that has centred on such issues as large-sized firms (Leifer et al., 2001; O'Connor and Rice, 2001), high-tech start-ups (Park, 2005); radical innovation (Rice et al., 2001) and lead users (Lettl et al., 2008). With respect to entrepreneurial opportunity recognition, Ardichvili and Cardozo (2000) argue based on their study that such opportunities are unearthed by entrepreneurs through recognition rather that "purposeful search", and an entrepreneurial aware-ness in addition to knowledge, social networks and an understanding of customers' problems contribute to entrepreneurial opportunity recognition. Ardichvili et al. (2003) also posit that the entrepreneur's personality traits also contribute to entre-preneurial opportunity recognition while Singh et al. (1999) suggest that an exten-sive personal social network is essential to leveraging the best possible insights necessary to support a new venture creation.

Within the emerging PI literature, opportunity recognition and the associated visioning has been the focus of some discussion. Romano et al. (2017) suggest that visioning is intertwined with the PIs' opportunity recognition. Its exploitation is equated with invention disclosure and academic patenting. Furthermore, Romano et al. (2017) argue that the opportunity recognition for PIs is industry focused. Based on their empirical study of PIs in France, Casati and Genet (2014) provide some insights into how PIs envision and shape science through four main prac-tices: focusing on the scientific discipline; innovating and problem solving; shaping new paradigms and models; and brokering science. They also posit that shaping and brokering practices are akin to "entrepreneurial activities". This would suggest that PIs need to be actively engaged in opportunity recognition and exploitation activities in order shape new scientific directions and to broker exploration and exploitation of scientific knowledge effectively with key stakeholders.

To create value for publicly funded science requires the PI to have strong sim-melian ties with key stakeholders to balance individual stakeholder self-interest and motives against that of the wider funded project (Cunningham et al., 2018). This means that PIs need to be attuned with the value motives of their project stakeholders coupled with the ability to be able to adapt to emerging research and marketing opportunities to meet the overall funded project value objectives as well as individual value objectives. This requires an understanding of the current and future value needs of stakeholders combined with the PIs' entrepreneurial opportunity recognition capability to shape and respond to specific public science funding calls or to shape existing public funding projects. As Casati and Genet (2014) state:

> Academic institutions need PIs with entrepreneurial capabilities to develop their activities within academia, to shape scientific avenues, to engage stakeholders and make sense to them . . . Shaping scientific field demands that they experiment, interact with a wider range of different partners (firms, policy makers and the society), and participate in the construction of meaning and theory.

Strategic posture and motives

Aligned to opportunity recognition is how do PIs position, respond and adopt to opportunities that arise in their environment? O'Kane et al. (2015), examining strategic posture and behaviour, identified four categories of strategic behaviours adopted by PIs – research designers, research adapter, research supporter and research pursuer. Moreover, O'Kane et al. (2015) also found that PIs are proactive and want to realise their long-term vision consistently to strategise and adopt non-conformist strategies. This would suggest that proactive PIs are consistently opportunity-seeking within their wider networks. At a fundamental level, PIs' opportunity recognition may be linked to their primary motivation to become a PI. Becoming a PI brings prestige to the individual scientist (see Cunningham et al., 2014; Romano et al., 2017). However, the primary motivations for becoming a PI are influenced by push factors – project dependencies and institutional pressures – and pull factors – control, career ambition and advancement, personal drive and ambition (see Cunningham et al., 2016a). Specific PI motivation factors add to the existing body of literature on scientists' motivations which centre on the prioritisation of new knowledge (see Merton, 1986). Becoming a PI gives a scientist control over the scientific direction that they wish to pursue and means that, as Cunningham et al. (2016a) note: "PIs were concerned that they would 'lose out' if they did not compete for publicly funded research and as such there could be a loss of scientific direction, influence and resources." The PI role provides status, an enhanced network and scientific knowledge that complements the boundary spanning entrepreneurial opportunity recognition they need to undertake in academic research funding and industry environments in order to be effective in the role. Through opportunity recognition the PI role means they can identify new opportunities that are relevant to creating value for multiple stakeholders (see Cunningham et al., 2018) to support their research ambitions as well as to appropriate the necessary resources through further funding proposals with the optimal research team and industry partners.

In studying senior R&D managers and team members Wang et al. (2013) found that entrepreneurial opportunity recognition: "contributed significantly to individual-level innovation performance". An emerging theme from the literature on PIs and empirical studies is that PIs need to have a threshold knowledge and expertise in entrepreneurship and innovation in order to continue to secure ongoing public funding to pursue their research agenda. The PI role involves being a technology transfer agent and, through their boundary spanning activities, acting as a bridge between science and industry, and therein supporting the exploitation of scientific knowledge (Cunningham et al., 2016a). There is an expectation that through their research leadership of large-scale publicly funded projects, PIs pursue technology transfer based on the generated scientific knowledge. The technology transfer mechanisms and potential industrial recipients are typically described in a funding proposal that is evaluated through peer review and realised during or after project completion. In making a convincing and credible commercialisation case, the PI needs to align anticipated scientific outcomes with market opportunities that are refined and validated through boundary spanning entrepreneurial opportunity recognition. These market opportunities can be made with the support of an industry partner who seeks to exploit the scientific discovery through their own innovation strategy.

Irrespective of the commercialisation strategy outlined that exploits the entrepreneurship and innovation potential of the scientific discovery, PIs need to have the capacity and capability to demonstrate market shaping (see Mangematin et al., 2014). This is becoming a more common evaluation criteria for publicly funded science and, increasingly, membership of peer review panels includes relevant industry representatives. Therefore, the exploitation of publicly funded science as the core expected outcome is that the PI will create value and not destroy it, for multiple stakeholders in a simultaneous manner (Cunningham et al., 2018). The realisation of value creation is described by Cunningham et al. (2018) as:

> PIs that have created strong simmelian ties with other helix actors mobilise resources, capabilities and actors to address such public science calls. The informal activities that PIs have done such as networking and bridging activities with other helix actors such as the sharing of knowledge and expertise contributes to building strong simmelian ties and enables them to assemble the best possible group of helix actors to respond effectively to meeting the envisaged outcomes of public science research calls.

The ability of PIs to exploit scientific knowledge can also contribute to the growth of entrepreneurial ecosystems (see Cunningham et al., 2017a).

Enablers and barriers

In attempting to exploit scientific knowledge, PIs experience barriers to technology transfer. In collaborating with SMEs, O'Reilly and Cunningham (2017) found that PIs reported the importance of personal relationships, asset scarcity and proximity as enablers and barriers of technology transfer. More broadly, political, environmental, institutional and project-based factors also inhibit PIs (Cunningham et al., 2014). The implications of these inhibitors for PIs, as Cunningham et al. (2014) note, are that:

> based on the evidence from our study it can undermine scientists' prioritization of discovery and places even greater managerial and administrative constraints on the PI that

is not adequately supported ... However, the 'ethos of science' and the prioritization of discovery must be protected and nutured.

Furthermore, in their study of healthcare PIs in New Zealand, O'Kane et al. (2017) found that: "a lack of clarity on the expectations and review processes of funding bodies, as well as a lack of appropriate support and resources within the university, can deter PIs from initiating or completing commercialization activities". Their study also reported that PIs feel underprepared for the commercialisation process and that technology transfer offices (TTOs) lack the resources – particularly with respect to market analysis – to support their commercialisation efforts. Such findings also have implications for the time that PIs allocate to different activities of their publicly funded projects. PIs who allocated more time to research related activities allocated more of their time to technology transfer activities (see Cunningham et al., 2016b). For institutions, a clear finding emerges that they need to create environments where PIs can thrive (see Kidwell, 2014).

In summary, drawing from the extant literature and growing empirical studies of PIs it is evident that the role is complex, challenging and requires scientists to take on additional responsibilities and activities. PIs require an array of skills and capabilities to successfully fulfil the role. The PI role provides the control that is needed to drive scientific knowledge ambition. Boundary spanning is an essential element of the role, and having strong simmelian ties with industry and other stakeholders is critical to the success of individual PIs. The professional development of scientists means that they become expert at opportunity recognition in their scientific domain in terms of contributing new knowledge; the PI role means that they have to expand this expertise into other arenas and domains, hence the boundary spanning entrepreneurial opportunity recognition.

3.   PI entrepreneurial opportunity recognition: a conceptual model

The focus of this chapter is to explore some of the key factors that influence the boundary spanning entrepreneurial opportunity recognition of PIs through a conceptual framework. In developing this conceptual model there are two main category sources of influencing factors: antecedent and individual (see Figure 5.1). The antecedent factors have a broad shaping and influencing role for the individual scientist in the PI role or those who are considering becoming a PI through grant applications. Individual factors centre on the individual scientist, whereas commercialisation factors consider some of the mediating factors that will influence the technology transfer direction that individual PIs will pursue to exploit the entrepreneurial and innovation potential of their created scientific discovery.

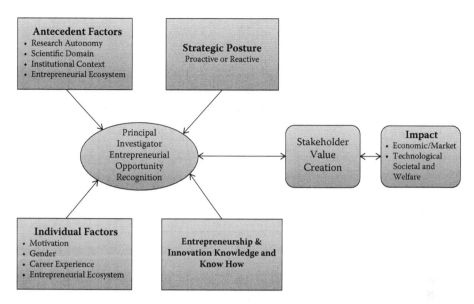

Figure 5.1   Principal investigator entrepreneurial opportunity recognition conceptual model

3.1   Antecedent factors

Research autonomy

Publicly funded research is considered the "freest from of support" (see Chubin and Hackett, 1990) and provides scientists with "structural holes" (see Burt, 2004) – the intellectual and research freedom – to pursue knowledge discovery. This is an essential element of entrepreneurial opportunity recognition. For PIs selecting research funding schemes – to focus their grant application and effort on – this is an important consideration in realising their scientific mission. For many scientific fields, particularly in the science, technology and engineering domains, there are a variety of funding instruments available that are publicly supported. Some of these schemes are designed to support specific research advancement coupled with clear economic and societal impact expectations. The individual scientist must consider what are the trade-offs he or she is willing to accept when it comes to securing some research autonomy that is necessary to realise the envisioned opportunity, as well as to further the scientific mission. In theory, publicly funded research traditionally provides greater levels of research autonomy for scientists in the PI role. This can be complemented effectively with the scientists' own entrepreneurial opportunity recognition focused on scientific and commercialisation arenas based on the potential for substantive knowledge discovery. The empirical studies on PIs to date would suggest this affirms some research autonomy and supports scientific opportunity recognition. However, the danger is that this is potentially being eroded and constrained due to the expanded and often prescriptive outcomes and beneficiary groups that are sought by public funding agencies administering public funds (Cunningham et al., 2014). The PI has to be able to manage to deliver on commercialisation objectives as well as scientific objectives and be able to manage the associated tensions and divisions that emerge around the publicly funded research programmes that they lead (see Nelson, 2004). This has forced scientists to reconceptualise what research autonomy for publicly funded science actually is, and how they position themselves through their career to be a successful serial PI. PIs also have to consider what actual trade-offs they have to make in order to satisfy growing stakeholder expectations and their own scientific mission.

Scientific domain

The norms and practices within scientific domains shape and influence the range of entrepreneurial opportunity recognition that scientists need to engage in as part of their role of being a PI. All scientific fields hone the research capabilities of individual scientists, particularly through the early formation career period. This capability is centred on the ability to recognise opportunity in the form of contributing original knowledge to a scientific domain. The doctoral process in the early career formation period provides a focal point in developing this essential research capability. This is then developed and refined further through the publication of scientific work such as journal papers, book chapters, monographs, etc. In some scientific domains in science, engineering and technology this opportunity recognition is expanded beyond the scientific arena. In order to conduct research, scientists need to secure funding and this requires them to extend their entrepreneurial opportunity recognition to the commercial and societal arenas. In essence, this pushes scientists in the PI role to consider how their original scientific knowledge can be used to support entrepreneurial opportunities for commercial and societal ends. This requires scientists – even those who are undertaking basic research – to consider value creation, and to consider who is going to benefit from their scientific discoveries. Moreover, the new norms for publicly funded research in science, technology and engineering domains require that individual PIs would be active and would have the capabilities to deliver scientific and commercialisation outcomes – spin-offs, licensing, etc. – as part of their publicly funded research programme. This can be a challenging expansion of entrepreneurial opportunity recognition for scientists who have honed their capabilities focused solely on the scientific arena. For other scientific domains such as the humanities and social sciences, the scientific opportunity recognition is centred on the scientific norms, with the commercialisation outcomes more focused on consultancy, contract research and societal impacts (see Olmos-Peñuela et al., 2014).

Institutional context

Several studies of PIs to date (Boehm and Hogan, 2014; Casati and Genet, 2014; Cunningham et al., 2014; Del Giudice et al 2017; Kidwell, 2014) have highlighted the importance of the institutional context for the individual PI. The institutional supports – formal and informal – that PIs draw on to deliver scientific, commercialisation and societal outcomes influence their strategic behaviours with respect to entrepreneurial opportunity recognition and ultimately their participation in publicly funded research. Findings from these studies highlight the frustrations PIs experience in dealing with their institutions, particularly with respect to technology transfer, human resources and finance. The available rather than the notional institutional context supports and influences the nature and extent of the entrepreneurial opportunities that PIs will pursue. This may lead to situations where PIs informally exploit scientific discovery through the back door, rather than through the formal institutional channels (see Markman et al., 2005). Therefore, institutions need to consider carefully how they actually support a scientist pre-becoming a PI and when they are in a PI role in to order to avoid sub-optimal outcomes for the individual scientist and the publicly funded project. The institutional context can enable and inhibit the activities and roles that scientists need to undertake in the PI capacity to fulfill and further develop their opportunity recognition scope and ambition. Kidwell (2014) best sums this up as:

Based on these findings, PIs are looking for an environment where their work is recognized and appropriately supported (by the technology transfer offices in particular) and where these and tenure committees are cognizant about the goals of the PI when considering their careers and those of their students and team members. There are also indications that training programs along these boundary lines might be helpful for researchers, in particularly around IP strategy and the implications of developing IP in sponsored research agreements.

Entrepreneurial ecosystem

While there has been some criticism of the entrepreneurial ecosystem (see Stam and Spigel, 2016; Alvedalen and Boschma, 2017; Audretsch et al. 2018), the scientists' engagement with other actors and supporting institutions within an entrepreneurial ecosystem can further enhance their entrepreneurial opportunity recognition capacity. Given the new norms associated with publicly funded research, wider engagement is essential to enhancing boundary spanning opportunity recognition. This enables a PI to select and mobilise a wider community within an entrepreneurial ecosystem to support his or her conceptualised opportunity in order to secure competitive public funding. This also provides the PI with insights into the value drivers and motives of potential collaborators and this can also support putting in place effective governance systems for the funded research programme (Cunningham et al., 2017a; Cunningham et al., 2018). Proximity and access to industry partners, levels of firm-level R&D investment, and access to a variety of sources of funding and human capital provides access to the resources and capabilities that scientists need to mobilise and engage with in order to support their scientific discovery in the PI role.

3.2   Individual factors

Motivation

Several studies have been undertaken on what motivates scientists (see Melin, 2000; Sauermann et al., 2010). The only study of what motives a scientist to become a PI to date found that one of the main motivational factors was control, as Cunningham et al. (2016a) note: "PIs were more confident that a proposal would get funded if it was under their stewardship, and obviously for reputational reasons were keen to keep a healthy 'success rate'." This is additional to the underlying motivation of knowledge discovery. To pursue boundary spanning entrepreneurial opportunities, and with a dependency on other actors to be successful, PIs have to retain and gain control. Applying for and leading publicly funded research programmes is a necessary approach for PIs to realise boundary spanning opportunity recognition. Maintaining control over their long-term scientific mission and objectives is essential to realise this.

Gender

Studies on the role of gender with respect to opportunity recognition in the entrepreneurship field such as that of DeTienne and Chandler (2007): "found that women and men utilise their unique stocks of human capital to identify opportunities and that they use fundamentally different processes of opportunity identification". The only study of gender differences between male and female PIs to date, set in an Irish context, found no significant differences with respect to commercialisation and impact (Cunningham et al., 2017b) and suggested that there is a need to conduct further empirical studies on this theme. Research on gender differences among scientists on issues such as family characteristics, scientific productivity, career stage, patenting (see Bordons et al., 2003; Fisher, 2005; Fox, 2005; Ding et al., 2006; Borrego et al., 2010) have relevant implications and considerations for scientists in the PI role. Consequently, the logical follow-on assumption is that gender differences may influence and shape boundary spanning opportunities of male and female PIs that are used to develop scientific knowledge supported by publicly funded research. Moreover, gender difference may also influence the commercialisation choices made by male and female PIs with respect to entrepreneurship and innovation.

Career experience

The career experience of PIs contributes to boundary spanning opportunity recognition (Cunningham et al., 2014; Cunningham et al., 2017b). In particular, Cunningham et al. (2017b: 239) note that "Male PIs had nearly worked on average as long in commercial organisations compared to female PIs." Kidwell (2014), drawing on research of scientists' careers, posits that: "PIs are activity managing their careers through carefully chosen paths and developing research agendas out of those experiences." It is these career experiences in different organisational settings that can enhance the capacity of the PI for boundary spanning opportunity recognition. In situations where PIs have exclusively academic and research experience in a university or public research organisation, while this may be considered a constraint in terms of broader opportunity recognition it can be mitigated by their engagement and interaction with industry partners. Experience in different organisational environments will broaden and hone the boundary spanning entrepreneurial opportunity recognition that is necessary at an individual level to consistently generate the originality that is required to be a serial PI.

The other factors that influence entrepreneurial opportunity recognition of PIs is their strategic posture – reactive or proactive – and entrepreneurship and innovation knowledge and know how. Given the boundary spanning nature of the PI role, scientists through their interaction with industry partners, technology transfer offices etc they are acquiring new knowledge about entrepreneurship and innovation particularly with respect to processes, practices and approaches. This in turn can influence the manner in which they respond and deal with opportunities that arise in their domain area. In summary, collectively these factors contribute to entrepreneurial opportunity recognition of PIs that in turn contributes to stakeholder value creation and ultimately to impact.

4.   Some concluding thoughts

This chapter outlines some of the key factors that influence the boundary spanning entrepreneurial opportunity recognition of PIs through a conceptual framework against the backdrop of the growing body of literature and empirical studies of PIs. There is a need for this conceptual framework to be tested and other factors identified as this goes to the heart of originality and novelty in publicly funded science. While there may be a tacit and an intuitive understanding of how PIs generate ideas that are novel and original there is a need for studies using different methodological approaches in order to better understand how this is generated through boundary spanning entrepreneurial opportunity recognition. This requires an interdisciplinary approach, and such empirical studies can contribute in a significant way to help shape the actual professional and formational support of scientists in the PI role in order to be effective given the increasing demands and challenges that they face in the role. Conducting studies across different scientific domains and organisational setting (universities, public and private research organisations) is essential. There are also opportunities to further understand how boundary spanning entrepreneurial opportunity recognition contributes to economic, technological and societal impacts. Measuring this is challenging but necessary in further providing robust empirical evidence of the significant and multidimensional contributions scientists in the PI role make to creating value for different stakeholders. Examining where boundary spanning entrepreneurial opportunity recognition fails to deliver the expected impacts is worthy of further studies as the focus to date has been on examining successful PIs and projects. In reality, not all publicly funded science projects deliver on the desired outcomes and impacts given the unpredictable nature of scientific discovery and rapidly changing market conditions. This impacts on individual PIs, and understanding how they cope with such project failure is worth examining given the significance of the role they play in stimulating and driving scientific discovery. Scientists in the PI role have a transformative function in universities and publicly funded research labs and what they achieve in terms of scientific discoveries tends to be invisible to wider society. This is a first step to beginning to examine one of the core dimensions of publicly funded science – that is the generation of novelty and originality through boundary spanning entrepreneurial recognition.

Acknowledgement

The author wishes to acknowledge the funding support of Science Foundation Ireland (SFI) and co-funding under the European Regional Development Fund under Grant Number 13/RC/2073.

References

Alvedalen, J., and Boschma, R. (2017), 'A critical review of entrepreneurial ecosystems research: towards a future research agenda'. *European Planning Studies*, **25** (6), 887–903.

Ambos, T., Makela, K., Birkinshaw, J. and D'Este, P. (2008), 'When does university research get commercialized? Creating ambidexterity in research institutions'. *Journal of Management Studies*, **45**, 1425–47.

Ardichvili, A., and Cardozo, R. N. (2000), 'A model of the entrepreneurial opportunity recognition process'. *Journal of Enterprising Culture*, **8** (2), 103–19.

Ardichvili, A., Cardozo, R., and Ray, S. (2003), 'A theory of entrepreneurial opportunity identification and development'. *Journal of Business Venturing*, **18** (1), 105–23.

Audretsch, D. B., Cunningham, J. A., Kuratko, D. F., Lehmann, E. E., and Menter, M. (2018), 'Entrepreneurial ecosystems: economic, technological, and societal impacts'. *The Journal of Technology Transfer*, 1–13.

Baglieri, D., and Lorenzoni, G. (2014), 'Closing the distance between academia and market: experimentation and user entrepreneurial processes'. *The Journal of Technology Transfer*, **39** (1), 52–74.

Baron, R. A. (2006), 'Opportunity recognition as pattern recognition: how entrepreneurs "connect the dots" to identify new business opportunities'. *The Academy of Management Perspectives*, **20** (1), 104–19.

Boehm, D., and Hogan, T. (2014), '"A jack of all trades": the role of PIs in the establishment and management of collaborative networks in scientific knowledge commercialisation'. *The Journal of Technology Transfer*, **39** (1), 134–49.

Bordons, M., Morillo, F., Fernández, M. T., and Gómez, I. (2003), 'One step further in the production of bibliometric indicators at the micro level: differences by gender and professional category of scientists'. *Scientometrics*, **57** (2), 159–73.

Borrego, Á., Barrios, M., Villarroya, A., and Ollé, C. (2010), 'Scientific output and impact of postdoctoral scientists: a gender perspective'. *Scientometrics*, **83** (1), 93–101.

Burt, R. S. (2004), 'Structural holes and good ideas'. *American Journal of Sociology*, **110** (2), 349–99.

Casati, A., and Genet, C. (2014), 'Principal investigators as scientific entrepreneurs'. *The Journal of Technology Transfer*, **39** (1), 11–32.

Chiesa, V., and Piccaluga, A. (2000), 'Exploitation and diffusion of public research: the case of academic spin-off companies in Italy'. *R&D Management*, **30** (4), 329–40.

Chubin, D. E., and Hackett, E. J. (1990), *Peerless Science: Peer Review and US Science Policy*, SUNY Press: New York.

Cockburn, I. M., and Henderson, R. M. (2000), 'Publicly funded science and the productivity of the pharmaceutical industry'. *Innovation Policy and the Economy*, **1**, 1–34.

Cunningham, J., and Harney, B. (2006), *Strategic Management of Technology Transfer: A New Challenge on Campus*, Oak Tree Press: Cork, Ireland.

Cunningham, J., O'Reilly, P., O'Kane, C., and Mangematin, V. (2014), 'The inhibiting factors that principal investigators experience in leading publicly funded research'. *Journal of Technology Transfer*, **39** (1), 93–110.

Cunningham, J. A., and Link, A. N. (2015), 'Fostering university-industry R&D collaborations in European Union countries'. *International Entrepreneurship and Management Journal*, **11** (4), 849–60.

Cunningham, J. A., O'Reilly, P., O'Kane, C., and Mangematin, V. (2015), 'Managerial challenges of publicly funded principal investigators'. *International Journal of Technology Management*, **68** (3–4), 176–202.

Cunningham, J. A., Mangematin, V., O'Kane, C., and O'Reilly, P. (2016a), 'At the frontiers of scientific advancement: the factors that influence scientists to become or choose to become publicly funded principal investigators'. *The Journal of Technology Transfer*, **41** (4), 778–97.

Cunningham, J. A., O'Reilly, P., Dolan, B., O'Kane, C., and Mangematin, V. (2016b), 'Publicly funded principal investigators allocation of time for public sector entrepreneurship activities'. *Economia e Politica Industriale*, **43** (4), 383–408.

Cunningham, J. A., O'Reilly, P., O'Kane, C., and Mangematin, V. (2016c), 'Publicly funded principal investigators as transformative agents of public sector entrepreneurship'. In David Audretsch and Albert N. Link (eds), *Essays in Public Sector Entrepreneurship*, pp. 67–94, Springer: Cham, Switzerland.

Cunningham, J. A., Menter, M., and Wirsching, K. (2017a), Entrepreneurial ecosystem governance: a principal investigator-centered governance framework'. *Small Business Economics*, 1–18.

Cunningham, J. A., O'Reilly, P., Dolan, B., O'Kane, C., and Mangematin, V. (2017b), 'Gender different and academic entrepreneurship: a study of scientists in the principal investigator role'. In Albert N. Link (ed.), *Gender and Entrepreneurial Activity*, pp. 221–51, Edward Elgar: Cheltenham, UK and Northampton, MA, USA.

Cunningham, J. A., Menter, M., and O'Kane, C. (2018), 'Value creation in the quadruple helix: a micro level conceptual model of principal investigators as value creators'. *R&D Management*, **48** (1), 136–47.

Del Giudice, M., Nicotra, M., Romano, M., and Schillaci, C. E. (2017), 'Entrepreneurial performance of principal investigators and country culture: relations and influences'. *The Journal of Technology Transfer*, **42** (2), 320–37.

DeTienne, D. R., and Chandler, G. N. (2007), 'The role of gender in opportunity identification'. *Entrepreneurship Theory and Practice*, **31** (3), 365–86.

Ding, W. W., Murray, F., and Stuart, T. E. (2006), 'Gender differences in patenting in the academic life sciences'. *Science*, **313** (5787), 665–7.

Feeney, M. K., and Welch, E. W. (2014), 'Academic outcomes among principal investigators, co-principal investigators, and non-PI researchers'. *The Journal of Technology Transfer*, **39** (1), 111–33.

Fisher, R. L. (2005), *The Research Productivity of Scientists: How Gender, Organization Culture, and the Problem Choice Process Influence the Productivity of Scientists*, University Press of America: Lanham, MD.

Fox, M. F. (2005). 'Gender, family characteristics, and publication productivity among scientists', *Social Studies of Science*, **35** (1), 131–50.

Geoghegan, W., and Pontikakis, D. (2008), 'From ivory tower to factory floor? How universities are changing to meet the needs of industry'. *Science and Public Policy*, **35** (7), 462–74.

Geoghegan, W., O'Kane, C., and Fitzgerald, C. (2015), 'Technology transfer offices as a nexus within the triple helix: the progression of the university's role'. *International Journal of Technology Management*, **68** (3–4), 255–77.

Kidwell, D. K. (2013), 'Principal investigators as knowledge brokers: a multiple case study of the creative actions of PIs in entrepreneurial science'. *Technological Forecasting and Social Change*, **80** (2), 212–20.

Kidwell, D. (2014), 'Navigating the role of the principal investigator: a comparison of four cases'. *The Journal of Technology Transfer*, **39** (1), 33–51.

Laursen, K., and Salter, A. (2004), 'Searching high and low: what types of firms use universities as a source of innovation?' *Research Policy*, **33** (8), 1201–15.

Lee, Y. (2000), 'The sustainability of university-industry research collaboration: an empirical assessment'. *Journal of Technology Transfer*, **25** (2), 111–31.

Leifer, R., O'connor, G. C., and Rice, M. (2001), 'Implementing radical innovation in mature firms: the role of hubs'. *The Academy of Management Executive*, **15** (3), 102–13.

Lettl, C., Hienerth, C., and Gemuenden, H. G. (2008), 'Exploring how lead users develop radical innovation: opportunity recognition and exploitation in the field of medical equipment technology'. *IEEE Transactions on Engineering Management*, **55** (2), 219–33.

Leyden, D. P., and Link, A. N. (2013), 'Knowledge spillovers, collective entrepreneurship, and economic growth: the role of universities'. *Small Business Economics*, **41**, 797–817.

Link, A. N., and Rees, J. (1990), 'Firm size, university-based research, and the returns to R&D'. *Small Business Economics*, **2**, 25–31.

Mangematin, V., O'Reilly, P., and Cunningham, J. (2014), 'PIs as boundary spanners, science and market shapers'. *The Journal of Technology Transfer*, **39** (1), 1–10.

Markman, G. D., Phan, P. H., Balkin, D. B., and Gianiodis, P. T. (2005), 'Entrepreneurship and university-based technology transfer'. *Journal of Business Venturing*, **20** (2), 241–63.

Martin, B. R., and Tang, P. (2007), 'The benefits from publicly funded research'. Science Policy Research Unit, University of Sussex.

Melin, G. (2000), 'Pragmatism and self-organization: research collaboration on the individual level'. *Research Policy*, **29** (1), 31–40.

Menter, M. (2016), 'Principal investigators and the commercialization of knowledge'. In D. B. Audretsch, E. Lehmann, M. Meoli, and S. Vismara (eds), *University Evolution, Entrepreneurial Activity and Regional Competitiveness*, pp. 193–203. Springer: Cham, Switzerland.

Merton, R. K. (1986 [1942]), 'The ethos of science'. In R. K. Merton, *On Social Structure and Science*. University of Chicago Press: Chicago, IL.

Nelson, R. R. (2004), 'The market economy, and the scientific commons'. *Research Policy*, **33** (3), 455–71.

O'Connor, G. C., and Rice, M. P. (2001), 'Opportunity recognition and breakthrough innovation in large established firms'. *California Management Review*, **43** (2), 95–116.

O'Kane, C., Cunningham, J., Mangematin, V., and O'Reilly, P. (2015), 'Underpinning strategic behaviours and posture of principal investigators in transition/uncertain environments'. *Long Range Planning*, **48** (3), 200–14.

O'Kane, C., Zhang, J. A., Cunningham, J. A., and O'Reilly, P. (2017), 'What factors inhibit publicly funded principal investigators' commercialization activities?' *Small Enterprise Research*, **24** (3), 215–32.

Olmos-Peñuela, J., Castro-Martínez, E., and D'Este, P. (2014), 'Knowledge transfer activities in social sciences and humanities: explaining the interactions of research groups with non-academic agents'. *Research Policy*, **43** (4), 696–706.

O'Reilly, P., and Cunningham, J. A. (2017), 'Enablers and barriers to university technology transfer engagements with small-and medium-sized enterprises: perspectives of Principal Investigators'. *Small Enterprise Research*, **24** (3), 274–89.

Park, J. S. (2005), 'Opportunity recognition and product innovation in entrepreneurial hi-tech start-ups: a new perspective and supporting case study'. *Technovation*, **25**(7), 739–52.

Rice, M., Kelley, D., Peters, L., and Colarelli O'Connor, G. (2001), 'Radical innovation: triggering initiation of opportunity recognition and evaluation'. *R&D Management*, **31** (4), 409–20.

Romano, M., Elita Schillaci, C., and Nicotra, M. (2017), 'Principal investigators in entrepreneurial universities: a research framework'. In James A. Cunningham, Maribel Guerrero, and David Urbano (eds), *The World Scientific Reference on Entrepreneurship. Volume 1: Entrepreneurial Universities, Technology and Knowledge Transfer*, pp. 165–84, World Scientific Publishing: Singapore.

Sauermann, H., Cohen, W., and Stephan, P. (2010), 'Doing well or doing good? The motives, incentives and commercial activities of academic scientists and engineers'. In *DRUID Summer Conference*, **200**, 16–18.

Sheehan, J., and Wyckoff, A. (2003), 'Targeting R&D: economic and policy complications of increasing R&D spending'. STI Working Paper 2003/8, Science and Innovation Unit, OECD, Paris.

Singh, R. P. (2001), 'A comment on developing the field of entrepreneurship through the study of opportunity recognition and exploitation'. *Academy of Management Review*, **26** (1), 10–12.

Singh, R. P., Hills, G. E., Lumpkin, G. T., and Hybels, R. C. (1999, August), 'The entrepreneurial opportunity recognition process: examining the role of self-perceived alertness and social networks'. In *Academy of Management Proceedings*, No. 1, August: G1–G6, Briarcliff Manor, NY 10510: Academy of Management.

Stam, E., and Spigel, B. (2016), 'Entrepreneurial ecosystems and regional policy'. In R. Blackburn, D. De Clercq, J. Heinonen, and Z. Wang (eds), *Sage Handbook for Entrepreneurship and Small Business*, SAGE: London.

Wang, Y. L., Ellinger, A. D., and Jim Wu, Y. C. (2013) 'Entrepreneurial opportunity recognition: an empirical study of R&D personnel'. *Management Decision*, **51** (2), 248–66.

6 The regional emergence of innovative start-ups: a research agenda[1]

Michael Fritsch[2]

1. Introduction

There is good reason to believe that innovative new businesses are of key importance for regional development (Schumpeter 1934; Fritsch 2011; Colombelli, Krafft and Vivarelli 2016). The huge variation in the number of such innovative start-ups across space clearly indicates that region-specific factors are important in this respect.[3] The role of regional conditions in the emergence of innovative new businesses is, however, still not well understood. What is mostly unclear is the effect of higher education institutions, of other public research institutes as well as of research and development (R&D) activities of incumbent firms. How is the knowledge of these organizations transferred to new businesses, and where are these new businesses located? What other local conditions may play a role? Valid responses to such questions are especially important for the design of policies that aim at stimulating the emergence of innovative start-ups, particularly policies that want to foster knowledge spillovers and improve the ability of academic institutions to positively impact the economy.

The following sections briefly summarize existing theory (section 2) and outline the key results of empirical research about the emergence and location of innovative start-ups (section 3). Section 4 derives a number of important research questions, and section 5 discusses research designs that are suited to provide answers to these questions. The final section (section 6) concludes. Since the focus of this contribution is on regional analyses, I will not discuss factors that may determine the emergence of innovative start-ups at the national level, such as the protection of intellectual property rights, administrative entry barriers, competition policy, labor market regulation, the tax regime, health insurance, etc. (see Feldman, Lanahan, and Miller 2011; Henrekson and Johansson 2011; Elert, Henrekson, and Stenkula 2017). Such regulations typically do not vary across the regions of a country, and an empirical analysis of their effect requires international comparisons.

---

1 I am indebted to Alina Sorgner, Michael Stuetzer, and Michael Wyrwich for helpful comments on an earlier version of this chapter.

2 Friedrich Schiller University Jena, School of Economics and Business Administration, Carl-Zeiss-Str. 3, 07743 Jena, Germany. m.fritsch@uni-jena.de; www.m-fritsch.de. ORCID 0000-0003-0337-4182.

3 See, for example, Bonaccorsi et al. (2014) and Colombelli (2016) for Italy, and Audretsch. Lehmann. and Warning (2005) and Fritsch and Aamoucke (2013, 2017) for Germany.

2.   The emergence and location of innovative start-ups: theory

The theory of occupational choice (Lucas 1978; for an overview see Parker 2018) suggests that someone will start their own business if he or she expects higher returns in self-employment than in paid employment. Based on this notion, the decision to start a business does not just depend on a person's entrepreneurial abilities, but on the monetary and non-monetary benefits of applying personal knowledge and skills in self-employment instead of paid employment.

The knowledge spillover theory of entrepreneurship (Acs et al. 2009, 2013) builds on this basic calculus. The theory asserts that knowledge that is generated by incumbent firms, universities, non-university public research institutes, or other sources may empower someone to generate a business idea based on an innovation that he or she believes to be economically valuable. Since the economic value of new knowledge is highly uncertain, the expectations about the returns of any new idea will vary across economic agents. Hence, if an employee in a firm assigns a much higher economic value to a new idea than does the management of that firm, the employee may be motivated to start a business based on this idea because he or she expects higher returns in self-employment than in paid employment (Acs et al. 2009, 2013).

A main reason why an employee becomes the founder of a new innovative firm is that new knowledge and business ideas cannot be easily communicated or traded on a market. Hence, to start a firm may be the only feasible way to see the idea realized, which can represent a considerable non-pecuniary return of being self-employed. This motivation may particularly hold for research staff in universities and other public research organizations where legal restrictions for the commercialization of knowledge apply. Via spin-offs, knowledge of the incubator organization spills over to the newly founded firm, and, thus, the knowledge base of the incubator firm can have a significant effect on the number and the success of its spin-offs (Klepper 2009, 2016).

In this process of entrepreneurial knowledge spillover, the regional dimension is relevant for at least three reasons. First, new knowledge and ideas do not flow freely across space but tend to be regionally bounded (Asheim and Gertler 2006; Boschma 2005). Second, founders show a pronounced tendency to locate their firm in close spatial proximity to their former workplace, or their residence (Figueiredo, Guimaraes, and Woodward 2002; Dahl and Sorenson 2009). Hence, innovative entrepreneurship is, in most cases, a "regional event" (Feldman 2001; Sternberg 2009). Third, because entrepreneurship tends to be a regional event, the local conditions for entrepreneurship are important factors in the emergence and the success of innovative new businesses. This includes the regional knowledge stock, knowledge spillovers, as well as the availability of appropriate labor, finance, and other resources that the start-ups need to survive and grow. Market success and the growth of spin-offs can create agglomeration economies that may be conducive to their future performance (Klepper 2010, 2016; Boschma 2015). A fourth reason why region-specific factors can be important is that certain places may attract potential founders from other regions to settle down and eventually start a firm. Reasons why certain regions attract entrepreneurial people could be the existence of favorable conditions for innovative entrepreneurship, but it may also be other factors such as a climate of creativity and tolerance (Florida 2002; Florida, Adler, and Mellander 2017), or simply that it is the place "to be."

3.   What we know about the regional emergence of innovative start-ups

3.1   Identification of innovative start-ups

A key problem confronting empirical studies investigating the formation of innovative new businesses is the identification of this type of start-up. In order to qualify as a start-up, the respective economic entity must be a new organization, not just a takeover of an already existing company. Spin-offs that emerge from existing firms or research organizations should, of course, be classified as start-ups. In the broadest sense an innovative start-up is any new business that supplies new products, uses new methods of production, or accesses new markets of suppliers or customers (Schumpeter 1934). Applying such a broad definition of innovation leaves room for distinguishing between different types of innovation (e.g., product, process, organizational, procurement, and marketing innovation), as well as different degrees of innovativeness. According to such a wide definition, there may be countless varieties of innovative new businesses based on one or another category, or on the degree of "newness" introduced.

Since innovation is a process, the innovativeness of start-ups may be captured by information about their inputs or outputs. Input and output are, of course, linked, but the relationship tends to be fairly stochastic. Accordingly, there are some cases where innovative effort does not lead to any innovative output, and other cases where innovative output requires little significant innovative input in terms of R&D. Hence, using either measure of innovativeness involves considerable problems.

First, it is not entirely clear what types of inputs (in terms of effort or activities) should be considered R&D (OECD 2015). The innovativeness of an output (the product or the respective production process) involves the problem of assessing its newness.[4] Given that the key motivation for investigating and analyzing innovative start-ups is their effect on the economy, one may conclude that it is probably more appropriate to assess their innovativeness on the output side of the innovation process. However, because the problems of measuring innovative input tend to be

---

4   The European Community Innovation Survey (CIS) is a prominent example of an attempt to assess the innovativeness of innovation on the output side (OECD 2017). The underlying questionnaire asks for type of innovations (e.g., product, process, procurement, marketing), and their market scope (new to the market vs. new to the enterprise).

less severe than measuring innovative output, most classifications of innovative start-ups are based on information about the input side.

A common criterion to identify and classify the innovativeness of firms is based on the amount of resources that they devote to R&D. Accordingly, firms or industries are regarded as "innovative" if they devote more than 3.5 percent of their inputs to R&D, and they are considered to be high-tech if this share is more than 8.5 percent (OECD 2005, 166–71). Since information about the R&D input of individual firms is frequently not available, it is common practice to identify innovative businesses based on their industry affiliation. The OECD (2005) has proposed a widely accepted classification that is based on the knowledge requirements and R&D intensity of industries, as well as the innovativeness of their product programs. This classification distinguishes between "high-technology," "medium-high-technology," "medium-low-technology," and "low-technology" industries. While this typology is limited to manufacturing industries, it is common practice to also classify certain service sector industries as being "knowledge-intensive" (see, for example, Eurostat 2018).

Classifying an industry based on its innovativeness also has a number of problems. First, what may be a non-innovative product or industry in one country may be quite innovative in another. It may, therefore, be appropriate to adjust this classification to the specific characteristics of countries. Second, the innovativeness of industries and products may change over time and require respective adjustments. Third, industry affiliation is a rather fuzzy distinction because there are innovative and not so innovative firms in all industries. Hence, even a well-developed and up-to-date industry classification listing leads to a somewhat diffuse picture of innovative and non-innovative entries. Given the limited availability of data on innovation activity, this is, however, often the only feasible way to identify such new businesses, at least in aggregate level analyses.

Another criterion for the identification of innovative start-ups is their ability to attract venture capital (VC) (Azoulay et al. 2018; Breschi, Lassébie, and Menon 2018). VC is equity financing earmarked for promising young businesses. VC investors normally make a detailed assessment of the prospects of a project before they invest their money. Using this approach outsources the decision of what might or might not be considered innovative to VC firms. Since start-ups that receive VC should be of relatively high quality, especially with regard to their growth prospects and profitability, this approach is similar to assessing the output side of the innovation process. One weakness of using this approach to identify innovative start-ups is that it identifies only those new businesses that have good prospects for growth and profitability. Although one may expect a relatively pronounced role of these entries for economic development, other new businesses that may not appear to be so obviously promising, but may also make a significant contribution to growth, are completely disregarded. Another weakness is that, although high growth prospects and profitability frequently include an innovation in the broadest sense, firms that attract VC may not be particularly innovative. But, even if these start-ups are innovative, VC investment does not tell us anything about the type of innovation. Moreover, it is not entirely clear if VC firms prefer to invest in a certain venture simply because of the spatial proximity of the venture (Sorenson and Stuart 2001; Fritsch and Schilder 2008, 2012).

It may also be important to distinguish between VC originating from exclusively private firms and VC from public or semi-public financiers, because public investors frequently use different criteria for evaluating investments. Generally, private VC investors tend to be more interested in gaining a high return than public investors. Hence, private investors often offer more support and consulting in an attempt to make the firm more profitable and encourage growth. Another critical difference is that private VC firms are very hesitant to invest in the early stages of an innovative start-up, while public VC financing may have the purpose of supporting innovative start-ups during the early stages of business development (Lerner 2002; Grilli and Murtinu 2014).

A further way of identifying innovative new businesses is based on intellectual property rights, specifically patents, that are involved in a start-up (Azoulay et al. 2018; Breschi, Lassébie, and Menon 2018). Accordingly, a new business is regarded as innovative or knowledge intensive if the firm or its founder owns such property rights.[5] Again, there are several problems involved in such a definition. First, classifying only those start-ups as innovative that own intellectual property rights disregards many innovative firms that do not fulfill this criterion. Second, there are types of inventions that cannot be patented (e.g., basic research), and there are inventions for which patent protection may not be regarded as appropriate (Hall et al. 2014; Walter, Schmidt, and Walter 2011). Third, firms in the early stages of development may not have the financial resources to provide comprehensive protection for their intellectual property, or it may just appear to be too expensive to them.

Attempting to classify spin-offs from universities and other research institutes as innovative may hold for most firms founded by faculty, but it could be completely misleading by ignoring that start-ups by former students include many businesses such as medical practices, law offices, accounting firms, etc., that are knowledge intensive but not particularly innovative. Hence, more information about the nature of a business is needed in order to identify innovative university spin-offs.

3.2   The macro-level pattern

Empirical research that relates the number of innovative start-ups in a certain region to the specific characteristics of that region, has found pronounced correlations between the emergence of innovative new businesses and the level of private sector R&D activities (i.e., presence of innovative incumbent firms), as well as the

---

5 Since intellectual property rights, such as patents, constitute an intermediate result of an innovation process that can hardly be traded, they could be classified as an input as well as an output of the innovation process.

presence, size, and type of higher education institutions (HEIs).[6] Regions with large numbers of innovative start-ups also tend to host numerous VC investors (Fritsch and Schilder 2008). Most of the aggregate-level analyses that distinguish between different fields of knowledge find a pronounced correlation of higher education and research in engineering and natural sciences with the numbers of innovative new businesses, while activities in social sciences or arts turn out to be hardly significant (Fritsch and Aamoucke 2017).

Fritsch and Wyrwich (2018) find that many German regions with high start-up rates in innovative and knowledge intensive industries today also had high levels of science-based self-employment more than 80 years early. They conclude that such a long-lasting tradition of innovative entrepreneurship has resulted in a regional culture of entrepreneurship, i.e., a high level of social acceptance of entrepreneurs and entrepreneurial behavior that is conducive to new business formation and growth (for details see Fritsch and Wyrwich 2019). Consistent with this interpretation, it is found that individuals living in regions with a pronounced tradition of self-employment tend to have a personality profile that is similar to the profile of entrepreneurs (Fritsch, Obschonka, and Wyrwich 2018).

Based on a rich data set about several types of activities of German HEIs, Fritsch and Aamoucke (2013, 2017) investigate the relationships of different measures of the activities of HEIs with the numbers of high-tech start-ups. They find that the correlation between the number of innovative start-ups and HEIs is based more on the number of professors than the number of students or graduates. This result may be, at first glance, rather surprising, because there are more start-ups initiated by students or graduates than by faculty simply due to the fact that the number of students is much larger. Moreover, members of faculty, especially if they have tenure, show a considerably lower propensity to set up their own business than graduates (Astebro, Bazzazian and Braguinsky 2012; see also Fritsch and Krabel 2012).

The correct interpretation of this result may be that the number of professors represents the knowledge stock of HEIs that resides in their scientific staff. Since it is mainly the professors who are key to organizing research and applying for research funds, the number of professors can be viewed as a main indicator for the amount and the quality of available knowledge. Hence, the high correlation between the number of professors and the number of innovative start-ups suggests that the size and the quality of the regional knowledge base is more important than the number of students and graduates. However, because of rather high correlations between the different indicators for characteristics and activities of HEIs, Fritsch and Aamoucke (2013, 2017) warn that this result should be regarded with considerable caution.

---

6 Harhoff (1999), Bade and Nerlinger (2000), Audretsch and Lehmann (2005), Audretsch. Lehmann, and Warning (2005), Baptista, Lima, and Mendonça (2011), Fritsch and Aamoucke (2013, 2017), Bonaccorsi et al. (2014), Hülsbeck and Pickavé (2014), Colombelli (2016).

Many studies find that most high-tech start-ups are located in close proximity to HEIs, and that their numbers sharply decrease as the geographic distance from a HEI increases. This pattern is consistent with the idea that it is the spillovers of spatially-bounded knowledge from HEIs that lead to the emergence of the new businesses, and that the process of transforming knowledge into innovative new businesses is highly localized. In particular, it may be concluded that the local HEIs are the sources of the innovative start-ups in the region.

This interpretation of the empirical evidence could, however, be somewhat misleading because the correlation between the local HEIs and the number of innovative start-ups does not necessarily indicate a causal relationship. The main reason why the correlation between local HEIs and the number of innovative start-ups may not represent a causal relationship is that most founders work as paid employees before starting their own venture. Due to the spatial mobility of founders before they switch into entrepreneurship, significant pieces of the knowledge that is used to start up an innovative business may not necessarily stem from the same region where the new business is set up. Founders of innovative firms are highly qualified, most of them holding an academic degree, and tend to live in or around larger cities because this is where most of the respective jobs are located.[7] Since founders have a strong tendency to set up their businesses close to their place of residence (Figueiredo, Guimaraes, and Woodward 2002; Stam 2007; Dahl and Sorenson 2009), innovative start-ups are most likely to emerge in or close to larger cities because this is where most of the potential founders reside.

A recent study by Konon, Fritsch, and Kritikos (2018) investigated the effect of the business cycle on start-up activity in different industries in Germany. The study revealed that new business formation in innovative manufacturing industries is countercyclical, meaning that more businesses in these industries are set up in recessions than in boom periods.[8] The authors speculate that perhaps relatively low labor costs and the exceptional availability of resources (i.e., qualified labor and available floor space) motivates this timing of a start-up. Another explanation could be that highly qualified employees with a business idea are more likely to react to real or expected unemployment by founding a firm than less qualified persons.

3.3   Micro-level evidence

The public discourse about the emergence of innovative start-ups is often biased by reports about some exceptionally successful new ventures that include the biographies of their founders. In spite of a possible bias, it is undisputed that most of

---

7 Firms with multiple branches typically base their headquarters and conduct most of their R&D activities in larger cities. It is also the case that larger cities host more and often larger HEIs.

8 This is particularly remarkable because new business formation in small-scale industries where entry costs are relatively low (e.g., personal services, hospitality) and where one would expect higher levels of necessity-motivated start-ups during recessions does not show such a countercyclical pattern.

the founders of innovative businesses had at least some contact with universities, and that most of these founders hold an academic degree. However, some of the well-known entrepreneurial superstars whose stories are a topic for the media (e.g., Bill Gates, Mark Zuckerberg) did not complete their university degree but dropped out of academia in order to establish their business venture at an early age.[9] These types of examples have fueled the myth of the young founder of innovative businesses who has at least some academic training. This myth may be one reason why a number of countries have introduced policy programs that are designed to support university students and graduates to start up their own business (e.g., the EXIST program in Germany).

However, the broader empirical evidence about the founders of innovative new businesses contradicts the picture of the young high-tech entrepreneur who spins off directly from a university. In contrast to this popular image, most founders of innovative firms in countries such as Germany and the US do not set up their business directly after completing a university education, but first work for a longer time period as paid employees (Metzger et al. 2010; Müller 2010; Azoulay et al. 2018; Breschi, Lassébie, and Menon 2018). This is well reflected in the fact that the age of the average founder of an innovative firm in Germany and in the US is about 40 years or older, which is not significantly different from the average age of people who set up businesses that are not particularly innovative.

The fact that most founders of innovative firms first work as paid employees for a period of more than ten years has a number of important implications.

- First, they add considerable practical experience and knowledge to their university education before they become founders. While working as paid employees, they may accumulate business skills and improve their abilities to recognize entrepreneurial opportunities through their contact with customers. This knowledge and experience may not only affect their decision to start up and the relative success of the business, but also the type of business that they found (Braguinsky, Klepper, and Ohyama 2012). As a result, many of these founders set up firms with business models that are quite similar to those of their former employers, and the knowledge base of the incubator firm has a significant impact on the success of the spin-off (Klepper 2009).
- Second, given that university graduates tend to show a relatively high degree of spatial mobility (Faggian, Rajbhandari, and Dotzel 2017) combined with the observation that founders have a strong tendency to locate their venture close to their place of residence, many innovative businesses will not be set up in the same region where the founders received their academic education. Hence, the academic knowledge that they acquired during their study may be commercialized in a different location. Florida (2002) claims that creative

---

9 Steve Jobs, the founder of Apple, is a famous borderline case in this respect because he was enrolled for a short period of time but did not attend classes.

people have a pronounced preference to work in regions with high shares of other people with creative activities, especially in large cities (see also Florida, Adler, and Mellander 2017).

- Third, assessing whether or not academic institutions are fertile ground for the formation of new businesses requires information about the entrepreneurial activities of former students and employees that covers a longer period of time, i.e., their whole professional life (one such example is the MIT Alumni Study; see Roberts, Murray, and Kim 2015). Most current assessments, however, are based only on the relatively small number of start-ups that are direct spin-offs of an academic institution, or only on those foundings for which the academic institution consciously provided support. Because this type of evaluation disregards the far larger share of new businesses that are set up by alumni long after they have left their university or research institute, it is only of rather limited value for deriving any policy conclusions.
- Fourth, at the time of start up (usually more than ten years after leaving their university), most founders have lost contact with their alma mater. If academic knowledge is an important input for their venture, contact and cooperation with academic knowledge sources have to be newly established. These sources of knowledge may be different from those where the founder received his academic education.

Astebro and Thompson (2011) found that independent inventors in Canada who have been self-employed for some period of time do change their employers, their occupational field, and the industry they work in more often than those who remain in paid employment. This observation may suggest that innovative entrepreneurs have a special taste for variety. Elfenbein, Hamilton, and Zenger (2010) show that innovative founders in the US tend to switch from larger firms to smaller firms before setting up their own business. The authors argue that this labor market mobility pattern may be explained by a preference of potential founders for autonomy that tends to be higher in smaller firms than in larger firms. The results of Elfenbein, Hamilton, and Zenger (2010) also suggest that innovative start-ups tend to be economically more successful if the founder worked in a small firm before becoming self-employed.

The public discourse about entrepreneurial superstars also touches upon a specific entrepreneurial personality profile of these people. Recent research has, indeed, identified certain personality profiles that are more conducive to starting a business (Caliendo, Fossen, and Kritikos 2014; Obschonka and Stuetzer 2017). This research is mainly based on the Big Five approach to personality measurement, and suggests that entrepreneurs score relatively high on "extraversion," "openness to experience," and "conscientiousness," but relatively low on "agreeableness," and "neuroticism (emotional instability)" (Obschonka and Stuetzer 2017).[10] Although

---

10 It is, however, an open question whether or not (and if yes, to what extent) the personality profile of innovative founders differs from the profile of non-innovative founders.

such personality traits may be partly genetic, a considerable part of a person's personality is influenced by socialization and education, meaning that entrepreneurs can also be "nurtured." Socialization and a person's personality profile can have an effect on career choices, i.e., what kind of interests and qualifications someone develops (e.g., field of study), what type of occupation that person chooses, etc. (Sorgner and Fritsch 2018). However, it remains largely unclear how schools and universities could affect the personality profiles of their students and improve their entrepreneurial abilities (see Martin, McNally, and Kay 2013).

3.4   Intermediate summary

Summarizing the state of the art of what we know about the emergence and location of innovative new businesses, it can be said that academic knowledge plays a role in most cases, but that it is not necessarily the knowledge of HEIs, other public research institutes, and private businesses in the region where an innovative firm is established. Hence, empirical analyses that relate the number and performance of innovative start-ups to knowledge sources that are located in the respective region may be of limited value for understanding the emergence and location of innovative start-ups. In particular, such studies may provide a rather poor empirical basis for the design of policies that aim at increasing the number of innovative new businesses.

For developing appropriate policies, much more should be known about the personality, social environment, educational achievement, career paths, and spatial mobility patterns of innovative firm founders as compared to founders of non-innovative businesses (Sorgner and Fritsch 2018). Investigation of such questions, especially of the self-selection of people into certain occupational and regional environments, requires longitudinal analyses for representative samples of people at the micro level.

4.   Research questions

The current state of knowledge about the traits of innovative founders and where they are located leaves a number of unanswered questions that deserve further research. The following list is a selection of topics that may be relevant for policymakers who intend to design promotion programs that aim at increasing the regional number of innovative new businesses and improving their performance.

The first question pertains to the definition of innovative new businesses and is of key importance for everything that follows. Is it useful and empirically feasible to distinguish between different categories of innovative start-ups based on the type of market or industry, type of innovation (product, process, organization, procurement, or marketing), or the level of innovativeness? If it can be shown that these distinctions are useful and important, and if an appropriate solution to the empirical identification problem can be found, it would be interesting to determine if alternative methods of identification (such as industry affiliation, VC investment, or patents) create a bias that results in over- or underrepresentation of the different types of innovative start-ups?

It was argued in the previous section that a better understanding of the emergence and location of innovative start-ups requires micro-level analyses with representative longitudinal data sets. This type of analysis could enable us to find answers to a variety of questions:

- What is the main motivation for setting up an innovative business? What impact does a dispute with an employer, or frustration with not being able to realize one's own idea in an incumbent organization (Klepper 2009), have on the type of innovative start-ups?
- To what extent are the personality profiles of people who set up innovative firms different from the profiles of founders of not particularly innovative firms? For example, are innovative founders more willing and able to cope with risk than those who set up less innovative new businesses?
- How are founders who start their businesses immediately after graduating from an academic institution (students and scientists) different from those who spin off a private firm after having worked there for several years? Are there any systematic differences between the two types of innovative businesses with regard to the newness of their product or business concept, the type of innovation, and their economic success (Müller 2010)? Are innovative start-ups that are directly set up out of academia based on more recent research than firm spin-offs?
- In what field of activity (e.g., R&D, marketing, management) do founders of firm spin-offs work as paid employees before starting their venture? To what extent are different types of work experience of founders in private firms conducive to the survival and success of innovative entries?
- Do founders who set up an innovative business directly out of academia need more support in terms of coaching than firm spin-offs? Are they more responsive to such support? Should different policies be applied to these two types of innovative start-up?
- What are the typical labor market mobility patterns of those founders who set up their business after a considerable time as paid employee? Do these founders change their employer more often than non-innovative founders, or compared to people who remain in paid employment (Astebro and Thompson 2011)? Do potential founders of innovative businesses prefer to work in smaller firms before switching into entrepreneurship (as claimed by Elfenbein, Hamilton, and Zenger 2010)?
- What is the role of the regional social climate and a regional culture of entrepreneurship for the individual decision to start an innovative business (Obschonka et al. 2015; Fritsch and Wyrwich 2018)?
- Do potential founders of innovative firms have preferences for certain types of regional environments, such as large cities with a high share of creative people, a tolerant atmosphere, and a rich supply of artistic activities (Florida 2002; Florida, Adler, and Mellander 2017)? Does the

presence of VC corporations play a role in the locational choice of potential founders?

Alumni studies that follow former students over their entire careers or work experiences would allow for the assessment of how many innovative start-ups a certain HEI has generated. Based on such data one could analyze the factors that make universities good seedbeds for innovative start-ups and what characterizes an entrepreneurial university.

5. How to proceed?

A key task for future research should be to clarify the fuzzy issue of "innovativeness." Should different types and intensities of innovation be distinguished? What kind of information can and should be used for such a classification? This is important in order to bring the research and discussion about innovative start-ups into sharper focus. Having a valid and precise set of definitions might help us to determine whether or not different studies are actually researching the same fundamental questions.

In light of our discussion about the shortcomings of macro-level analyses concerning the emergence and location of innovative new businesses, it is clear that identification of the relevant causal relationships requires micro-level investigations based on comprehensive and representative data about founders and their firms. Preferably, such data have a panel structure and cover long periods of time. The longer the time period covered the better the possibilities of identifying long-term relationships, such as the effects of childhood and early education on a person's behavior and performance later in life. When exploring the role of regional conditions, and especially the self-selection of potential founders into certain regional environments, obviously the data should include information about the location of the founder and about spatial mobility over the covered period. To be able to analyze the relationship between the characteristics of the founder and the qualities of his venture, especially its performance, it should be possible to link the information about founders with the information about their firms.

Case studies of single founders and their firms may fulfill these demands and can lead to valuable insights. However, because such case studies typically comprise only a few examples (often just one case), it is questionable if the results can be generalized. Moreover, since case studies of innovative founders and their firms do not provide a systematic comparison with founders of non-innovative firms, nor with people who remain in self-employment, one cannot determine the extent to which innovative founders are special or face specific problems. Answers to such questions require statistical analyses of larger data sets.

Although the perfect database for investigating all the relevant questions does not exist, there is some publicly available information that allows the investigation of some specific issues. Important data sources for longitudinal micro-level analyses are the German Socio-Economic Panel (SOEP) (see Wagner, Frick, and Schupp 2007), the British Household Panel (BHP), and the available Panel Studies of Entrepreneurial Dynamics (PSED) (see Reynolds and Curtin 2008). Other valuable sources can be found in administrative data, such as employment statistics, social insurance statistics, or tax statistics. If such information can be organized as individual panel data it may be useful in analyzing the individual career paths of innovative founders and help us better understand the emergence of innovative new firms and the reasons why founders choose certain locations to establish their businesses.

6.   Concluding remarks

The emergence and location of innovative new businesses can have considerable economic effects. More knowledge about the issue may be especially important for the design of appropriate policies that aim at stimulating the commercialization of knowledge by innovative start-ups.

It is clear from our review of the available empirical evidence that macro-level analyses are largely unsuited for identifying the relevant causal relationships, especially the effect of regional characteristics on innovative start-ups. I believe that micro-level studies that investigate the career paths of potential founders, especially their spatial mobility, might be helpful in identifying causal links that will provide policymakers with the information they need to design effective policies that will support the growth of entrepreneurial activities.

Another shortcoming of studies in the field of innovative entrepreneurship is the lack of consensus among scholars about what constitutes an innovative start-up. In a similar vein, it is not clear how to differentiate between the various types of innovative start-ups. It is, therefore, of crucial importance to know more about the merits and deficiencies of different approaches used to identify and categorize innovative new businesses.

References

Acs, Zoltan J., Pontus Braunerhjelm, David B. Audretsch, and Bo Carlsson (2009), 'The knowledge spillover theory of entrepreneurship', *Small Business Economics*, **32**, 15–30. https://doi.org/10.1007/s11187-008-9157-3

Acs, Zoltan J., David B. Audretsch, and Erik Lehmann (2013), 'The knowledge spillover theory of entrepreneurship', *Small Business Economics*, **41**, 767–74. https://doi/org.10.1007/s11187-013-9505-9

Asheim, Björn T. and Meric S. Gertler (2006), 'The geography of innovation: Regional innovation systems', in Jan Fagerberg, David C. Mowery, and Richard R. Nelson (eds.), *The Oxford Handbook of Innovation*, Oxford: Oxford University Press, pp. 291–317. https://doi.org/10.1093/oxfordhb/9780199286805.003.0011

Astebro, Thomas and Peter Thompson (2011), 'Entrepreneurs, Jack of all trades or Hobos?', *Research Policy*, **40**, 637–49. https://doi.org/10.1016/j.respol.2011.01.010

Astebro, Thomas, Navid Bazzazian, and Serguey Braguinsky (2012), 'Startups by recent university graduates and their faculty: Implications for university entrepreneurship policy', *Research Policy*, **41**, 663–77. https://doi.org/10.1016/j.respol.2012.01.004

Audretsch, David B. and Erik Lehmann (2005), 'Does the knowledge spillover theory of entrepreneurship hold for regions?', *Research Policy*, **34**, 1191–202. https://doi.org/10.1016/j.respol.2005.03.012

Audretsch, David B., Erik Lehmann and Susanne Warning (2005), 'University spillovers and new firm location', *Research Policy*, **34**, 1113–22. https://doi.org/10.1016/j.respol.2005.05.009

Azoulay, Pierre, Benjamin F. Jones, J. Daniel Kim, and Javier Miranda (2018), 'Age and high-growth entrepreneurship', NBER Working Paper No. 24489, Cambridge, MA: National Bureau of Economic Research. https://doi.org/10.3386/w24489

Bade, Franz-Josef and Erik A. Nerlinger (2000), 'The spatial distribution of new technology-based firms: Empirical results for West-Germany', *Papers in Regional Science*, **79**, 155–76. https://doi.org/10.1007/s101100050041

Baptista, Rui, Francisco Lima, and Joana Mendonça (2011), 'Establishment of higher education institutions and new firm entry', *Research Policy*, **40**, 751–60. https://doi.org/10.1016/j.respol.2011.02.006

Bonaccorsi, Andrea, Massimo G. Colombo, Massimiliano Guerini, and Cristina Rossi Lamastra (2014), 'How universities contribute to the creation of knowledge intensive firms: Detailed evidence on the Italian case', in Andrea Bonaccorsi (ed.), *The European Higher Education Landscape – Diversity and Performance*, Cheltenham, UK and Northampton, MA, USA: Edward Elgar Publishing, pp. 205–30. https://doi.org/10.4337/9781783472000

Boschma, Ron (2005), 'Proximity and innovation: A critical assessment, *Regional Studies*, **39**, 61–74. https://www.tandfonline.com/doi/abs/10.1080/0034340052000320887

Boschma, Ron (2015), 'Do spinoff dynamics or agglomeration externalities drive industry clustering? A reappraisal of Steven Klepper's work', *Industrial and Corporate Change*, **24**, 859–73. https://doi.org/10.1093/icc/dtv024

Braguinsky, Serguey, Steven Klepper, and Atsushi Ohyama (2012), 'High-tech entrepreneurship', *Journal of Law and Economics*, **55**, 869–900. http://www.jstor.org/stable/10.1086/666488

Breschi, Stefano, Julie Lassébie, and Carlo Menon (2018), 'A portrait of innovative startups across countries', OECD Science, Technology and Industry Working Papers, 2018/02, Paris: OECD Publishing. http://dx.doi.org/10.1787/f9ff02f4-en

Caliendo, Marco, Frank Fossen, and Alexander Kritikos (2014), 'Personality characteristics and the decision to become and stay self-employed', *Small Business Economics*, **42**, 787–814. https://doi.org/10.1007/s11187-013-9514-8

Colombelli, Alessandra (2016), 'The impact of local knowledge bases on the creation of innovative start-ups in Italy', *Small Business Economics*, **47**, 383–96. https://doi.org/10.1007/s11187-016-9722-0

Colombelli, Alessandra, Jackie Krafft, and Marco Vivarelli (2016), 'To be born is not enough: the key role of innovative start-ups', *Small Business Economics*, **47**, 277–91. https://doi.org/10.1007/s11187-016-9716-y

Dahl, Michael S. and Olav Sorenson (2009), 'The embedded entrepreneur', *European Management Review*, **6**, 172–81. https://doi.org/10.1057/emr.2009.14

Elert, Niklas, Magnus Henrekson, and Mikael Stenkula (2017), *Institutional Reform for Innovation and Entrepreneurship – An Agenda for Europe*, Cham, Switzerland: Springer. https://doi.org/10.1007/978-3-319-55092-3

Elfenbein, Daniel W., Barton H. Hamilton, and Todd R. Zenger (2010), 'The small firm effect and the entrepreneurial spawning of scientists and engineers', *Management Science*, **56**, 659–81. https://doi.org/10.1287/mnsc.1090.1130

Eurostat (2018), Glossary: Knowledge-intensive services (KIS). http://ec.europa.eu/eurostat/statistics-explained/index.php/Glossary:Knowledge-intensive_services_(KIS) (accessed July 7, 2018).

Faggian, Alessandra, Isha Rajbhandari, and Kathryn R. Dotzel (2017), 'The interregional migration of human capital and its regional consequences: A review', *Regional Studies*, **51**, 128–43. https://www.tandfonline.com/doi/full/10.1080/00343404.2016.1263388

Feldman, Maryann (2001), 'The entrepreneurial event revisited: Firm formation in a regional context', *Industrial and Corporate Change*, **10**, 861–91. https://doi.org/10.1093/icc/10.4.861

Feldman, Maryann, P., Lauren Lanahan, and Jennifer M. Miller (2011), 'Inadvertent infrastructure and regional entrepreneurship policy', in Michael Fritsch (ed.), *Handbook of Research on Entrepreneurship and Regional Development*, Cheltenham, UK and Northampton, MA, USA: Edward Elgar Publishing, pp. 216–51.

Figueiredo O., P. Guimaraes, and D. Woodward (2002), 'Home-field advantage: Location decisions of Portuguese entrepreneurs', *Journal of Urban Economics*, **52**, 341–61. https://doi.org/10.1016/Soo 94-1190(02)00006-2

Florida, Richard (2002), *The Rise of the Creative Class*, New York: Basic Books.

Florida, Richard, Patrick Adler, and Charlotta Mellander (2017), 'The cita as innovation machine', *Regional Studies*, **51**, 86–96. https://doi.org/10.1080/00343404.2016.1255324

Fritsch, Michael (2011), 'start-ups in innovative industries – causes and effects', in David B. Audretsch, Oliver Falck, Stephan Heblich, and Adam Lederer (eds.), *Handbook of Innovation and Entrepreneurship*, Cheltenham, UK and Northampton, MA, USA: Edward Elgar Publishers, pp. 365–81.

Fritsch, Michael and Ronney Aamoucke (2013), 'Regional public research, higher education, and innovative start-ups—an empirical investigation', *Small Business Economics*, **41**, 865–885. https://doi.org/10.1007/s11187-013-9510-z

Fritsch, Michael and Ronney Aamoucke (2017), 'Fields of knowledge in higher education institutions, and innovative start-ups—an empirical investigation', *Papers in Regional Science*, **96**, S1–S27. https://doi.org/10.1111/pirs.12175

Fritsch, Michael and Stefan Krabel (2012), 'Ready to leave the ivory tower?—Academic scientists' appeal to work in the private sector', *Journal of Technology Transfer*, **37**, 271–96. https://doi.org/10.1007/s10961-010-9174-7

Fritsch, Michael and Dirk Schilder (2008), 'Does venture capital investment really require spatial proximity? An empirical investigation', *Environment and Planning A*, **40**, 2114–31. https://doi.org/10.1068/a39353

Fritsch, Michael and Dirk Schilder (2012), 'The regional supply of venture capital—can syndication overcome bottlenecks?', *Economic Geography*, **88**, 59–76. https://doi.org/10.1111/j.1944-8287.2011.01139.x

Fritsch, Michael and Michael Wyrwich (2018), 'Regional knowledge, entrepreneurial culture and innovative start-ups over time and space—an empirical investigation', *Small Business Economics*, **51** (2), 337–53. https://doi.org/10.1007/s11187-018-0016-6

Fritsch, Michael and Michael Wyrwich (2019), *Regional Trajectories of Entrepreneurship, Knowledge, and Growth—The Role of History and Culture*, Cham, Switzerland: Springer. https://doi.org/10.10 07/978-3-319-97782-9

Fritsch, Michael, Martin Obschonka, and Michael Wyrwich (2018), 'Historical roots of entrepreneurial culture and innovation activity — an analysis for German regions', Jena Economic Research Papers #2018-007, Jena: Friedrich Schiller University. http://pubdb.wiwi.uni-jena.de/pdf/wp_2018_007.pdf

Grilli, Luca and Samuele Murtinu (2014), 'Government, venture capital and the growth of European high-tech entrepreneurial firms', *Research Policy*, **43**, 1523–43. https://doi.org/10.1016/j.respol.2014.04.002

Hall, Bronwyn H., Christian Helmers, Mark Rogers, and Vania Sena (2014), 'The choice between formal and informal intellectual property: A review', *Journal of Economic Literature*, **52**, 375–423. http://dx.doi.org/10.1257/jel.52.2.375

Harhoff, Dietmar (1999), 'Firm formation and regional spillovers – evidence from Germany', *Economics of Innovation and New Technology*, **8**, 27–55. https://doi.org/10.1080/10438599900000003

Henrekson, Magnus and Dan Johansson (2011), 'Firm growth, institutions, and structural transformation', in Michael Fritsch (ed.), *Handbook of Research on Entrepreneurship and Regional Development*, Cheltenham, UK and Northampton, MA, USA: Edward Elgar Publishing, pp. 175–215.

Hülsbeck, Marcel and Elena N. Pickavé (2014), 'Regional knowledge production as determinant of high-technology entrepreneurship: Empirical evidence for Germany', *International Entrepreneurship Management Journal*, **10**, 121–38. https://doi.org/10.1007/s11365-011-0217-9

Klepper, Steven (2009), 'Spinoffs: A review and synthesis', *European Management Review*, **6**, 159–71. https://doi.org/10.1057/emr.2009.18

Klepper, Steven (2010), 'The origin and growth of industry clusters: The making of Silicon Valley and Detroit', *Journal of Urban Economics*, **67**, 15–32. https://doi.org/10.1016/j.jue.2009.09.004

Klepper, Steven (2016), *Experimental Capitalism—The Nanoeconomics of American High-Tech Industries*, Princeton, NJ: Princeton University Press. https://doi.org/10.2307/j.ctt2166864

Konon, Alexander, Michael Fritsch, and Alexander Kritikos (2018), 'Business cycles and start-ups across industries: An empirical analysis for Germany', *Journal of Business Venturing*, **33**, 742–61. https://doi.org/10.1016/j.jbusvent.2018.04.006

Lerner, Josh (2002), 'When bureaucrats meet entrepreneurs: The design of effective "public venture capital" programmes', *Economic Journal*, **112**, F73–F84. https://doi.org/10.1111/1468-0297.00684

Lucas, Robert E. (1978), 'On the size distribution of business firms', *Bell Journal of Economics*, **9**, 508–23. https://doi.org/10.2307/3003596

Martin, Bruce C., Jeffrey J. McNally, and Michael J. Kay (2013), 'Examining the formation of human capital in entrepreneurship: A meta-analysis of entrepreneurship education outcomes', *Journal of Business Venturing*, **28**, 211–24. https://doi.org/10.1016/j.jbusvent.2012.03.002

Metzger, Georg, Diana Heger, Daniel Höwer, and Georg Licht (2010), *High-Tech-Gründungen in Deutschland – Zum Mythos des jungen High-Tech-Gründers*, Mannheim: ZEW. http://ftp.zew.de/pub/zew-docs/gutachten/hightechgruendungen2_10.pdf

Müller, Kathrin (2010), 'Academic spin-offs transfer speed: Analyzing the time from leaving university to venture', *Research Policy*, **39**, 189–99. https://doi.org/10.1016/j.respol.2009.12.001

Obschonka, Martin and Michael Stuetzer (2017), 'Integrating psychological approaches to entrepreneurship: The Entrepreneurial Personality System (EPS)', *Small Business Economics*, **49**, 203–31. https://doi.org/10.1007/s11187-016-9821-y

Obschonka, Martin, Michael Stuetzer, Samuel D. Gosling, Peter J. Rentfrow, Michael E. Lamb, Jeff Potter, and David B. Audretsch (2015), 'Entrepreneurial regions: Do macro-psychological cultural characteristics of regions help solve the "knowledge paradox" of economics?' *PloS One*, **10** (6), e0129332. https://doi.org/10.1371/journal.pone.0129332

Organisation for Economic Co-operation and Development (OECD) (2005), *OECD Handbook on Economic Globalisation Indicators*, Paris: OECD Publishing.

Organisation for Economic Co-operation and Development (OECD) (2015), *Frascati Manual 2015 – Guidelines for Collecting and Reporting Data and Research and Experimental Development*, Paris: OECD Publishing.

Organisation for Economic Co-operation and Development (OECD) (2017), *OECD Science, Technology and Industry Scoreboard 2017*, Paris: OECD Publishing.

Parker, Simon (2018), *The Economics of Entrepreneurship*, 2nd edition, Cambridge: Cambridge University Press. https://doi.org/10.1017/9781316756706

Reynolds, Paul D. and Richard T. Curtin (2008), 'Business creation in the United States: Panel Study of Entrepreneurial Dynamics II—Initial Assessment', *Foundations and Trends in Entrepreneurship*, **4**, 155–307. https://doi.org/10.1561/0300000022

Roberts, Edward B., Fiona Murray, and J. Daniel Kim (2015), *Entrepreneurship and Innovation at MIT—Continuing Global Growth and Impact*, Boston, MA: Massachusetts Institute for Technology.

Schumpeter, Joseph A. (1934), *The Theory of Economic Development*, Cambridge, MA: Cambridge University Press.

Sorenson, O. and T. E. Stuart (2001), 'Syndication networks and the spatial distribution of venture capital investments', *American Journal of Sociology*, **106**, 1546–88. https://doi.org/10.1086/321301

Sorgner, Alina and Michael Fritsch (2018), 'Entrepreneurial career paths: Occupational context and the propensity to become self-employed', *Small Business Economics*, **51**, 129–52. https://doi.org/10.1007/s11187-017-9917-z

Stam, Erik (2007), 'Why butterflies don't leave: Locational behavior of entrepreneurial firms', *Economic Geography*, **83**, 27–50. https://doi.org/10.1111/j.1944-8287.2007.tb00332.x

Sternberg, Rolf (2009), 'Regional dimensions of entrepreneurship', *Foundations and Trends in Entrepreneurship*, **5**, 211–340. https://doi.org/10.1561/0300000024

Wagner, Gert G., Joachim R. Frick, and Jürgen Schupp (2007), 'The German socio-economic panel study (SOEP)—Scope, evolution and enhancements', *Journal of Applied Social Science Studies*, **127**, 139–69.

Walter, Sascha G., Arne Schmidt, and Achim Walter (2011), 'Do academic entrepreneurs patent their secrets? An empirical investigation of patent rationales', *Frontiers of Entrepreneurship Research*, **31**, 403–17.

7 Public and policy entrepreneurship research: a synthesis of the literature and future perspectives

Heike M. Grimm

1 Introduction

The term entrepreneurship has predominantly been used in a profit-oriented, economic sense referring to start-up activities in the private sector (Audretsch et al. 2005) or more generally speaking to professional independence and to the "discovery and exploitation of profitable opportunities" (Shane and Venkataraman 2000, p. 217). The many definitions of the term highlight very significant aspects, including personality aspects such as innovativeness; the willingness to take risks; the urge for action; the creative development of ideas and entrepreneurial implementation; furthermore, the functions and actions of entrepreneurial individuals, firms, or other organizations; traits and behaviors. Meanwhile, the term has been defined in many and different ways across academic disciplines and applied to the public, social, and non-profit sectors as well (Leyden and Link 2015; Leyden 2016). Audretsch et al. (2015) underline that constricting the field and meaning of entrepreneurship may be the wrong approach for future research and identify an emerging eclectic view of entrepreneurship across disciplines. The following contribution carries on these thoughts and focuses specifically on two categories of entrepreneurship: public and policy entrepreneurship.

Currently, no literature review exists that specifically focuses on public and policy entrepreneurship (PPE). Conceptualization is missing to pursue research in both fields more systematically. The chapter offers a review of refereed articles published in the Web of Science from 2000 until 2017 with a focus on PPE. Such a synthesis of the literature is a worthwhile methodology to further advance in this specific field of research through the development of a categorization scheme. The approach also aims at making the field of PPE more accessible to researchers and policymakers (Rothaermel et al. 2007, p. 706).[1]

Although the activities of public and policy entrepreneurs have received some attention in several studies (Roberts and King 1996; Bernier and Hafsi 2007),

---

[1] The approach was developed by Rothaermel et al. 2007 in the context of university entrepreneurship and is adapted with regard to the research focusing on public and private entrepreneurship in this chapter.

the concept of both forms of entrepreneurship is yet vaguely defined and, therefore, hardly integrated within analyses of change, problem-solving, development, and education. To facilitate more integration of both concepts, this chapter offers an initial overview of major publications with reference to PPE with the goal of answering the question: Do we observe an increasing academic interest in this field of research? If so, why should these concepts be taken into consideration in the context of the public policy process and policymaking? The question is grounded in the hypothesis that the number of publications in this field of research has increased within the last years, reflecting on a rising interest in entrepreneurship for policymaking and for the daily routine of public servants.

It is further assumed that entrepreneurship is an important asset and feature of public policymaking. Public servants need entrepreneurial skills to cope with challenges, design new policies and solutions, and to promote transformations in the public sector. Future public and policy entrepreneurs have the potential to support attitudes and activities for developing and implementing creative, innovative ideas, and solutions for overcoming social and institutional challenges. Such entrepreneurs are motivated by diverse interests including improving services to their own communities and increasing the level and quality of public goods – e.g. peace, safety, health, etc. – available to citizens (Ostrom 2005; Mintrom and Norman 2009).

Nonetheless, research about the interrelationships between entrepreneurship and public administrations, on the one hand, and policymakers and entrepreneurs, on the other hand, is still in short supply but is essential to better understand the key challenges in societies, to increase the level and quality of public goods, and to design innovative policies for sustainable and inclusive development. Silander (2016) further points out that entrepreneurship research has focused on entrepreneurs in the private, profit-oriented sector but is lacking in research on entrepreneurial activity in the public and political sector. This concern is linked to a research agenda presented by Audretsch et al. (2015, p. 709) who foresee "(. . .) the development of a dynamic theory of entrepreneurship to apply to decision making and behavior within the context of the public sector."

Therefore, this chapter aims at offering a first synthesis of the literature focusing on the keywords "public entrepreneurship" and "policy entrepreneurship" to gain a first-hand overview of the state of the art in this field of research. Section 2 will introduce the methodology of this chapter. In section 3, the role of entrepreneurship for public organizations is discussed. In section 4, the terms public and policy entrepreneurship will be operationalized; reference will be made to the importance of both for innovative and sustainable policymaking. Section 5 highlights the major findings from the taxonomy of the literature, followed by an outlook and recommendations for future research in section 6.

2   Methodology

The chapter offers an initial review of refereed articles published in the Social Science Citation Index of the Web of Science in the field of policy or public entrepreneurship and adapts the taxonomy of the literature developed by Rothaermel et al. in 2007 that focused on university entrepreneurship. To be included in the analysis, the research must have appeared between January 2000 and May 2017. I decided to focus on articles published in the 21st century knowing that a substantial number of pioneering articles appeared in the 1990s (e.g. Roberts and King 1991, 1996; Osborne and Gabler 1993; Mintrom 1997) and hypothesizing that the interest in PPE has increased only recently due to the complexity of global public policymaking. In a first step, I chose to run queries searching for the terms "public entrepreneurship" and "policy entrepreneurship" appearing consecutively and not separate in the title or abstracts of articles published within the above-specified time frame. I decided to narrow the first phase of research while excluding other relevant topic-related keywords such as "public sector entrepreneurship" or "political entrepreneurship" to find out whether the hypothesis can be confirmed that an increase of articles can be observed since 2000. Further, journal articles were differentiated from book chapters and contributions to conference proceedings. In a final step, I analyzed each article to make sure that "public entrepreneurship" and "policy entrepreneurship" were not only mentioned in the title and/or abstract but also turned out to be the major theme in the article to create a database in which I coded the following data: (i) author name(s), (ii) article title, (iii) journal of publication, (iv) year published, (v) total sum of citations (adapted according to Rothaermel et al. 2007, p.694). I received further information such as volume and issue of the journal, special issues, page numbers, years of citations, but did not include them in the first evaluation of data and graphical presentations.

The approach is highly exploratory and aims at grasping whether PPE gained in importance in academic research during the last years, whether there are specific journals publishing articles with reference to PPE and authors that write repeatedly about this topic. Further research needs to extend the chosen time frame (going back to the 1990s) and broaden and refine the categories, terms, and definitions (such as "public sector entrepreneurship," "policy entrepreneur," "political entrepreneurship," etc.), to narrow and specify the focus of research, and to provide guidance for future research to make this field of research more accessible to scholars and practitioners alike (see also Rothaermel et al. 2007, p.692). Recommendations for further research are summarized in the final section.

3   Why does entrepreneurship matter for public administrations?

Entrepreneurial, innovative, creative, and independent thinking and acting have become increasingly important for professionals in an innovation and knowledge society (Audretsch 2007; Grimm 2009; Karlsson et al. 2016). Neither governments nor politicians have room for policy and political experiments; both can, however, benefit from the creativity and innovativeness of public and policy entrepreneurs. And both have an interest in identifying efficient, sustainable solutions for social, economic, and political challenges. In this regard, the public and policy entrepreneur has the potential to serve as an important mediator and communicator while impacting institutional change.

New forms of governance demand high socio-political skills and the development of social capital to professionally and successfully act polycentric systems (Ostrom 2005; Audretsch 2017). As such, the focus on public entrepreneurship has been a logical consequence for meeting high standards in future public sector organizations. Nevertheless, the role of entrepreneurship for policymaking is not evident at first glance but while reconsidering the shift from traditional public administration to new public management (NPM) reforms that evolved into new forms of governance, the role of entrepreneurship within a public sector context appears to have evolved slowly. With their path-breaking volume on reinventing government, Osborne and Gaebler (1993) offered a variety of ideas on how to make bureaucracies more entrepreneurial without following the ideas of the NPM or the new steering model. Entrepreneurship is rather seen as an attitude and mindset promoting action to make bureaucracies more efficient, more innovative, and more attractive. Public and policy entrepreneurs are crucial to paving new paths for designing and implementing public policy. The study of entrepreneurship has also been acknowledged for acquiring practical and methodological competencies necessary for the promotion of transformative, progressive processes within public administrations and organizations.

By defining and applying entrepreneurship in a broader sense (Schumpeter 1934, 1997; Audretsch et al. 2015, p. 704), professionals grasp an idea that entrepreneurial skills and assets can promote institutional change. Today, policymakers need competences to draw lessons, understand context, align bottom-up and top-down approaches, communicate professionally, build up trust, and engage with an entrepreneurial attitude rather than to apply a one size fits all approach (Rose 1993). The complexity of public sector activity and the fast-rising challenges for public servants emerged from the 1970s onwards with the appearance of new forms of governance and multilevel, interlinked public policy frameworks. Public policy is a form of governing that adheres to certain motives for action and brings about change. The reference to action implies an entrepreneurial attitude. A policy is a consciously made government decision, particularly when not only the solution proposal but also the change affected by the policy is of interest (Howlett et al. 2009, p. 4).

4 Policy entrepreneurs in public sector organizations

In the context of public policymaking, entrepreneurship serves as a driving force to a better quality and delivery of public goods and services, as well as social change and development. The policy entrepreneur is a type of actor who not only develops ideas for solutions to political and social challenges but also designs measures and instruments for implementing and promoting change (Grimm 2010). Visionaries such as Schumpeter refer to personalities who "think the unthinkable" and initiate political as well as social transformation processes in a persistent and sustainable manner. In their book *Reinventing Government: How the Entrepreneurial Spirit is Transforming the Public Sector*, Osborne and Gaebler (1993) provide a large variety of examples of how entrepreneurship can overcome bureaucratic procrastination, as well as promote active citizenship and innovative action from state actors, resulting in the development of an efficient and effective bureaucracy that must adapt to a rapidly changing globalized knowledge economy. The complexity and extent of political action taken by decision makers, as well as the demands they face, have increased drastically over the past two decades. This has come with the diversification and professionalization of education and further training, owing to the increased demands in politics and administration, and helps to explain the rapid ascent of new academic courses in public policy and governance incorporating a specialization in entrepreneurship.

In other words, entrepreneurs do not only contribute to economic progress but also to overall societal change through entrepreneurial activity. Policy entrepreneurs focus on political change and learning processes. Such processes are driven by a type of actor who develops not only innovative and creative ideas for the solution of socio-political challenges but also provides tools and instruments to transfer and implement them in order to promote political and policy change. Policy entrepreneurs are frequently, in the Schumpeterian sense, visionaries who think the unthinkable (*Undenkbares denken*), set in motion rather unimaginable ideas and political processes by mobilizing the public, forming new coalitions, and accepting, if necessary, considerable costs in the form of time or money to reach their mission (Mintrom and Norman 2009). "Policy entrepreneurs represent actors that are capable of bringing about the implementation of their political ideas, even if material distribution conflicts have gained the upper hand in the political process and lead to the organization of powerful oppositional interests" (Kingdon 1995, p. 5). The policy entrepreneur overcomes political stagnation and inertia caused by the short-term, instrumentally rational, and even egoistic thinking of political actors who seek to maximize their own benefit in the political process. Consequently, the policy entrepreneur does not act according to routine (maximizing short-term interests), which would lead to political stagnation. He (or she) acts as a promoter of political change processes: He enters new paths, recognizes new political possibilities (windows of opportunities), and is not afraid of any resistance in the implementation of innovative ideas. "In public policy a new technology, a new service, a new administrative process or procedure might be examples of such innovation" (Roberts and King 1996, p. 5). Osborne and Gaebler (1993) provide a wealth of examples on how it is possible for policy entrepreneurs to overcome bureaucratic red tape, promote civil-society involvement, and convince government actors to pursue innovative actions. The result is the further development of an efficient and effective bureaucracy and the promotion of an innovative civil society that is subject to constant change and must adjust to a rapidly changing, globalized knowledge economy.

Link and Link (2007) regard government as entrepreneurial and dynamic in terms of the ability to act in new and innovative ways, and in its willingness to undertake policy actions that have uncertain outcomes. They discuss various policy actions and programs (such as the U.S. Small Business Innovation Program) that contributed successfully to development.

In their research on the role of policy entrepreneurs in political change processes, Roberts and King (1991, p. 168) have created a typology of their activities, which can be divided into four categories: creative/intellectual activities (such as developing and disseminating new policy ideas); strategic activities (such as formulating visions, developing political strategies and action plans); mobilization activities (such as building up lobby groups and media support, obtaining support from politicians); and administrative/evaluative activities (such as program evaluation).

In comparison to the rather broad and sometimes vague definition of a policy entrepreneur, Silander and Silander deduced a definition by first looking at the meaning of political entrepreneurship. "We define a political entrepreneur as a politician/bureaucrat/officer/department within the publicly funded sector who with innovative approaches encourages entrepreneurship/business and where the goals are growth, employment and common good" (Silander and Silander 2016, p. 3). This definition contextualizes the role of political entrepreneurs by relating them to the goal of promoting entrepreneurship and economic development. Entrepreneurship is, therefore, not defined as an attitude or personal characteristic or trait but rather as the economic outcome of innovative activities within the public sector. Whereas the political entrepreneur is limited to (inter)action in the public sector, he (inter) acts across all sectors and is, therefore, challenging traditional patterns, values, and norms in a more comprehensive and cutting-edge way. He does not only seek the promotion of entrepreneurship but of innovative paths and methods for policymaking in general.

5   Findings

In the following, an overview of findings is presented after running a query as specified in section 2 with a focus on the keywords and research areas "public entrepreneurship" and "policy entrepreneurship."

5.1   Public entrepreneurship

The Web of Science query reveals a total of 86 publications which have been published in a variety of academic journals and by various authors between 2000 and 2017. Despite the long time frame, most articles were published in more recent years. A total of 40 articles were published in peer-reviewed journals.

After investigating the hit list more thoroughly, there is surprising evidence that the topic gained high importance at international conferences that provided a bridge

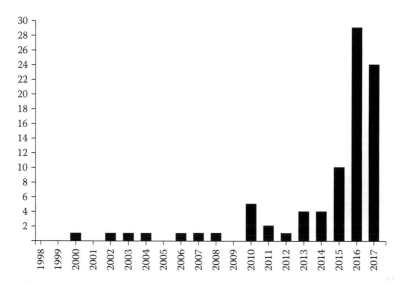

Source: Web of Science, accessed May 31, 2018.

Figure 7.1   Keyword "public entrepreneurship" published per year, 2000–2017 (including articles, book chapters, and conference proceedings)

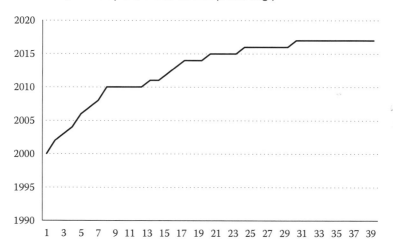

Source: Own calculation based on Web of Science, accessed May 31, 2018.

Figure 7.2   Keyword "public entrepreneurship" articles published, 2000–2017 (cumulative)

between academia, politics, and the private sector from 2013 onwards, with a focus on practical issues in relationship with management and education issues but also with regard to a mechanical, information, electronic, and digital society. While in 2013 and 2014 only one conference proceeding is listed in the Web of Science, the number increased in 2015 (five conference proceedings). In 2016, a total of

23 conference proceedings were published in the Web of Science; by end of June 2017, a total of 14 are available online. The topic seems specifically interesting in a Chinese and Asian context; a majority of authors coming from this region.

The 40 journal articles were published in 34 journals. The distribution among journals is highly scattered. There is no specific journal that had an emphasis or focus on public entrepreneurship since 2000 onwards and a low appearance in mainstream management and public administration journals. Only six journals covered the topic twice: *Administration & Society*; *Journal of Entrepreneurship and Public Policy*; *Journal of Management Inquiry*; *Local Government Studies*; *Public Administration Review*; *Public Performance & Management Review*. No author published more than one article with a focus on public entrepreneurship between 2000 and 2017. A total of 14 articles were published less than ten times and more than twice. Ten articles received high attention measured by a number of citations, as presented in Table 7.1 (more than ten total citations).

The initial findings show that the number of articles and conference proceedings increased substantially within the last years as well as the sum of citations per year. The majority of articles are rather qualitative due to the fact that theory development, either inductive or deductive, generally precedes empirical testing and validation in a new field of inquiry. Nonetheless, there seems no specific focus on a chosen topic within the research area; most authors do not publish frequently, and not in academic journals that attract most attention for authors.

5.2   Policy entrepreneurship

Whereas the findings for the query "public entrepreneurship" showed a slight increase in publications, the hits for the keyword "policy entrepreneurship" are significant by number. A total of 114 articles were published in refereed academic journals within the chosen time frame as reflected by Figure 7.3.

Table 7.2 introduces the most-often cited articles between January 2000 and May 2017 which were cited more than 20 times. Compared to the query on "public entrepreneurship," there is far more focus on policy entrepreneurship measured not only by the total number of articles but also by the sum of citations.

The article by Mintrom and Norman published in the *Policy Studies Journal* received a total of 224 citations and is ground-breaking for research in the field "policy entrepreneurship." Interestingly, there is again no specific academic journal which attracts a critical number of publications. Three articles were published in the journals *Public Administration* and *Journal of European Public Policy*; all of them were cited frequently and received significant attention from the research community. On the other hand, three articles published in the journal *Policy and Society* (in 2017) were not cited, although the topic seems more appropriate with regard to the aims and scope of the journal. The journal invites critical contributions "in policy theory and practice at the local, national and international levels and seeks

Table 7.1   Most often cited articles, keyword "public entrepreneurship," 2000–2017
(>10 total citations)[2]

Title	Authors	Source title	Total citations	Publication date
The political theory of reinvention	deLeon, L.; Denhardt, R.B.	*Public Administration Review*	120	2000
Toward a theory of public entrepreneurship	Klein, Peter G.; Mahoney, Joseph T.; McGahan, Anita M.; Pitelis, Christos N.	*European Management Review*	73	2010
The changing nature of public entrepreneurship	Bernier, Luc; Hafsi, Taieb	*Public Administration Review*	55	2007
Public sector innovation and entrepreneurship: Case studies from local government	Bartlett, D.; Dibben, P.	*Local Government Studies*	48	2002
Public entrepreneurship: Desiring social change, creating sociality	Hjorth, Daniel	*Entrepreneurship and Regional Development*	31	2013
Innovation and implementation in the public sector: An examination of public entrepreneurship	Mack, W.R.; Green, Deanna; Vedlitz, Arnold	*Review of Policy Research*	16	2008
What drives the diffusion of privatization policy? Evidence from the telecommunications sector	Schmitt, Carina	*Journal of Public Policy*	14	2011
Managerial values and accountability pressures: Challenges of crisis and disaster	Schwartz, R.; Sulitzeanu-Kenan, R.	*Journal of Public Administration Research and Theory*	11	2004
Stimulating entrepreneurial practices in the public sector: The roles of organizational characteristics	Kim, Younhee	*Administration & Society*	10	2010
Multilevel governance and EU structural funds: An entrepreneurial local government perspective	Zerbinati, Stefania	*Local Government Studies*	10	2012

2 The keywords "public entrepreneurship" and "policy entrepreneurship" must have appeared consecutively and not separately in the title or abstracts of the articles. In future research an extended number of keywords will be used (e.g. "public sector entrepreneurship") to incorporate articles that cover the topic but do not have the herewith narrow defined keywords in title or abstract.

Table 7.1   (continued)

Title	Authors	Source title	Total citations	Publication date
Public or private entrepreneurship? Revisiting motivations and definitions of success among academic entrepreneurs	Hayter, Christopher S.	*Journal of Technology Transfer*	10	2015

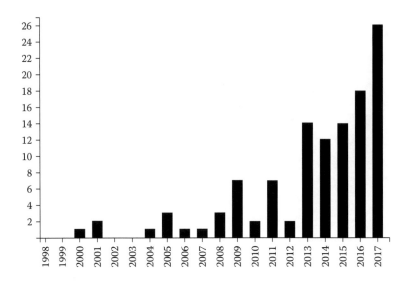

Source: Web of Science, accessed May 31, 2018.

Figure 7.3   Keyword "policy entrepreneurship" articles published per year, 2000–2017

to understand the origin, workings and implications of policies within their broader political, social and economic contexts." *Policy Studies Journal* published six articles between 2009 and 2017, all of them with considerable citation output.

6   Conclusion and outlook

This chapter offers initial findings of an exploratory synthesis of the literature with a focus on PPE. The Social Science Citation Index query shows that the interest in "public entrepreneurship"-related topics increased; the number of publications and sum of citations increased significantly in the context of the keyword "policy entrepreneurship" in the last ten years. Tables 7.2 and 7.3 present a synthesis of journals that have published more than two articles since 2000 with a focus on PPE. The overview shows that a significant variety of journals published only one article with a focus on PPE, which seems to be an indicator that the total number

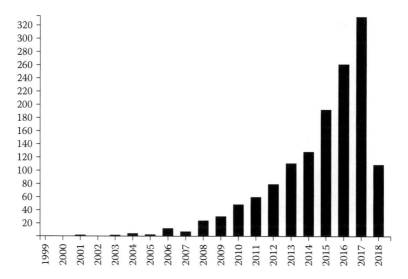

Source: Web of Science, accessed May 31, 2018.

Figure 7.4   Keyword "policy entrepreneurship" articles by the sum of citations per year, 2000–2017

of publications and total sum of citations increased, but it seems that research on PPE is, while an important and clearly relevant topic, still a speciality within the broader entrepreneurship research community. Another possible explanation for why research on PPE has not developed a more mainstream profile in public policy and public administration journals is that most studies on PPE tend to be more qualitative in nature and focus on theory building rather than theory testing. Finally, the lack of availability of systematic, longitudinal data and in-depth case studies that are needed to produce studies beyond qualitative aspects pose another drawback in order to be considered in premier journals more frequently. Further research has to investigate whether these findings can be confirmed.

Future research and additional systematic queries need to take into consideration further keywords including "public sector entrepreneurship," "public entrepreneur," "policy entrepreneur," "institutional entrepreneurship," or "political entrepreneurship." The differentiation amongst these terms is still not clear in academic research. Based on the above selected most-often cited articles, a better categorization of the terms public entrepreneurship versus policy entrepreneurship can be achieved – which should be the goal for future publications and research. Moreover, a systematic content-related review of the literature will offer better information about potential major themes and potential country foci. Furthermore, the time frame of systematic investigation needs to be extended; a 17-year history is considered a rather short time frame in academic research "(. . .) when compared with, for example, the 50-year history of strategy or the more than 225-year history of economics" (Rothaermel et al. 2007, p. 699).

Table 7.2 Most-often cited articles, keyword "policy entrepreneurship," 2000–2017
(>20 total citations)[3]

Title	Authors	Source title	Total citations	Publication date
Policy entrepreneurship and policy change	Mintrom, Michael; Norman, Phillipa	*Policy Studies Journal*	224	2009
Personal values as a catalyst for corporate social entrepreneurship	Hemingway, C.A.	*Journal of Business Ethics*	133	2005
Policy entrepreneurship and multilevel governance: A comparative study of European cross-border regions	Perkmann, Markus	*Environment and Planning C – Government and Policy*	83	2007
When ideas trump interests: Preferences, worldviews, and policy innovations	Rodrik, Dani	*Journal of Economic Perspectives*	51	2014
The action plan on combating terrorism: A flawed instrument of EU security governance	Bossong, Raphael	*Journal of Common Market Studies*	49	2008
Multiple streams in EU policy-making: The case of the 2005 sugar reform	Ackrill, Robert; Kay, Adrian	*Journal of European Public Policy*	41	2011
Ambiguity, multiple streams, and EU policy	Ackrill, Robert; Kay, Adrian; Zahariadis, Nikolaos	*Journal of European Public Policy*	39	2013
European Union energy policy integration: A case of European Commission policy entrepreneurship and increasing supranationalism	Maltby, Tomas	*Energy Policy*	39	2013
Explaining radical policy change: The case of climate change and energy policy under the British Labour Government 2006–10	Carter, Neil; Jacobs, Michael	*Public Administration*	37	2014

3 The keywords "public entrepreneurship" and "policy entrepreneurship" must have appeared consecutively and not separately in the title or abstracts of the articles. In future research an extended number of keywords will be used (e.g. "public sector entrepreneurship") to incorporate articles which cover the topic but do not have the herewith narrow defined keywords in title or abstract.

Table 7.2   (continued)

Title	Authors	Source title	Total citations	Publication date
Undocumented immigrants and state higher education policy: The politics of in-state tuition eligibility in Texas and Arizona	Dougherty, Kevin J.; Nienhusser, H. Kenny; Vega, Blanca E.	*Review Of Higher Education*	34	2010
Policy entrepreneurship in the development of public sector strategy: The case of London health reform	Oborn, Eivor; Barrett, Michael; Exworthy, Mark	*Public Administration*	v31	2011
Policy entrepreneurship and institutional change: Multilevel governance of central banking reform	Bakir, Caner	*Governance – An International Journal of Policy Administration and Institutions*	31	2009
Bureaucratic job mobility and the diffusion of innovations	Teodoro, Manuel P.	*American Journal of Political Science*	30	2009
Shifting resources and venues producing policy change in contested subsystems: A case study of Swedish signals intelligence policy	Nohrstedt, Daniel	*Policy Studies Journal*	28	2011
The WTO and food safety regulatory policy innovation in the European Union	Skogstad, G.	*Journal of Common Market Studies*	28	2001
Policy windows, ambiguity and Commission entrepreneurship: Explaining the relaunch of the European Union's economic reform agenda	Copeland, Paul; James, Scott	*Journal of European Public Policy*	26	2014
Taking on tobacco: Policy entrepreneurship and the tobacco litigation	Spill, R.L.; Licari, M.J.; Ray, L.	*Political Research Quarterly*	26	2001
Australian beach safety and the politics of shark attacks	Neff, Christopher	*Coastal Management*	25	2012
Public policy, entrepreneurship, and venture capital in the United States	Cumming, Douglas; Li, Dan	*Journal of Corporate Finance*	22	2013

Table 7.2   (continued)

Title	Authors	Source title	Total citations	Publication date
Policy entrepreneurship in the co-evolution of institutions, preferences, and technology. Comparing the diffusion of totally chlorine-free pulp bleaching technologies in the US and Sweden	Reinstaller, A.	*Research Policy*	21	2005

Table 7.3   Keyword "public entrepreneurship," articles published per academic journal, 2000–2017 (more than two publications per journal)

Academic journal	Articles published, 2000–2017
Energy Policy	2
Environment and Planning C – Politics and Space	4
Environment and Planning C – Government and Policy	2
Environmental Politics	2
Governance – An International Journal of Policy Administration and Institutions	2
Journal of Cleaner Production	2
Journal of Comparative Policy Analysis	3
Journal of European Public Policy	3
Journal of Health Politics Policy and Law	3
Policy and Society	3
Policy Studies Journal	6
Politics & Policy	2
Public Administration	3
Social Science & Medicine	2
West European Politics	2

These initial findings and thoughts give some directions for future research through which I hope to increase the number of scholars who will participate in the growing research on PPE, not least because the role of PPE will increase. More research about the interrelationship and linkages between PPE and sustainable development will bring about more acceptable and effective solutions for the most challenging social, economic, and political issues today. These solutions often demand drastic changes and, therefore, lack acceptance and support by societies and politicians alike. How can policy entrepreneurs contribute to (a) the development of innovative solutions and (b) a higher acceptance of drastic changes in policymaking? Drastic policy changes are needed for sustainable development in ageing societies as much as in emerging or fragile states. The pension system in Germany is just one randomly selected example. It will collapse in the long run if drastic reforms are not taken immediately. It offers privileges to an elite group of people (such as selected civil servants) and discriminates against other parts of the working population receiving lower pensions and fewer privileges. This lopsided distribution is already causing financial shortcomings in the pension system. Another example is climate change which will not be solved with short-sighted, national solutions but only by a global effort of private, public, and non-profit organizations and partnerships. Another example is the tragic warfare in Syria which seems to continue without international joint efforts to end a war against the poorest and most vulnerable of the global planet. Innovative solutions followed by drastic reforms will not emerge easily because they require a change in norms, habits, behaviors, and societal standards. Only by delivering more research about the role of PPE for overcoming and substituting old and rigid rules and standards in policymaking will societies and places be able to progress and improve sustainably.

The role of the public and policy entrepreneur is becoming more important. He or she tends to operate at the intersection of the three classical sectors and takes action in areas where the government, private, and non-profit sectors are not yet active or effective. Due to financial limitations of state and municipal budgets, but also due to government failure, for example in the areas of protecting global common goods or human rights, the engagement of policy entrepreneurs will rise (Stein 2008). In this context, policy entrepreneurs can uphold an important role because they create a balance between state and social-entrepreneurial action and make an important contribution to social change. The clear accentuation and support of transparent, effective social entrepreneurial projects could enable policy entrepreneurs to build a bridge across politics and society and serve as an important driver and also as a control element in the policy process. The potentials of policy but also social entrepreneurs lie in experimenting, developing, and implementing creative, innovative ideas and solutions for overcoming social (and also political) challenges, which is why he or she works as a provider of ideas to the government.

References

Audretsch, D.B. (2007), *The Entrepreneurial Society*, New York: Oxford University Press.

Audretsch, D.B. (2017), 'Entrepreneurship and universities', *International Journal of Entrepreneurship and Small Business*, **31** (1), 4–11.

Audretsch, D.B., Keilbach, M., and Lehmann, E. (2005), *Entrepreneurship and Economic Growth*, New York: Oxford University Press.

Audretsch, D.B., Kuratko, D.F., and Link, A.N. (2015), 'Making sense of the elusive paradigm of entrepreneurship', *Small Business Economics*, **45** (4), 703–12.

Bernier, L. and Hafsi, T. (2007), 'The changing nature of public entrepreneurship', *Public Administration Review*, **67**, 408–533.

Grimm, H.M. (2009), 'Creating an entrepreneurial economy: The role of public policy', in D.B. Audretsch and R. Strom (eds.), *Entrepreneurship, Growth, and Public Policy*, Cambridge: Cambridge University Press, pp. 299–318.

Grimm, H.M. (2010), 'Entrepreneur – Social Entrepreneur – Policy Entrepreneur. Typologische Merkmale und Perspektiven', *Zeitschrift für Politikberatung*, **3** (3–4), 441–56.

Howlett, M., Ramesh, M., and Perl, A. (2009), *Studying Public Policy. Policy Cycles and Policy Subsystems*, Oxford: Oxford University Press.

Karlsson, C., Silander, C., and Silander, D. (eds.) (2016), *Political Entrepreneurship. Regional Growth and Entrepreneurial Diversity in Sweden*, Cheltenham, UK and Northampton, MA, USA: Edward Elgar Publishing Limited.

Kingdon, J.W. (1995), *Agendas, Alternatives, and Public Policies*, 2nd ed., Boston, MA: Little, Brown & Company.

Leyden, D.P. (2016), 'Public-sector entrepreneurship and the creation of a sustainable innovative economy', *Small Business Economics*, **46** (4), 553–64.

Leyden, D.P. and Link, A.N. (2015), *Public Sector Entrepreneurship: US Technology and Innovation Policy*, New York: Oxford University Press.

Link, A.N. and Link, J.R. (2007), *Government as Entrepreneur*, New York: Oxford University Press.

Mintrom, M. (1997), 'Policy entrepreneurs and the diffusion of innovation', *American Journal of Political Science*, **41** (3), 738–70.

Mintrom, M. and Norman, P. (2009), 'Policy entrepreneurship and policy change', *Policy Studies Journal*, **37** (4), 649–67.

Osborne, D. and Gaebler, T. (1993), *Reinventing Government. How the Entrepreneurial Spirit is Transforming the Public Sector*, New York: Penguin Books.

Ostrom, E. (2005), 'Unlocking public entrepreneurship and public economies'. Working Paper DP2005/01, World Institute for Development Economic Research (UNU-WIDER).

Roberts, N. and King, P.J. (1991), 'Policy entrepreneurs: Their activity structure and function in the policy process', *Journal of Public Administration Research and Theory*, **1** (2), 147–75.

Roberts, N. and King, P.J. (1996), *Transforming Public Policy*, San Francisco, CA: Jossey-Bass Publishers.

Rose, R. (1993), *Lesson Drawing in Public Policy: A Guide to Learning across Time and Space*, Chatham, UK: Chatham House.

Rothaermel, F.T., Agung, S., and Jiang, L. (2007), 'University entrepreneurship: A taxonomy of the literature', *Industrial and Corporate Change*, **16** (4), 691–791.

Schumpeter, J.A. (1934), *The Theory of Economic Development: An Inquiry into Profits, Capital, Credit, Interest, and the Business Cycle*, 16th ed., New Brunswick, NJ: Transaction Publishers.

Schumpeter, J.A. (1997), *Theorie der wirtschaftlichen Entwicklung. Eine Untersuchung über Unternehmergewinn, Kapital, Kredit, Zins und den Konjunkturzyklus*, Neunte Auflage, Berlin: Duncker & Humblot.

Shane, S. and Venkataraman, S. (2000), 'The promise of entrepreneurship as a field of research', *The Academy of Management Review*, **25** (1), 217–26.

Silander, D. (2016), 'The Political Entrepreneur', in C. Karlsson, C. Silander and D. Silander (eds.), *Political Entrepreneurship. Regional Growth and Entrepreneurial Diversity in Sweden*, Cheltenham, UK and Northampton, MA, USA: Edward Elgar Publishing Limited, pp. 7–20.

Silander, D. and Silander, C. (2016), 'Introduction: The political entrepreneur for regional growth and entrepreneurial diversity', in C. Karlsson, C. Silander, and D. Silander (eds.), *Political Entrepreneurship. Regional Growth and Entrepreneurial Diversity in Sweden*, Cheltenham, UK and Northampton, MA, USA: Edward Elgar Publishing Limited, pp. 3–7.

Stein, T. (2008), 'Globale Wohltäter', *Die neuen Weltbürger und ihr Beitrag zum gesellschaftlichen Wandel. WZB-Mitteilungen*, **119** (March), 22–7.

8 A research agenda for entrepreneurship and innovation: the role of entrepreneurial universities

Maribel Guerrero and David Urbano

Introduction

Since the publication of Burton R. Clark's book (1998), the research about the phenomena of "entrepreneurial universities" and their core activities – teaching, research, technology transfer and entrepreneurship – has increased significantly. Traditionally, studies tend to take a narrow view about the role of universities in entrepreneurship and innovation activities analysing them like different phenomenon (Autio et al., 2014; Herrera et al., 2018). However, the role of a university is dichotomous focusing both innovation and entrepreneurship to contribute to competitiveness and economic growth via graduate entrepreneurship (Guerrero et al., 2018), academic entrepreneurship (Siegel et al., 2007; Wright et al., 2007; Guerrero et al., 2016), technology transfer/commercialization (Mosey et al., 2017) and being the intersection of entrepreneurship and innovation ecosystems (Autio et al., 2014; Herrera et al., 2018).

The most recent worldwide economic downturn and current socio-economic events (e.g., Brexit, the US elections, migration/refugees, digitalization) are representing a strategic game changer for most organizations. Severe resource constraints and unpredictable conditions created significant challenges for organizational survival, let alone growth through innovation and entrepreneurial initiatives. Universities are also facing challenges such as higher rates of unemployment, the reduction of public budgets, reduction in the demand of higher education studies, etc. In this new socio-economic landscape, universities try to connect teaching/research activities with real practices/challenges where their students/researchers not only capture new knowledge but also participate in the strengthening of local socio-economic development. Consequently, we may expect new transformation and evolutionary processes of universities in the most reflective entrepreneurial/knowledge-based societies, calling for a new research agenda.

This chapter examines the academic research about entrepreneurial universities that has been published in the major journals and identifies trends for future research in this phenomenon. To achieve this objective, we examine articles published on entrepreneurial universities from several domains that comprise their roles on entrepreneurship and innovation. Our findings serve as the foundation, the boundaries and direction of research in this domain. More specifically, we examine what might be emerging as a distinctive domain of entrepreneurial universities research. We also explore the implications of boundary and areas of opportunities for exchange new advances in entrepreneurship and innovation in multidisciplinary fields.

This chapter is organized as follows. Section 2 presents the link between entrepreneurship and innovation. Section 3 integrates the methodological design. Section 4 describes the radiography of entrepreneurial university research. Section 5 describes the role of higher education organizations such as drivers of innovation and entrepreneurship in the light of existent studies. Section 6 discusses the emerging areas in entrepreneurial university research. Finally, section 7 summarizes some concluding remarks.

Entrepreneurship, innovation and universities

The configurations of new knowledge-intensive environments required fertile settings for innovative and entrepreneurial activities. Innovation and entrepreneurship are multidimensional processes and both types of activities play a crucial role in the economy. Since the seminal work of Schumpeter, entrepreneurship and innovation have been strongly related when the creative destruction is present when entrepreneurs introduce radically new products, services and processes to the marketplace (Schumpeter, 1934). In this vein, Baumol (2002) also argued that entrepreneurship and innovation are the main sources of national competitive advantage when new ventures broke the established development paths and undermined established competencies. As a result, many nations/regions/cities have implemented several policies to stimulate innovation by entrepreneurial firms to foster economic growth (Autio et al., 2014); particularly, policies to promote technology-based entrepreneurship (Mustar and Wright, 2010; Grimaldi et al., 2011). It explains why the Triple or Quadruple Helix concepts have been operationalized in different ways (with/without government/social intervention, closed/opened, administrated/entrepreneurially, etc.) in different spaces (global, national, regional, local) and in different contexts (organizational, institutional, technological, social, etc.).

Because of this diversity, there has been growing interest in the study of how organizations transform their roles and practices in the development and strengthening of entrepreneurship and innovation. However, the majority of research has analysed both activities separately. Zahra and Wright (2011) argue that innovation literature has been mostly oriented on the structure and institutions while entrepreneurship literature has been mostly about the individual or the firm. On one side, innovation literature focused on the complex relationships of cooperation, communication and feedback among institutions in both the process of innovation and the innovative performance across countries (Carlsson et al., 2002). On the other side, the entrepreneurship literature traditionally focused on independent ventures as well as on the organizational mode within which entrepreneurial initiatives took place (Parker, 2011). Following these perspectives, universities are key agents for entrepreneurship and innovation by their significant intersection of both scenarios through the development of core activities such as education, research, transference/commercialization of knowledge, and start-up creation. By nature, entrepreneurial and innovative universities tend to adopt an entrepreneurial management style, with members who act entrepreneurially, who interact with the outside environment in an entrepreneurial manner (Audretsch, 2014), and who incorporate an entrepreneurial orientation into their core activities/ missions (Kirby et al., 2011). As a result, the entrepreneurial university configures an adequate environment for nurturing innovation and entrepreneurship within its community (students, faculty, academics and alumni) and simultaneously acts like a intersection in the regional innovation systems and entrepreneurship ecosystems (Herrera et al., 2018).

Methods

We examined entrepreneurship articles published in the Web of Science database to identify articles based on the following criteria: (1) one or more keywords related to entrepreneurial and/or innovative universities in the article title or abstract (i.e., university missions, academic entrepreneurship, graduate entrepreneurship, university-industry collaboration, technology transfer, innovation and entrepreneurial ecosystems); and (2) publication between 1993 and 2018, inclusive. As a result, 726 articles were identified and coded. Each article was coded into one of five categories: core missions/activities; graduate entrepreneurship; academic entrepreneurship; main outputs/outcomes/impacts; and involvement in innovation/entrepreneurship ecosystems. The rationale for these categories was put forward by Shane (2004), O'Shea et al. (2005, 2007), Guerrero and Urbano (2012b) and Autio et al. (2014) in their proposed conceptual model about entrepreneurial universities.

Radiography of entrepreneurial university research

Over the past 25 years – and especially in the last decade – research on "the entrepreneurial university" has increased dramatically (see Figure 8.1). According with Web of Science (June, 2018), 726 papers have studied this phenomena adopting different academic perspectives – for example, business economics, education research, public administration, engineering, operation management, environmental sciences, geography, information science, social science, science technology, psychology, urban studies, sociology, agriculture, government law, biotechnology, computer science, history, women's studies, among others.

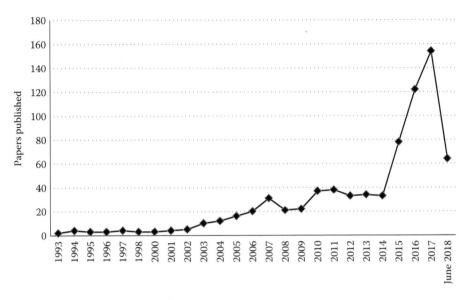

Source: Web of Science (June, 2018).

Figure 8.1   Entrepreneurial university research, January 1993–June 2018

Concerning publishers, entrepreneurial university research has been published by academic journals such as *Research Policy* (45), *Journal of Technology Transfer* (40), *Higher Education* (22), *Technovation* (21), *Small Business Economics* (16), *Education and Training* (14), *Scientometrics* (13), *Journal of Management Development* (12), *International Journal of Technology Management* (11), *Journal of Business Venturing* (10), *Entrepreneurship and Regional Development* (9), *Journal of Small Business Management* (9), *Technological Forecasting and Social Change* (9), *Science and Public Policy* (8), *European Planning Studies* (8), *International Entrepreneurship and Management Journal* (8), *International Journal of Engineering Education* (7), *International Journal of Entrepreneurial Behavior & Research* (7), *R&D Management* (7), *Entrepreneurship Research Journal* (6), *International Journal of Innovation and Technology Management* (6), *International Journal of Innovation Science* (6), *Journal of Small Business and Entrepreneurship Development* (6), *Science, Technology and Society* (6) and *Studies in Higher Education* (6), among others (Table 8.1).

The phenomena of entrepreneurial universities has analysed different higher education systems (Table 8.2). *The American university system* analysed the cases of Berkeley University, Duke University, Georgia Institute of Technology, Georgetown University, Kent State University, MIT, Ohio State University, Rutgers University, Stanford University, St Louis University, University of California, University of Michigan, University of Missouri, University of North Carolina-Chapel Hill, University of South Carolina and University of Texas, among others. *The British university system* explored the entrepreneurial orientation of Cambridge

Table 8.1 Main publishers of entrepreneurial universities research

45 Research Policy	21 Technovation	12 Journal of Management Development	9 Journal of Small Business Management	9 Technological Forecasting and Social Change	8 European Planning Studies	8 International Entrepreneurship and Management
	16 Small Business Economics	11 International Journal of Technology Management	8 Science and Public Policy	7 R&D Management	6 Entrepreneurship Research Journal	6 International Journal of Innovation and Technology Management
40 Journal of Technology Transfer	14 Education and Training	10 Journal of Business Venturing	7 International Journal of Engineering Education	6 International Journal of Innovation Science	6 Science Technology and Society	6 Studies in Higher Education
22 Higher Education	13 Scientometrics	9 Entrepreneurship and Regional Development	7 International Journal of Entrepreneurial Behavior & Research	6 Journal of Small Business and Enterprise Development		

Source: Web of Science (June, 2018).

Table 8.2   Analysed higher education systems

172 USA	57 Italy	29 Belgium	24 Canada	18 South Africa	17 Malaysia	17 Norway
	48 Germany	29 The Netherlands	17 Portugal	13 France	13 Iran	13 Poland
106 England	32 China	27 Russia	16 Brazil	13 Taiwan	12 Ireland	
75 Spain	29 Australia	26 Sweden	16 Finland	12 Austria	10 Denmark	

Source: Web of Science (June, 2018).

University, the London universities, Newcastle University, Oxford University, Sussex University and Scotland's universities, among others. *The Spanish university system* analysed the entrepreneurial stages of the Autonomous University of Barcelona, the Technical University of Catalonia, the Technical University of Valencia, University of Huelva, University of Navarra, University of Sevilla and Valencia University, among others. *The Italian university system* explored the cases of Florence University, Milan University, Turin University, Polytechnic of Milano, the University of Ferrara and the University of Pisa, among others. Other *European entrepreneurial universities* examples have been Katholieke Universiteit Leuven and University of Flanders (Belgium), Aalto University, University of Jyvaskyla, University of Turku, and Lappeenranta University of Technology (Finland) and the Universities of Chalmers, Linkoping and Twente (Sweden), among others.

Moreover, several studies have developed comparative studies within continents/countries and across such systems as American and European universities, American and Asian universities, American and Latin-American universities, European and African universities, among others.

The cited works in each of these 726 articles were analysed to count the number of references to articles published in journals listed in the Web of Science dataset. Table 8.3 shows the highest paper cited from January 1993 to June 2018. In this regard, the most cited authors who focused exclusively on entrepreneurial universities have been: Etzkowitz (1998) who explored the links between university and industry; Vohora et al. (2004) who analysed the development of high-tech companies; Thursby and Thursby (2002) who explored the main basis of academic entrepreneurship; O'Shea et al. (2005) who established the main basis of the entrepreneurial orientation of universities, technology transfer and spin-off performance; Audretsch and Lehmann (2005) who explained the spillover effect of

Table 8.3   The highest-impact articles

Authors	Publisher	Year	Citations
Etzkowitz, H.	*Research Policy*	1998	436
Vohora, A.; Wright, M.; Lockett, A.	*Research Policy*	2004	364
Thursby, Jg; Thursby, Mc	*Management Science*	2002	342
Blumenthal, D.; Campbell, Eg; Anderson, Ms; Causino, N.; Louis, Ks	*Jama-Journal of the American Medical Association*	1997	339
O'Shea, Rp; Allen, Tj; Chevalier, A.; Roche, F.	*Research Policy*	2005	320
Luthje, C.; Franke, N.	*R & D Management*	2003	237
Deem, R.	*Comparative Education*	2001	230
Audretsch, Db; Lehmann, Ee	*Research Policy*	2005	224
Robinson, Pb; Sexton, Ea	*Journal of Business Venturing*	1994	220
Wright, Mike; Lockett, Andy; Clarysse, Bart; Binks, Martin	*Research Policy*	2006	187
Cooke, P.	*Research Policy*	2005	172
Powell, W.W.	*Journal of Institutional and Theoretical Economics*	1996	164
Van Looy, B.; Ranga, M.; Callaert, J.; Debackere, K.; Zimmermann, E.	*Research Policy*	2004	163
Siegel, Donald S.; Veugelers, Reinhilde; Wright, Mike	*Oxford Review of Economic Policy*	2007	159
Jacob, M.; Lundqvist, M.; Hellsmark, H.	*Research Policy*	2003	143
Shane, S.	*Journal of Business Venturing*	2004	142
Rasmussen, Ea; Sorheim, R.	*Technovation*	2006	140
Bramwell, Allison; Wolfe, David A.	*Research Policy*	2008	139
Kenney, M.; Goe, Wr	*Research Policy*	2004	137
Van Looy, B.; Callaert, J.; Debackere, K.	*Research Policy*	2006	132
Youtie, Jan; Shapira, Philip	*Research Policy*	2008	130
Ndonzuau, Fn; Pirnay, F.; Surlemont, B.	*Technovation*	2002	121
Lowe, Ra; Ziedonis, Aa	*Management Science*	2006	115
Blank, Steve	*Harvard Business Review*	2013	111
Kuckertz, Andreas; Wagner, Marcus	*Journal of Business Venturing*	2010	110
Siegel, Donald S.; Wright, Mike; Lockett, Andy	*Industrial and Corporate Change*	2007	110
Djokovic, Djordje; Souitaris, Vangelis	*Journal of Technology Transfer*	2008	101
Markman, Gideon D.; Siegel, Donald S.; Wright, Mike	*Journal of Management Studies*	2008	100
Philpott, Kevin; Dooley, Lawrence; O'Reilly, Caroline; Lupton, Gary	*Technovation*	2011	98
Barnett, R.	*Higher Education*	2000	98
Lam, Alice	*Research Policy*	2011	96
Van Looy, Bart; Landoni, Paolo; Callaert, Julie; Van Pottelsberghe, Bruno; Sapsalis, Eleftherios; Debackere, Koenraad	*Research Policy*	2011	89

Table 8.3   (continued)

Authors	Publisher	Year	Citations
O'Shea, Rory P.; Allen, Thomas J.; Morse, Kenneth P.; O'Gorman, Colm; Roche, Frank	*R & D Management*	2007	89
Landry, Rejean; Amara, Nabil; Rherrad, Imad	*Research Policy*	2006	89
Chrisman, Jj; Hynes, T.; Fraser, S.	*Journal of Business Venturing*	1995	89
Martinelli, Arianna; Meyer, Martin; Von Tunzelmann, Nick	*Journal of Technology Transfer*	2008	87
Meyer, Martin	*Research Policy*	2006	87
Eun, Jong-Hak; Lee, Keun; Wu, Guisheng	*Research Policy*	2006	86
Boardman, P. Craig; Ponomariov, Branco L.	*Technovation*	2009	84
Stromquist, Nelly P.	*Higher Education*	2007	84
Ylijoki, OH	*Higher Education*	2003	84
Guerrero, Maribel; Urbano, David	*Journal of Technology Transfer*	2012	80
Harmon, B.; Ardishvili, A.; Cardozo, R.; Elder, T.; Leuthold, J.; Parshall, J.; Raghian, M.; Smith, D.	*Journal of Business Venturing*	1997	80
Clarysse, Bart; Tartari, Valentina; Salter, Ammon	*Research Policy*	2011	79
Lam, Alice	*Social Studies of Science*	2010	77
Wong, Poh-Kam; Ho, Yuen-Ping; Singh, Annette	*World Development*	2007	77
Fini, Riccardo; Grimaldi, Rosa; Sobrero, Maurizio	*Journal of Technology Transfer*	2009	74
Perkmann, Markus; King, Zella; Pavelin, Stephen	*Research Policy*	2011	71
Baldini, Nicola; Grimaldi, Rosa; Sobrero, Maurizio	*Scientometrics*	2007	71
Chlosta, Simone; Patzelt, Holger; Klein, Sabine B.; Dormann, Christian	*Small Business Economics*	2012	70
Clarysse, Bart; Wright, Mike; Van De Velde, Els	*Journal of Management Studies*	2011	70
Rasmussen, Einar; Borch, Odd Jar	*Research Policy*	2010	70
Baldini, Nicola; Grimaldi, Rosa; Sobrero, Maurizio	*Research Policy*	2006	70

Source: Web of Science (June, 2018)

universities in regions; Wright et al. (2006) who started to highlight the relationship of universities with venture capitalists; Siegel et al. (2007) who explained the link between technology transfer offices, commercialization and intellectual property; and Shane (2004) who established the main fundaments of the existence of entrepreneurial universities as a result of the Bayh-Dole Act.

What we do know about the role of entrepreneurial universities on innovation and entrepreneurship activities

Core activities

The so-called entrepreneurial university simultaneously fulfills three different activities – teaching, research and entrepreneurship – while providing an adequate atmosphere in which the university community can explore and exploit ideas and contribute to the creation of a sustained competitive advantage that could be transformed into social and economic impacts (Guerrero and Urbano, 2012a, b). The revised literature includes 71 papers that clearly evidenced some trends concerning the interaction of entrepreneurship and innovation across the core activities in several educational systems (Figure 8.2).

In the North American higher educational context, the main analyses were oriented to recognize the core activities based on the most representative examples of entrepreneurial universities (Shane, 2004; O'Shea et al., 2005; Wright et al., 2006; Siegel et al., 2007; O'Shea et al., 2007), to understand the socialization process (Mendoza, 2007), the emergence of entrepreneurship across university organizational structures (French and Miller, 2012; Wolf, 2017), the critical conjectures about the missions (Vohora et al., 2004; Grandi and Grimaldi, 2005), the analysis of research ambidexterity (Chang et al., 2016) and reflecting about social sustainability (Karpov, 2017; Fichter and Tiemann, 2018; Tiemann et al., 2018).

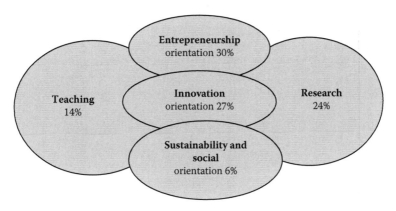

Source: Authors.

Figure 8.2 Core entrepreneurial university activities, N=71

In the European higher educational context, the literature provides insights about the institutional transformation (Barnett, 2000; Baldini et al., 2006; Van Looy et al., 2006; Liyanage and Andrade, 2012) regarding the excellence in teaching for fostering start-up creation (Sanchez-Canizares and Rodriguez-Gutierrez, 2015) as well as the dynamics of academic knowledge production (Ranga et al., 2003; Kalar and Antoncic, 2015), knowledge transfer (Guerrero and Urbano, 2012a; Berbegal-Mirabent et al., 2013) and commercialization (Baldini, 2006; Wigren-Kristoferson et al., 2011; Jacobsson et al., 2013; Berggren, 2017). Interestingly, the most up-to-date papers are questioning ethics and values (Loi and Di Guardo, 2015), evaluating the quality of value creation (Di Berardino and Corsi, 2018) of entrepreneurial universities in and for peripheral areas (Addie et al., 2018) as well as the vision of the future of these missions (Sperrer et al., 2016).

In the emerging economies higher education context, the research emerges for identifying characteristics of entrepreneurial universities (Bernasconi, 2005) as well as evidencing how university stimulates entrepreneurship and innovation via courses transforming mindsets (Araújo et al., 2005; Digby, 2005; Abou-Warda, 2015; Hassanzadeh et al., 2015; Jabeen et al., 2017) as well as adopting an entrepreneurial orientation during knowledge generation (Wong et al., 2007; Cantu et al., 2009; Kamunyori et al., 2010; Luna et al., 2017). Interestingly, several papers try to identify synergies or differences contrasting with current entrepreneurial universities' models (Kwon and Martin, 2012; Carayannis et al., 2016).

Graduate/academic innovative entrepreneurs

The entrepreneurial university core activities are oriented to transform the mindset and actions of the community (students and academics). The revised literature includes 190 papers that clearly evidenced the main characteristics of graduate entrepreneurs and academic entrepreneurs across higher education systems (Figure 8.3).

Regarding graduate entrepreneurship, in the context of developed economies, during the 2000s the focus was on delighting the design of entrepreneurship programmes (McMullan and Gillin, 1998), the entrepreneurial intention of university students (Lüthje and Franke, 2003), and the entrepreneurial mindset (Toledano and Urbano, 2008). Afterwards, the research was oriented to explore the link with

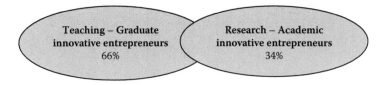

Source: Authors.

Figure 8.3   Entrepreneurial university community, N=190

career choices (Ilouga et al., 2014), understanding the main competences, passion, emotions (May et al., 2016; Costa et al., 2018), the role of mentors (St-Jean et al., 2017), institutional determinants (Urbano et al., 2017), programmes across different campuses/locations (Katz et al., 2014; Larsson et al., 2017), as well as introducing online promotion (Pizarro and Gurrisi, 2017; Trevitt et al., 2017). In the context of developing and emerging economies, the number of publications regarding graduate entrepreneurship has increased radically during the last five to ten years. Nevertheless, the majority of these studies still focused on exploring the entrepreneurial intention of university students applying traditional models, paying attention to the influence of university via entrepreneurship education (Lima et al., 2015; Karimi et al., 2016; Sun et al., 2017) as well as certain university support mechanisms (Guerrero et al., 2017, 2018; Mamun et al., 2017; Xiao and North, 2017). Interestingly, the analysis of minority groups is also included in this research, in particular the focus on disabled graduate students (Johnmark et al., 2016) and gender (Szelényi et al., 2016).

Regarding academic entrepreneurship in developing economies, the existent research provides insights about the recognition of the relevance of entrepreneurial capacity (Etzkowitz, 1998; Markman et al., 2008; Clarysse et al., 2011; Holley and Watson, 2017), team composition (Visintin and Pittino, 2014), organizational and environmental conditions (Fox and Xiao, 2013; Davey et al., 2016), social embeddedness (Kenney and Goe, 2004) to incentive and motivate (Lam, 2011) the scientific performance (Van Looy et al., 2004) and high-growth intentions (Knockaert et al., 2015). In emerging economies, the publications are recent and focused on basic/foundational elements regarding career development with regard to gender (Riordan and Louw-Potgieter, 2011), academic experience and capacity (Lubango and Pouris, 2007), required resources (Ryu, 1998; Shibayama et al., 2012), and evaluation of effectiveness (Ahmadzadeh et al., 2017).

Outputs, outcomes and impacts

Associated with the university missions and community, we found 158 papers related to the main outputs, outcomes and impacts of entrepreneurial universities (Table 8.4). The majority of research regarding entrepreneurial university outputs focused on venture creation (Landry et al., 2006; Wright et al., 2006; Djokovic and Souitaris, 2008; Kroll and Liefner, 2008; Åstebro et al., 2012; Baltzopoulos and Broström, 2013; Epure et al., 2016; van Stijn et al., 2018) and commercialization processes (Meyer, 2006; Landry et al., 2007; Baldini, 2010; Carayannis et al., 2015). Concerning outcomes, the existent research provides insights about intensity, performance (O'Shea et al., 2005; Gittelman, 2006; Smith and Ho, 2006; Chang et al., 2009; Abramo et al., 2012; Zhang et al., 2016), success (Siegel and Wessner, 2012), effectiveness (Van Looy et al., 2011), growth (Mueller, 2007) and visibility.

In the long term, the expected impact of entrepreneurial university outputs could be transformed into the predominant production factors that contribute to social and economic development, which are: *human capital* through the

Table 8.4   Entrepreneurial university's outputs, outcomes and impacts, N=158

Outputs (44%)	Outcomes (13%)	Impacts (43%)
Venture creation	Spin-offs	Human capital
● Start-up	● Performance	● Work-ready graduates
● Spin-offs, spin-outs	● Growth	● Self-employment
● Biotech/High-tech firms	● Revenues	● Job creation/Employability
● Hybrid firms		● Productivity
● Science-based	Commercialization	
entrepreneurship	● Innovation/Research/	Knowledge
● Social entrepreneurship	IP/Technology	● Production
	transfer performance	● Spillovers
Commercialization	● Effectiveness, success	● Innovation capacity
● Licensing		
● Patenting	Others	Region
● Social innovations	● Visibility and	● Social and economic development
● High-tech inventors	reputation	● Sustainability
	● Brand image	● Competitiveness
		● Well-being
		● Community capacity
		● Specialization

Source: Authors.

generation, attraction and retention of job seekers and entrepreneurs (Robinson and Sexton, 1994; Allen et al., 2007; Chlosta et al., 2012; Carree et al., 2015); *knowledge capital* produced by the generation, attraction and retention of prestigious researchers who facilitate knowledge transfer/commercialization that produces innovation capacities, spillovers and specializations (Audretsch and Lehmann, 2005; Aharonson et al., 2007; Hsu et al., 2007; Audretsch et al., 2012; Theodorakopoulos et al., 2012; Kim, 2013; Bonaccorsi et al., 2014; Drucker, 2016; Del Giudice et al., 2017; Fini et al., 2018; Trequattrini et al., 2018); *entrepreneurship capital* with the creation of new ventures that promote competitiveness, and diversity (Chrisman et al., 1995; Bramwell and Wolfe, 2008; Bathelt et al., 2010; Harrison and Leitch, 2010; Urbano and Guerrero, 2013; Carree et al., 2014; Guerrero et al., 2015; Guerrero et al., 2016; Budyldina, 2018).

Strategies, resources and capabilities

Exploring within the entrepreneurial universities, we found 136 papers that analysed this phenomena from a managerial and strategic perspective (Table 8.5).

Several authors have paid attention to the strategic implementations within these organizations in terms of entrepreneurial orientation (Jacob et al., 2003; Todorovic

Table 8.5   Entrepreneurial universities' strategies, resources and capabilities, N=136

Strategies (35%)	Resources (46%)	Capabilities (18%)
Orientation	Resources	● Alliances
● Diversification	● Financial	● Joint ventures
● Internationalization	● Staff and faculty	● Collaborations
● Entrepreneurial		● Open innovation
● Transformation processes	Infrastructures	
● Business model	● Technology transfer offices	
● Value creation	● Incubators	
	● Business creation offices	
	● Scientific parks	

Source: Authors.

et al., 2011), international orientation (Minola et al., 2016), diversification orientation (Guri-Rozenblit, 1993), value creation, and new business models (Madichie
and Gbadamosi, 2017; Abdelkafi et al., 2018). Entrepreneurial universities are
characterized by certain resources and capabilities (Guerrero and Urbano, 2012a,
b). First, concerning managing human resources, the literature explores how the
university managed career development, incentives, motivation and satisfaction
(Fini et al., 2009; Philpott et al., 2011; Leih and Teece, 2016). Second, regarding
infrastructures, there is a mature analysis about the main infrastructures developed by the university to support innovation and entrepreneurship; particularly
the literature about technology transfer offices (Harmon et al., 1997; Shane, 2002),
incubators, scientific parks (Mian, 1994; Salvador, 2011) and business creation
offices (Smilor et al., 2007). Third, the capacities associated with joint ventures with
international partners (Allen and Link, 2015). Only a few papers have explored the
entrepreneurial university as an innovative and entrepreneurial ecosystem (Miller
and Acs, 2017; Herrera et al., 2018; Huang-Saad et al., 2017). Therefore, the revised
literature about these issues provides the foundations of the entrepreneurial university's entrepreneurial and innovative ecosystem.

Relationships with external agents

We found 171 papers that have explored the relationship of the entrepreneurial
university with external agents (see Figure 8.4). Following the basis of an entrepreneurial and innovation ecosystem, we observed that the majority of papers focused
on analysing the relation between the university and the industry for engaging
entrepreneurship and innovation (Perkmann et al., 2011; Callaert et al., 2015;
Cunningham and Link, 2015), for creating value (Cunningham et al., 2018) and for
contributing to regional wealth (Lehmann and Menter, 2016). They also analysed
the role of culture expressed in terms of values, ethics (Slaughter and Rhoades,
2010), behaviours, beliefs (Bergmann, 2017; Iorio et al., 2017) and national culture/
climate (Huyghe and Knockaert, 2015; Huyghe et al., 2016; Bergmann et al., 2018;

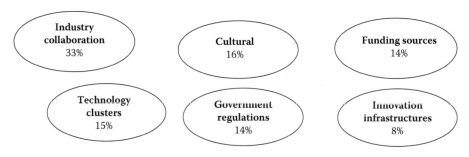

Source: Authors.

Figure 8.4   Entrepreneurial university community, N=171

Shirokova et al., 2018) that influence the emergence of entrepreneurship and innovation opportunities within the university, and the opportunities to have access to
diverse sources of funding as seed capital and venture capital (Croce et al., 2014;
Munari et al., 2015), and the interaction of university and external organization/
stakeholders to support/promote entrepreneurial innovations via technological clusters, scientific parks, and as being part of innovation systems (Youtie and
Shapira, 2008; Sohn and Kenney, 2007; Motoyama and Knowlton, 2017). Finally,
there is a strong link between regulations associated with intellectual property,
entrepreneurship, innovation and higher education (Shane, 2004; Wright and Katz,
2016; Oliver and Sapir, 2017).

What we do not know about the role of entrepreneurial universities on innovation and entrepreneurship activities

After reviewing the published research, several questions about the following two
themes are still unexplored.

University leadership, governance and strategic design for entrepreneurship and innovation

Despite relevance, however, surprisingly few studies of entrepreneurial universities
have focused on leadership, governance and broader design issues of contextual
fit with the environment (Leih and Teece, 2016). These managerial and strategic
characteristics are critical to the development of the entrepreneurial and innovative higher education sector. Leadership must be positive and responsive for
an organization to be dynamic and successful – to survive and thrive – during
unpredictable, complex times. All innovation and entrepreneurship will flourish
in a university that is united under a shared vision and culture, that does not allow
managerial systems to suffocate for lack of new ideas, that does not constantly strive
for autonomy circuitously via stakeholders. In the changing socio-economic landscape, environmental and contextual regional strategic management has gained

prominence warranting innovative organizational designs to realize sustained growth. These are the emerging, essential strategic tasks of university leadership, governance and design in the pursuit of entrepreneurialism and innovativeness.

Simultaneously, entrepreneurial and innovative higher education organizations are also influenced by technological and digital revolutions; for example, the digital economy that represents opportunities/challenges and compulsory transformation of routines into new ways of managing, teaching, learning and working. The academic literature of entrepreneurial universities doesn't provide enough answers about how digitalization influences organizational processes as well as the fostering innovative, disruptive and entrepreneurial activities. Plausible examples could include that of distance education, particularly the new revolution of massive online open courses, as well as online platforms oriented to support digital entrepreneurship and innovation initiatives. However, this is an explored area in the field of entrepreneurial universities.

Therefore, original (conceptual and empirical) research should be focused on the internal/external strategic challenges that are facing universities and exploring how those could be faced from an entrepreneurial and innovative orientation. A suggested research agenda around this theme could contribute to: (i) the integration of entrepreneurial universities' missions with societal needs, environmental/economic pressures, stakeholder expectations, and new digital trends; (ii) understanding the link between the new entrepreneurial university models/archetypes and university governance; (iii) understanding the inverse relationships between the strategic orientations of entrepreneurial universities and institutional context (e.g., in the development of policies); (iv) the identification, prevention and management of opportunist behaviours from academics as well as other internal/external agents; (v) the exploration of catalysts, leaders, champions to develop successful university driven entrepreneurship and innovation in various regions/countries; and (vi) the advantages/disadvantages of digitalization for supporting entrepreneurship and innovation.

Innovation and entrepreneurship higher education ecosystems

Despite the fact that in practice there is an inexistent dividing line between entrepreneurship and innovation, the existent literature confirms that entrepreneurial and innovative ecosystems continue to be analysed as independent phenomenon and with only a small emphasis on the higher educational context. As was evidenced in the previous section, the entrepreneurial university research recognizes and legitimizes the efforts of universities in the configuration of favourable conditions for fostering/developing both entrepreneurial and innovative activities. To achieve that, universities have developed capabilities, invested in support infrastructures, and fostered strong connections with different stakeholders. Therefore, one component in the research agenda to explore the role of universities in entrepreneurship and innovation is to explore the university as an ecosystem (Miller and Acs, 2017).

Conceptually, entrepreneurship ecosystems involve a set of individual, organizational, industrial and environmental elements such as leadership, dynamic capabilities, culture, capital markets, networks and open-minded customers that combine in complex ways (Isenberg, 2010, p. 2). Mason and Brown (2014, p. 5) argue that the entrepreneurial ecosystem is an interconnected set of entrepreneurial actors and organizations that are part of any entrepreneurial process and that determine the entrepreneurial environment of their localities or territories. Similarly, innovation ecosystems are focused on the complex relationships of cooperation, communication and feedback among organizations (Carlsson et al., 2002). The research on entrepreneurial and innovation ecosystems is increasing considerably but has several gaps to cover linked with governance (Colombo et al., 2017), digitalization (Sussan and Acs, 2017) and the metrics of success/impacts (Acs et al., 2018), among others.

In the university context, an entrepreneurial and innovation university ecosystem could be composed by educational programmes, infrastructures (incubators, research parks, technology transfer offices, business creation offices, employment offices, etc.), regulations (business creation normative, property rights, etc.), culture (role models, attitudes towards entrepreneurship, etc.), as well as relationships with government, investors, industry and other socio-economic agents (Guerrero and Urbano, 2012a, b; Herrera et al., 2018). This ecosystem supports the university community (students, alumni, academics, staff, etc.) in the identification, development and commercialization of innovative and entrepreneurial initiatives (Guerrero et al., 2018). The analysis of these interconnections is relevant because both ecosystems regulate the nature and the quality of entrepreneurial activity by shaping rewards linked to opportunity identification/generation and the pursuit of organizational forms/strategies (Wright et al., 2017).

In order to understand entrepreneurial and innovation higher education ecosystems it is still necessary to explore conceptually (adopting different perspectives: behavioural, organizational, network, economic and institutional) and empirically (using different methodological approaches: cross-section, multilevel, longitudinal, experimental, cases, action-research, narrative, meta-analysis, mixed). A suggested research agenda around this theme could contribute to: (i) concepts, elements, typologies and appropriate design; (ii) required organizational resources and dynamic capabilities involved in the creation/development process; (iii) the informal and formal institutions that affect the life-cycles in diverse contexts (advanced, developing, emerging economies), socio-economic scenarios (stable, turbulent, uncertainty) and higher educational systems (open, closed, regulated); (iv) the most adequate metrics and evaluation methods of outputs/impacts; (v) evidencing learning and knowledge exchange based on experiences of success and failure; (vi) policy formulation and managerial implications; among others.

Conclusions

The data and analysis reported in this chapter points towards the field of entrepreneurship and innovation continuing to advance in several meaningful ways. First, the pattern of entrepreneurial university research in the well-known journals shows significant increases in not only the volume of research published but also its impact in terms of citations (a signal of legitimation as a field of research). Second, researchers have strengthened our understanding of the core domains around the role of entrepreneurial universities (missions, graduate entrepreneurship, academic entrepreneurship, strategic side, outputs/outcomes/impacts, and ecosystems) in entrepreneurship and innovation, and they are forging new directions for future research based on the new societal, economic, technological and digital challenges. Third, the sizeable expansion in the number of entrepreneurship articles published in multidisciplinary fields also indicates the broadening contribution of the entrepreneurial university community as well as the opening of a door for creating value in themes such as: academic entrepreneurship (Hayter et al., 2016) and the economic, societal and technological contributions of the university (Guerrero et al., 2015, 2016); individual/organizational/institutional factors affecting entrepreneurial universities (Guerrero and Urbano, 2012); the emergence of opportunities (Busenitz et al., 2014; Bergmann et al., 2016); conceptual clarification of entrepreneurial and innovative ecosystems (Autio et al., 2014); the nature and effectiveness of higher entrepreneurship education in preparing students to become successful (intra)entrepreneurs (Martin et al., 2013; Wright el al., 2017); exploration of new/adequate research methods in entrepreneurship (McDonald et al., 2015); higher education graduate employability (Holmes, 2017; Tomlinson, 2017); regional collaboration between firms in a Penta Helix context; and firms (small and large), academy, the public sector, labour organizations and civil society actors (Tonkovic et al., 2015).

A better understanding about the role of universities in entrepreneurship and innovation also generates some implications. For *university managers*: a learning process based on experiences of successful/failure related to the design, implementation and sustainability of entrepreneurial university models (Wright et al., 2017). In both temporal and spatial contexts, this chapter also contributes to the identification of the main competences required to renovate/reinforce the change process to be more active actors in the ecosystems based on experimentation, capacity building, collaboration with key stakeholders, and entrepreneurial and innovative perspectives. It could be translated into the well-being of the university community and society. For *policy makers*: to design/implement policies in different spheres (regional competitiveness, higher university systems, employment, R&D, industry restructuring, etc.) and support individuals/organizations in each stage of the entrepreneurial process (Åstebro et al., 2012). Many countries have adopted policies to stimulate innovation, entrepreneurship and higher education systems (Grimaldi et al., 2011). However, entrepreneurship and innovation are two themes strongly related in practice but strongly disconnected in the theory (Guerrero et al., 2016). Based on this gap, this chapter aims to evidence the relevance of university activities and to build theoretical bridges between entrepreneurship and innovation as a part of university transformation and regional transformation. In addition, the debates around how "work ready" graduates are and what economic contribution they can make have been around for many decades, but interest in this area has exploded since the start of this century (Holmes, 2017; Tomlinson, 2017).

Acknowledgements

David Urbano acknowledges the financial support from projects ECO2017-87885-P [Spanish Ministry of Economy & Competitiveness], and 2017-SGR-1056 [Economy & Knowledge Department – Catalan Government], and ICREA-Academia program [Catalan Government].

References[1]

* Abdelkafi, N., Hilbig, R., and Laudien, S. M. (2018). Business models of entrepreneurial universities in the area of vocational education – an exploratory analysis. *International Journal of Technology Management*, **77** (1–3), 86–108.
* Abou-Warda, S. H. (2015). Entrepreneurial orientation in business schools: a comparative study of higher education systems in Egypt. *International Journal of Educational Management*, **29** (2), 192–212.
* Abramo, G., D'Angelo, C. A., Ferretti, M., and Parmentola, A. (2012). An individual-level assessment of the relationship between spin-off activities and research performance in universities. *R&D Management*, **42** (3), 225–42.
Acs, Z. J., Estrin, S., Mickiewicz, T., and Szerb, L. (2018). Entrepreneurship, institutional economics, and economic growth: an ecosystem perspective. *Small Business Economics*, **51** (2), 501–14.
* Addie, J. P. D., Angrisani, M., and De Falco, S. (2018). University-led innovation in and for peripheral urban areas: new approaches in Naples, Italy and Newark, NJ, US. *European Planning Studies*, **26** (6), 1181–201.
* Aharonson, B. S., Baum, J. A., and Feldman, M. P. (2007). Desperately seeking spillovers? Increasing returns, industrial organization and the location of new entrants in geographic and technological space. *Industrial and Corporate Change*, **16** (1), 89–130.
* Ahmadzadeh, M., Salarzahi, H., Yaghoubi, N. M., Zaei, M. E., Pelekh, O., and Kapil, P. (2017). Ranking and evaluating effectiveness of teaching methods in academic entrepreneurship by using satisfaction matrix model. *Pacific Business Review International*, **10** (4), 103–11.
* Allen, S. D., and Link, A. N. (2015). US research joint ventures with international partners. *International Entrepreneurship and Management Journal*, **11** (1), 169–81.
* Allen, S. D., Link, A. N., and Rosenbaum, D. T. (2007). Entrepreneurship and human capital: evidence of patenting activity from the academic sector. *Entrepreneurship Theory and Practice*, **31** (6), 937–51.
* Araújo, M. H., Lago, R. M., Oliveira, L. C., Cabral, P. R., Cheng, L. C., and Filion, L. J. (2005). Stimulating entrepreneurship in chemistry courses: the formation of entrepreneurial chemists. *Química Nova*, **28**, S18–S25.
* Åstebro, T., Bazzazian, N., and Braguinsky, S. (2012). Startups by recent university graduates and their faculty: implications for university entrepreneurship policy. *Research Policy*, **41** (4), 663–77.

---

1 * Papers included in the analysis.

* Audretsch, D. B. (2014). From the entrepreneurial university to the university for the entrepreneurial society. *The Journal of Technology Transfer*, **39** (3), 313–21.

* Audretsch, D. B., and Lehmann, E. E. (2005). Does the knowledge spillover theory of entrepreneurship hold for regions? *Research Policy*, **34** (8), 1191–202.

* Audretsch, D. B., Hülsbeck, M., and Lehmann, E. E. (2012). Regional competitiveness, university spillovers, and entrepreneurial activity. *Small Business Economics*, **39** (3), 587–601.

Autio, E., Kenney, M., Mustar, P., Siegel, D., and Wright, M. (2014). Entrepreneurial innovation: the importance of context. *Research Policy*, **43** (7), 1097–108.

* Baldini, N. (2006). The Act on inventions at public research institutions: Danish universities' patenting activity. *Scientometrics*, **69** (2), 387–407.

* Baldini, N. (2010). Do royalties really foster university patenting activity? An answer from Italy. *Technovation*, **30** (2), 109–16.

* Baldini, N., Grimaldi, R., and Sobrero, M. (2006). Institutional changes and the commercialization of academic knowledge: a study of Italian universities' patenting activities between 1965 and 2002. *Research Policy*, **35** (4), 518–32.

* Baltzopoulos, A., and Broström, A. (2013). Attractors of entrepreneurial activity: universities, regions and alumni entrepreneurs. *Regional Studies*, **47** (6), 934–49.

* Barnett, R. (2000). University knowledge in an age of supercomplexity. *Higher Education*, **40** (4), 409–22.

* Bathelt, H., Kogler, D. F., and Munro, A. K. (2010). A knowledge-based typology of university spin-offs in the context of regional economic development. *Technovation*, **30** (9–10), 519–32.

Baumol, W. J. (2002). *The Free-Market Innovation Machine: Analyzing the growth miracle of capitalism*. Princeton, NJ: Princeton University Press.

* Berbegal-Mirabent, J., Lafuente, E., and Solé, F. (2013). The pursuit of knowledge transfer activities: an efficiency analysis of Spanish universities. *Journal of Business Research*, **66** (10), 2051–9.

* Berggren, E. (2017). Researchers as enablers of commercialization at an entrepreneurial university. *Journal of Management Development*, **36** (2), 217–32.

* Bergmann, H. (2017). The formation of opportunity beliefs among university entrepreneurs: an empirical study of research- and non-research-driven venture ideas. *The Journal of Technology Transfer*, **42** (1), 116–40.

* Bergmann, H., Hundt, C., and Sternberg, R. (2016). What makes student entrepreneurs? On the relevance (and irrelevance) of the university and the regional context for student start-ups. *Small Business Economics*, **47** (1), 53–76.

* Bergmann, H., Geissler, M., Hundt, C., and Grave, B. (2018). The climate for entrepreneurship at higher education institutions. *Research Policy*, **47** (4), 700–716.

* Bernasconi, A. (2005). University entrepreneurship in a developing country: the case of the P. Universidad Católica de Chile, 1985–2000. *Higher Education*, **50** (2), 247–74.

* Bonaccorsi, A., Colombo, M. G., Guerini, M., and Rossi-Lamastra, C. (2014). The impact of local and external university knowledge on the creation of knowledge-intensive firms: evidence from the Italian case. *Small Business Economics*, **43** (2), 261–87.

* Bramwell, A., and Wolfe, D. A. (2008). Universities and regional economic development: the entrepreneurial University of Waterloo. *Research Policy*, **37** (8), 1175–87.

* Budyldina, N. (2018). Entrepreneurial universities and regional contribution. *International Entrepreneurship and Management Journal*, **14** (2), 265–77.

Busenitz, L. W., Plummer, L. A., Klotz, A. C., Shahzad, A., and Rhoads, K. (2014). Entrepreneurship research (1985–2009) and the emergence of opportunities. *Entrepreneurship Theory and Practice*, **38** (5), 981–1000.

* Callaert, J., Landoni, P., Van Looy, B., and Verganti, R. (2015). Scientific yield from collaboration with industry: the relevance of researchers' strategic approaches. *Research Policy*, **44** (4), 990–98.

* Cantu, F. J., Bustani, A., Molina, A., and Moreira, H. (2009). A knowledge-based development model: the research chair strategy. *Journal of Knowledge Management*, **13** (1), 154–70.

* Carayannis, E. G., Dubina, I. N., and Ilinova, A. A. (2015). Licensing in the context of entrepreneurial university activity: an empirical evidence and a theoretical model. *Journal of the Knowledge Economy*, **6** (1), 1–12.
* Carayannis, E. G., Cherepovitsyn, A. Y., and Ilinova, A. A. (2016). Technology commercialization in entrepreneurial universities: the US and Russian experience. *The Journal of Technology Transfer*, **41** (5), 1135–47.
Carlsson B., Jacobsson S., Holmén M., and Rickne A. (2002). Innovation systems: analytical and meth odological issues. *Research Policy*, **31** (2), 233–45.
* Carree, M., Della Malva, A., and Santarelli, E. (2014). The contribution of universities to growth: empirical evidence for Italy. *The Journal of Technology Transfer*, **39** (3), 393–414.
* Carree, M., Congregado, E., Golpe, A., and van Stel, A. (2015). Self-employment and job generation in metropolitan areas, 1969–2009. *Entrepreneurship & Regional Development*, **27** (3–4), 181–201.
* Chang, Y. C., Yang, P. Y., and Chen, M. H. (2009). The determinants of academic research commercial performance: towards an organizational ambidexterity perspective. *Research Policy*, **38** (6), 936–46.
* Chang, Y. C., Yang, P. Y., Martin, B. R., Chi, H. R., and Tsai-Lin, T. F. (2016). Entrepreneurial universities and research ambidexterity: a multilevel analysis. *Technovation*, **54**, 7–21.
* Chlosta, S., Patzelt, H., Klein, S. B., and Dormann, C. (2012). Parental role models and the decision to become self-employed: the moderating effect of personality. *Small Business Economics*, **38** (1), 121–38.
* Chrisman, J. J., Hynes, T., and Fraser, S. (1995). Faculty entrepreneurship and economic development: the case of the University of Calgary. *Journal of Business Venturing*, **10** (4), 267–81.
Clark, B. R. (1998). *Creating Entrepreneurial Universities: Organizational Pathways of Transformation*. Issues in Higher Education. Oxford and New York: Pergamon.
* Clarysse, B., Tartari, V., and Salter, A. (2011). The impact of entrepreneurial capacity, experience and organizational support on academic entrepreneurship. *Research Policy*, **40** (8), 1084–93.
* Colombo, M. G., Dagnino, G. B., Lehmann, E. E., and Salmador, M. (2017). The governance of entrepreneurial ecosystems. *Small Business Economics*, **52** (2), 419–28.
* Costa, S. F., Santos, S. C., Wach, D., and Caetano, A. (2018). Recognizing opportunities across campus: the effects of cognitive training and entrepreneurial passion on the business opportunity prototype. *Journal of Small Business Management*, **56** (1), 51–75.
* Croce, A., Grilli, L., and Murtinu, S. (2014). Venture capital enters academia: an analysis of university-managed funds. *The Journal of Technology Transfer*, **39** (5), 688–715.
* Cunningham, J. A., and Link, A. N. (2015). Fostering university-industry R&D collaborations in European Union countries. *International Entrepreneurship and Management Journal*, **11** (4), 849–60.
* Cunningham, J. A., Menter, M., and O'Kane, C. (2018). Value creation in the quadruple helix: a micro level conceptual model of principal investigators as value creators. *R&D Management*, **48** (1), 136–47.
* Davey, T., Rossano, S., and van der Sijde, P. (2016). Does context matter in academic entrepreneurship? The role of barriers and drivers in the regional and national context. *The Journal of Technology Transfer*, **41** (6), 1457–82.
* Del Giudice, M., Nicotra, M., Romano, M., and Schillaci, C. E. (2017). Entrepreneurial performance of principal investigators and country culture: relations and influences. *The Journal of Technology Transfer*, **42** (2), 320–37.
* Di Berardino, D., and Corsi, C. (2018). A quality evaluation approach to disclosing third mission activities and intellectual capital in Italian universities. *Journal of Intellectual Capital*, **19** (1), 178–201.
* Digby, A. (2005). Early black doctors in South Africa. *The Journal of African History*, **46** (3), 427–54.
* Djokovic, D., and Souitaris, V. (2008). Spinouts from academic institutions: a literature review with suggestions for further research. *The Journal of Technology Transfer*, **33** (3), 225–47.
* Drucker, J. (2016). Reconsidering the regional economic development impacts of higher education institutions in the United States. *Regional Studies*, **50** (7), 1185–202.
* Epure, M., Prior, D., and Serarols, C. (2016). Assessing technology-based spin-offs from university support units. *Regional Studies*, **50** (3), 411–28.

* Etzkowitz, H. (1998). Entrepreneurial scientists and entrepreneurial universities in American academic science. *Minerva*, **21** (2–3), 198–233.

* Fichter, K., and Tiemann, I. (2018). Factors influencing university support for sustainable entrepreneurship: insights from explorative case studies. *Journal of Cleaner Production*, **175**, 512–24.

* Fini, R., Grimaldi, R., and Sobrero, M. (2009). Factors fostering academics to start up new ventures: an assessment of Italian founders' incentives. *The Journal of Technology Transfer*, **34** (4), 380–402.

* Fini, R., Rasmussen, E., Siegel, D., and Wiklund, J. (2018). Rethinking the commercialization of public science: from entrepreneurial outcomes to societal impacts. *Academy of Management Perspectives*, **32** (1), 4–20.

* Fox, M. F., and Xiao, W. (2013). Perceived chances for promotion among women associate professors in computing: individual, departmental, and entrepreneurial factors. *The Journal of Technology Transfer*, **38** (2), 135–52.

* French, M., and Miller, F. A. (2012). Leveraging the "living laboratory": on the emergence of the entrepreneurial hospital. *Social Science & Medicine*, **75** (4), 717–24.

* Gittelman, M. (2006). National institutions, public–private knowledge flows, and innovation performance: a comparative study of the biotechnology industry in the US and France. *Research Policy*, **35** (7), 1052–68.

* Grandi, A., and Grimaldi, R. (2005). Academics' organizational characteristics and the generation of successful business ideas. *Journal of Business Venturing*, **20** (6), 821–845.

* Grimaldi, R., Kenney, M., Siegel, D., and Wright, M. (2011). 30 years after Bayh-Dole: reassessing academic entrepreneurship. *Research Policy*, **40** (8), 1045–57.

* Guerrero, M., and Urbano, D. (2012a). Knowledge and technology transfer strategies: best practices in Spanish entrepreneurial universities. *Gestión y Política Pública*, **21** (1), 107–39.

* Guerrero, M., and Urbano, D. (2012b). The development of an entrepreneurial university. *The Journal of Technology Transfer*, **37** (1), 43–74.

* Guerrero, M., Cunningham, J. A., and Urbano, D. (2015). Economic impact of entrepreneurial universities' activities: an exploratory study of the United Kingdom. *Research Policy*, **44** (3), 748–64.

* Guerrero, M., Urbano, D., and Fayolle, A. (2016). Entrepreneurial activity and regional competitiveness: evidence from European entrepreneurial universities. *The Journal of Technology Transfer*, **41** (1), 105–31.

* Guerrero, M., Urbano, D., and Gajón, E. (2017). Higher education entrepreneurial ecosystems: exploring the role of business incubators in an emerging economy. *International Review of Entrepreneurship*, **15** (2), 175–202.

* Guerrero, M., Urbano, D., Cunningham, J. A., and Gajón, E. (2018). Determinants of graduates' start-ups creation across a multi-campus entrepreneurial university: the case of Monterrey Institute of Technology and Higher Education. *Journal of Small Business Management*, **56** (1), 150–78.

* Guri-Rozenblit, S. (1993). Trends of diversification and expansion in Israeli higher education. *Higher Education*, **25** (4), 457–72.

* Harmon, B., Ardishvili, A., Cardozo, R., Elder, T., Leuthold, J., Parshall, J., . . . and Smith, D. (1997). Mapping the university technology transfer process. *Journal of Business Venturing*, **12** (6), 423–34.

* Harrison, R. T., and Leitch, C. (2010). Voodoo institution or entrepreneurial university? Spin-off companies, the entrepreneurial system and regional development in the UK. *Regional Studies*, **44** (9), 1241–62.

* Hassanzadeh, Z. S., Hosseini, S. R., and Honarbakhsh, F. (2015). Study of the educational factors contributing to realization of the objectives of entrepreneurial university. *International Journal of Advanced and Applied Sciences*, **2** (10), 1–12.

* Hayter, C. S., Lubynsky, R., and Maroulis, S. (2016). Who is the academic entrepreneur? The role of graduate students in the development of university spinoffs. *The Journal of Technology Transfer*, 1–18.

Herrera, F., Guerrero, M., and Urbano, D. (2018). Entrepreneurship and innovation ecosystems drivers:

the role of higher education organizations. In J. Leitão, H. Alves, N. Krueger, and J. Park (eds), *Entrepreneurial, Innovative and Sustainable Ecosystems* (pp. 109–28). Cham, Switzerland: Springer.

* Holley, A. C., and Watson, J. (2017). Academic entrepreneurial behavior: birds of more than one feather. *Technovation*, **64**, 50–57.

Holmes, L. (2017). Graduate employability: future directions and debate. In M. Tomlinson and L. Holmes (eds), *Graduate Employability in Context* (pp. 359–69). London: Palgrave Macmillan.

* Hsu, D. H., Roberts, E. B., and Eesley, C. E. (2007). Entrepreneurs from technology-based universities: evidence from MIT. *Research Policy*, **36** (5), 768–88.

* Huang-Saad, A., Fay, J., and Sheridan, L. (2017). Closing the divide: accelerating technology commercialization by catalyzing the university entrepreneurial ecosystem with I-Corps™. *The Journal of Technology Transfer*, **42** (6), 1466–86.

* Huyghe, A., and Knockaert, M. (2015). The influence of organizational culture and climate on entrepreneurial intentions among research scientists. *The Journal of Technology Transfer*, **40** (1), 138–60.

* Huyghe, A., Knockaert, M., and Obschonka, M. (2016). Unraveling the "passion orchestra" in academia. *Journal of Business Venturing*, **31** (3), 344–64.

* Ilouga, S. N., Mouloungni, A. N., and Sahut, J. M. (2014). Entrepreneurial intention and career choices: the role of volition. *Small Business Economics*, **42** (4), 717–28.

* Iorio, R., Labory, S., and Rentocchini, F. (2017). The importance of pro-social behaviour for the breadth and depth of knowledge transfer activities: an analysis of Italian academic scientists. *Research Policy*, **46** (2), 497–509.

Isenberg, D. J. (2010). How to start an entrepreneurial revolution. *Harvard Business Review*, **88** (6), 40–50.

* Jabeen, F., Faisal, M. N., and I. Katsioloudes, M. (2017). Entrepreneurial mindset and the role of universities as strategic drivers of entrepreneurship: evidence from the United Arab Emirates. *Journal of Small Business and Enterprise Development*, **24** (1), 136–57.

* Jacob, M., Lundqvist, M., and Hellsmark, H. (2003). Entrepreneurial transformations in the Swedish university system: the case of Chalmers University of Technology. *Research Policy*, **32** (9), 1555–68.

* Jacobsson, S., Lindholm-Dahlstrand, Å., and Elg, L. (2013). Is the commercialization of European academic R&D weak? A critical assessment of a dominant belief and associated policy responses. *Research Policy*, **42** (4), 874–85.

* Johnmark, D. R., Wummen Soemunti, T., Laura, O., Munene, J. C., and Balunywa, W. (2016). Disabled students' entrepreneurial action: the role of religious beliefs. *Cogent Business & Management*, **3** (1), 1252549.

* Kalar, B., and Antoncic, B. (2015). The entrepreneurial university, academic activities and technology and knowledge transfer in four European countries. *Technovation*, **36**, 1–11.

* Kamunyori, S., Al-Bader, S., Sewankambo, N., Singer, P. A., and Daar, A. S. (2010). Science-based health innovation in Uganda: creative strategies for applying research to development. *BMC International Health and Human Rights*, **10** (1), S5.

* Karimi, S., Biemans, H. J., Lans, T., Chizari, M., and Mulder, M. (2016). The impact of entrepreneurship education: a study of Iranian students' entrepreneurial intentions and opportunity identification. *Journal of Small Business Management*, **54** (1), 187–209.

* Karpov, A. O. (2017). University 3.0–social mission and reality. *Sociological Studies*, **9** (9), 114–24.

* Katz, J. A., Roberts, J., Strom, R., and Freilich, A. (2014). Perspectives on the development of cross campus entrepreneurship education. *Entrepreneurship Research Journal*, **4** (1), 13–44.

* Kenney, M., and Goe, W. R. (2004). The role of social embeddedness in professorial entrepreneurship: a comparison of electrical engineering and computer science at UC Berkeley and Stanford. *Research Policy*, **33** (5), 691–707.

* Kim, Y. (2013). The ivory tower approach to entrepreneurial linkage: productivity changes in university technology transfer. *The Journal of Technology Transfer*, **38** (2), 180–97.

* Kirby, D., Guerrero, M, and Urbano, D. (2011). Making universities more entrepreneurial: development of a model. *Canadian Journal of Administrative Sciences*, **28**, 302–16.

* Knockaert, M., Der Foo, M., Erikson, T., and Cools, E. (2015). Growth intentions among research scientists: a cognitive style perspective. *Technovation*, **38**, 64–74.

* Kroll, H., and Liefner, I. (2008). Spin-off enterprises as a means of technology commercialisation in a transforming economy – evidence from three universities in China. *Technovation*, **28** (5), 298–313.

* Kwon, K. S., and Martin, B. R. (2012). Synergy or separation mode: the relationship between the academic research and the knowledge-transfer activities of Korean academics. *Scientometrics*, **90** (1), 177–200.

* Lam, A. (2011). What motivates academic scientists to engage in research commercialization: "gold", "ribbon" or "puzzle"? *Research Policy*, **40** (10), 1354–68.

* Landry, R., Amara, N., and Rherrad, I. (2006). Why are some university researchers more likely to create spin-offs than others? Evidence from Canadian universities. *Research Policy*, **35** (10), 1599–615.

* Landry, R., Amara, N., and Saïhi, M. (2007). Patenting and spin-off creation by Canadian researchers in engineering and life sciences. *The Journal of Technology Transfer*, **32** (3), 217–49.

* Larsson, J. P., Wennberg, K., Wiklund, J., and Wright, M. (2017). Location choices of graduate entrepreneurs. *Research Policy*, **46** (8), 1490–504.

* Lehmann, E. E., and Menter, M. (2016). University–industry collaboration and regional wealth. *The Journal of Technology Transfer*, **41** (6), 1284–307.

* Leih, S., and Teece, D. (2016). Campus leadership and the entrepreneurial university: a dynamic capabilities perspective. *Academy of Management Perspectives*, **30** (2), 182–210.

* Lima, E., Lopes, R. M., Nassif, V., and da Silva, D. (2015). Opportunities to improve entrepreneurship education: contributions considering Brazilian challenges. *Journal of Small Business Management*, **53** (4), 1033–51.

* Liyanage, S., and Andrade, A. D. (2012). The changing role of research and education in New Zealand universities. *Science, Technology and Society*, **17** (2), 201–32.

* Loi, M., and Di Guardo, M. C. (2015). The third mission of universities: an investigation of the espoused values. *Science and Public Policy*, **42** (6), 855–70.

* Lubango, L. M., and Pouris, A. (2007). Industry work experience and inventive capacity of South African academic researchers. *Technovation*, **27** (12), 788–96.

* Luna, L. G., Ojeda, M. O., and Ruenes, A. R. (2017). Axes and driving forces for the scientific development in the Luis Vargas Torres Technical University, Esmeraldas, Ecuador. *Revista Gestion de la Educacion*, **7** (1), 99–136.

* Lüthje, C., and Franke, N. (2003). The "making" of an entrepreneur: testing a model of entrepreneurial intent among engineering students at MIT. *R&D Management*, **33** (2), 135–47.

* Madichie, N. O., and Gbadamosi, A. (2017). The entrepreneurial university: an exploration of "value-creation" in a non-management department. *Journal of Management Development*, **36** (2), 196–216.

* Mamun, A. A., Nawi, N. B. C., Mohiuddin, M., Shamsudin, S. F. F. B., and Fazal, S. A. (2017). Entrepreneurial intention and startup preparation: a study among business students in Malaysia. *Journal of Education for Business*, **92** (6), 296–314.

* Markman, G. D., Gianiodis, P. T., and Phan, P. H. (2008). Full-time faculty or part-time entrepreneurs. *IEEE Transactions on Engineering Management*, **55** (1), 29–36.

Martin, B. C., McNally, J. J., and Kay, M. J. (2013). Examining the formation of human capital in entrepreneurship: a meta-analysis of entrepreneurship education outcomes. *Journal of Business Venturing*, **28** (2), 211–24.

Mason, C., and Brown, R. (2014). Entrepreneurial ecosystems and growth-oriented entrepreneurship. Final Report to OECD, Paris, 1–38.

* May, J., Delahunty, J., O'Shea, S., and Stone, C. (2016). Seeking the passionate career: first-in-family enabling students and the idea of the Australian University. *Higher Education Quarterly*, **70** (4), 384–99.

McDonald, S., Gan, B. C., Fraser, S. S., Oke, A., and Anderson, A. R. (2015). A review of research methods in entrepreneurship 1985–2013. *International Journal of Entrepreneurial Behavior & Research*, **21** (3), 291–315.

* McMullan, W. E., and Gillin, L. M. (1998). Industrial Viewpoint–Entrepreneurship Education–Developing technological start-up entrepreneurs: a case study of a graduate entrepreneurship programme at Swinburne University. *Technovation*, **4** (18), 275–86.
* Mendoza, P. (2007). Academic capitalism and doctoral student socialization: a case study. *The Journal of Higher Education*, **78** (1), 71–96.
* Meyer, M. (2006). Are patenting scientists the better scholars?: an exploratory comparison of inventor-authors with their non-inventing peers in nano-science and technology. *Research Policy*, **35** (10), 1646–62.
* Mian, S. A. (1994). US university-sponsored technology incubators: an overview of management, policies and performance. *Technovation*, **14** (8), 515–28.
* Miller, D. J., and Acs, Z. J. (2017). The campus as entrepreneurial ecosystem: The University of Chicago. *Small Business Economics*, **49** (1), 75–95.
* Minola, T., Donina, D., and Meoli, M. (2016). Students climbing the entrepreneurial ladder: does university internationalization pay off? *Small Business Economics*, **47** (3), 565–87.
* Mosey, S., Guerrero, M., and Greenman, A. (2017). Technology entrepreneurship research opportunities: insights from across Europe. *The Journal of Technology Transfer*, **42** (1), 1–9.
* Motoyama, Y., and Knowlton, K. (2017). Examining the connections within the startup ecosystem: a case study of St. Louis. *Entrepreneurship Research Journal*, **7** (1).
* Mueller, P. (2007). Exploiting entrepreneurial opportunities: the impact of entrepreneurship on growth. *Small Business Economics*, **28** (4), 355–362.
* Munari, F., Pasquini, M., and Toschi, L. (2015). From the lab to the stock market? The characteristics and impact of university-oriented seed funds in Europe. *The Journal of Technology Transfer*, **40** (6), 948–75.
* Mustar, P., and Wright, M. (2010). Convergence or path dependency in policies to foster the creation of university spin-off firms? A comparison of France and the United Kingdom. *Journal of Technology Transfer*, **35** (1), 42–65.
* Oliver, A. L., and Sapir, A. (2017). Shifts in the organization and profession of academic science: the impact of IPR and technology transfer. *Journal of Professions and Organization*, **4** (1), 36–54.
* O'Shea, R. P., Allen, T. J., Chevalier, A., and Roche, F. (2005). Entrepreneurial orientation, technology transfer and spinoff performance of US universities. *Research Policy*, **34** (7), 994–1009.
* O'Shea, R. P., Allen, T. J., Morse, K. P., O'Gorman, C., and Roche, F. (2007). Delineating the anatomy of an entrepreneurial university: The Massachusetts Institute of Technology experience. *R&D Management*, **37** (1), 1–16.
Parker, S. C. (2011). Intrapreneurship or entrepreneurship? *Journal of Business Venturing*, **26** (1), 19–34.
* Perkmann, M., King, Z., and Pavelin, S. (2011). Engaging excellence? Effects of faculty quality on university engagement with industry. *Research Policy*, **40** (4), 539–52.
* Philpott, K., Dooley, L., O'Reilly, C., and Lupton, G. (2011). The entrepreneurial university: examining the underlying academic tensions. *Technovation*, **31** (4), 161–70.
* Pizarro Milian, R., and Gurrisi, M. (2017). The online promotion of entrepreneurship education: a view from Canada. *Education + Training*, **59** (9), 990–1006.
* Ranga, L., Debackere, K., and Tunzelmann, N. (2003). Entrepreneurial universities and the dynamics of academic knowledge production: a case study of basic vs. applied research in Belgium. *Scientometrics*, **58** (2), 301–20.
* Riordan, S., and Louw-Potgieter, J. (2011). Career success of women academics in South Africa. *South African Journal of Psychology*, **41** (2), 157–72.
* Robinson, P. B., and Sexton, E. A. (1994). The effect of education and experience on self-employment success. *Journal of Business Venturing*, **9** (2), 141–56.
* Ryu, M. (1998). A muted voice in academe: the Korean version of entrepreneurial scholarship. *Higher Education*, **35** (1), 9–26.
* Salvador, E. (2011). Are science parks and incubators good "brand names" for spin-offs? The case study of Turin. *The Journal of Technology Transfer*, **36** (2), 203–32.

* Sanchez-Canizares, S. M., and Rodriguez-Gutierrez, P. (2015). Promoting entrepreneurship by university teaching innovation in the subject Business Creation. *IJERI – International Journal of Educational Research and Innovation*, **4**, 41–50.

Schumpeter, J. A. (1934). *The Theory of Economic Development: An Inquiry into Profits, Capital, Credit, Interest and the Business Cycle*. Cambridge, MA: Harvard University Press.

* Shane, S. (2002). Executive forum: university technology transfer to entrepreneurial companies. *Journal of Business Venturing*, **17** (6), 537–52.

* Shane, S. (2004). Encouraging university entrepreneurship? The effect of the Bayh-Dole Act on university patenting in the United States. *Journal of Business Venturing*, **19** (1), 127–51.

* Shibayama, S., Walsh, J. P., and Baba, Y. (2012). Academic entrepreneurship and exchange of scientific resources: material transfer in life and materials sciences in Japanese universities. *American Sociological Review*, **77** (5), 804–30.

* Shirokova, G., Tsukanova, T., and Morris, M. H. (2018). The moderating role of national culture in the relationship between university entrepreneurship offerings and student start-up activity: an embeddedness perspective. *Journal of Small Business Management*, **56** (1), 103–30.

* Siegel, D. S., and Wessner, C. (2012). Universities and the success of entrepreneurial ventures: evidence from the small business innovation research program. *The Journal of Technology Transfer*, **37** (4), 404–15.

* Siegel, D. S., Veugelers, R., and Wright, M. (2007). Technology transfer offices and commercialization of university intellectual property: performance and policy implications. *Oxford Review of Economic Policy*, **23** (4), 640–60.

* Slaughter, S., and Rhoades, G. (2010). The social construction of copyright ethics and values. *Science and Engineering Ethics*, **16** (2), 263–93.

* Smilor, R., O'Donnell, N., Stein, G., and Welborn III, R. S. (2007). The research university and the development of high-technology centers in the United States. *Economic Development Quarterly*, **21** (3), 203–22.

* Smith, H. L., and Ho, K. (2006). Measuring the performance of Oxford University, Oxford Brookes University and the government laboratories' spin-off companies. *Research Policy*, **35** (10), 1554–68.

* Sohn, D. W., and Kenney, M. (2007). Universities, clusters, and innovation systems: the case of Seoul, Korea. *World Development*, **35** (6), 991–1004.

* Sperrer, M., Müller, C., and Soos, J. (2016). The concept of the entrepreneurial university applied to universities of technology in Austria: already reality or a vision of the future? *Technology Innovation Management Review*, **6** (10), 37–44.

* St-Jean, É., Tremblay, M., Janssen, F., Baronet, J., Loué, C., and Nafa, A. (2017). May business mentors act as opportunity brokers and enablers among university students? *International Entrepreneurship and Management Journal*, **13** (1), 97–111.

* Sun, H., Lo, C. T., Liang, B., and Wong, Y. L. B. (2017). The impact of entrepreneurial education on entrepreneurial intention of engineering students in Hong Kong. *Management Decision*, **55** (7), 1371–93.

* Sussan, F., and Acs, Z. J. (2017). The digital entrepreneurial ecosystem. *Small Business Economics*, **49** (1), 55–73.

* Szelényi, K., Bresonis, K., and Mars, M. M. (2016). Who am I versus who can I become?: Exploring women's science identities in STEM Ph. D. programs. *The Review of Higher Education*, **40** (1), 1–31.

* Theodorakopoulos, N., Preciado, D. J. S., and Bennett, D. (2012). Transferring technology from university to rural industry within a developing economy context: the case for nurturing communities of practice. *Technovation*, **32** (9–10), 550–59.

Thursby, J. G., and Thursby, M. C. (2002). Who is selling the ivory tower? Sources of growth in university licensing. *Management Science*, **48** (1), 90–104.

* Tiemann, I., Fichter, K., and Geier, J. (2018). University support systems for sustainable entrepreneurship: insights from explorative case studies. *International Journal of Entrepreneurial Venturing*, **10** (1), 83–110.

* Todorovic, Z. W., McNaughton, R. B., and Guild, P. (2011). ENTRE-U: an entrepreneurial orientation scale for universities. *Technovation*, **31** (2–3), 128–37.

* Toledano, N., and Urbano, D. (2008). Promoting entrepreneurial mindsets at universities: a case study in the South of Spain. *European Journal of International Management*, **2** (4), 382–99.

Tomlinson, M. (2017). Introduction: graduate employability in context: charting a complex, contested and multi-faceted policy and research field. In M. Tomlinson and L. Holmes (eds), *Graduate Employability in Context* (pp. 1–40). London: Palgrave Macmillan.

Tonkovic, A. M., Veckie, E., and Veckie, V. W. (2015). Applications of Penta Helix Model in economic development. *Economy of Eastern Croatia Yesterday, Today, Tomorrow*, **4**, 385–93.

* Trequattrini, R., Lombardi, R., Lardo, A., and Cuozzo, B. (2018). The impact of entrepreneurial universities on regional growth: a local intellectual capital perspective. *Journal of the Knowledge Economy*, **9** (1), 199–211.

* Trevitt, C., Steed, A., Du Moulin, L., and Foley, T. (2017). Leading entrepreneurial e-learning development in legal education: a longitudinal case study of "universities as learning organisations". *The Learning Organization*, **24** (5), 298–311.

* Urbano, D., and Guerrero, M. (2013). Entrepreneurial universities: socioeconomic impacts of academic entrepreneurship in a European region. *Economic Development Quarterly*, **27** (1), 40–55.

* Urbano, D., Aparicio, S., Guerrero, M., Noguera, M., and Torrent-Sellens, J. (2017). Institutional determinants of student employer entrepreneurs at Catalan universities. *Technological Forecasting and Social Change*, **123**, 271–82.

* Van Looy, B., Ranga, M., Callaert, J., Debackere, K., and Zimmermann, E. (2004). Combining entrepreneurial and scientific performance in academia: towards a compounded and reciprocal Matthew-effect? *Research Policy*, **33** (3), 425–41.

* Van Looy, B., Callaert, J., and Debackere, K. (2006). Publication and patent behavior of academic researchers: conflicting, reinforcing or merely co-existing? *Research Policy*, **35** (4), 596–608.

* Van Looy, B., Landoni, P., Callaert, J., Van Pottelsberghe, B., Sapsalis, E., and Debackere, K. (2011). Entrepreneurial effectiveness of European universities: an empirical assessment of antecedents and trade-offs. *Research Policy*, **40** (4), 553–64.

* van Stijn, N., van Rijnsoever, F. J., and van Veelen, M. (2018). Exploring the motives and practices of university–start-up interaction: evidence from Route 128. *The Journal of Technology Transfer*, **43** (3), 674–713.

* Visintin, F., and Pittino, D. (2014). Founding team composition and early performance of university-based spin-off companies. *Technovation*, **34** (1), 31–43.

* Vohora, A., Wright, M., and Lockett, A. (2004). Critical junctures in the development of university high-tech spinout companies. *Research Policy*, **33** (1), 147–75.

* Wigren-Kristoferson, C., Gabrielsson, J., and Kitagawa, F. (2011). Mind the gap and bridge the gap: research excellence and diffusion of academic knowledge in Sweden. *Science and Public Policy*, **38** (6), 481–92.

* Wolf, G. (2017). Entrepreneurial university: a case study at Stony Brook University. *Journal of Management Development*, **36** (2), 286–94.

* Wong, P. K., Ho, Y. P., and Singh, A. (2007). Towards an "entrepreneurial university" model to support knowledge-based economic development: the case of the National University of Singapore. *World Development*, **35** (6), 941–58.

* Wright, M., Lockett, A., Clarysse, B., and Binks, M. (2006). University spin-out companies and venture capital. *Research Policy*, **35** (4), 481–501.

Wright, M., Clarysse, B., Mustar, P., and Lockett, A. (2007). *Academic Entrepreneurship in Europe*. Cheltenham, UK and Northampton, MA, USA: Edward Elgar Publishing.

Wright, M., Siegel, D. S., and Mustar, P. (2017). An emerging ecosystem for student start-ups. *The Journal of Technology Transfer*, **42** (4), 909–22.

* Wright, S. L., and Katz, J. A. (2016). Protecting student intellectual property in the entrepreneurial classroom. *Journal of Management Education*, **40** (2), 152–69.

* Xiao, L., and North, D. (2017). The graduation performance of technology business incubators in China's three tier cities: the role of incubator funding, technical support, and entrepreneurial mentoring. *The Journal of Technology Transfer*, **42** (3), 615–34.

* Youtie, J., and Shapira, P. (2008). Building an innovation hub: a case study of the transformation of university roles in regional technological and economic development. *Research Policy*, **37** (8), 1188–1204.

Zahra, S., and Wright, M. (2011). Entrepreneurship's next act. *Academy of Management Perspectives*, **25**, 67–83.

* Zhang, Q., MacKenzie, N. G., Jones-Evans, D., and Huggins, R. (2016). Leveraging knowledge as a competitive asset? The intensity, performance and structure of universities' entrepreneurial knowledge exchange activities at a regional level. *Small Business Economics*, **47** (3), 657–75.

9 Corporate governance and innovation

Hezun Li, Timurs Uman, and Siri Terjesen

Introduction

Corporate governance is typically defined as the mechanisms by which a firm is directed and controlled (Gabrielsson 2017). While corporate boards of directors (BODs) are at the apex of entrepreneurial firms' hierarchy and can significantly influence major decisions, corporate governance focuses beyond boards, to include the mechanisms through which shareholders, entrepreneurs, and top management teams (TMTs) are involved in start-ups (Wirtz 2011). This book chapter extends the discussion of findings in Li, Terjesen, and Umans' (2019) review of corporate governance in entrepreneurial firms.

Before discussing future research directions for corporate governance of entrepreneurial firms, we conduct a literature review of 135 papers in this field and identified 30 frequently cited empirical studies in recent decades (see Appendix 1 and Li, Terjesen, and Umans (2019)). We summarize the research questions, findings, and theories applied in each of the 30 studies and identify important themes (see Appendix 2). In the next section, we briefly discuss current research status of these themes, and find that while previous studies investigate various stakeholders' roles in corporate governance, they do not fully address the relations and interactions among various stakeholders or groups of stakeholders, especially between boards and TMTs. Therefore, we propose future research directions focus on BOD-TMT interactions.

Current themes and topics

In this section, we briefly summarize the current status of three interrelated research themes: the role of key stakeholders, governance processes, and outcomes of corporate governance. Given the importance of corporate boards, we first discuss the role of directors, particularly outside directors. Next we discuss how venture capitalists affect entrepreneurial firms beyond providing financial resources. Then we discuss how entrepreneurs get involved in corporate governance mechanisms. We identify two corporate governance processes frequently discussed in previous literature: social networking and strategic decision making. We also find that apart from financial performance, three aspects are frequently addressed when research-ers investigate the outcomes of corporate governance: innovation, growth, and internationalization.

The role of key stakeholders

Directors

Playing a crucial role in entrepreneurial firms' functioning and survival (e.g. Charas and Perelli 2013), the BOD is responsible for monitoring managerial decisions on behalf of the shareholders and for providing resources for firm strategic devel-opment (Finkelstein et al. 2009). BOD engagement in monitoring is important for effective functioning of the firm as it reduces the agency costs of managerial opportunism (Fama and Jensen 1983). At the same time BOD engagement in the resource provision role can bring value to the firm in terms of growth and stra-tegic adaptation (Pearce and Zahra 1992). Board composition is discussed in the literature in terms of outside directors (Pollock et al. 2010; e.g. Boone et al. 2007). It is also noteworthy that boards are entrepreneurs' potential "battlefield" against outsiders (e.g. Charas and Perelli 2013). For example, a venture capitalist (VC) who sits on a venture's board can shape the firm's HR policy and replace the founder with an outside CEO (Hellmann and Puri 2002).

Venture capitalists

VCs add more value than just financial support for their portfolio companies. Sapienza et al.'s (1996) four-country study describes how VCs provide additional advisory support and mentorship. VCs typically professionalize their ventures by instituting processes related to human resources, stock option plan adoption, and external hiring, particularly for marketing and CEO (Hellmann and Puri 2002).

Entrepreneurs

Top managers are responsible for the formulation and the implementation of firm strategy (Finkelstein et al. 2009). Due to incomplete separation of ownership and control, many entrepreneurial firms have a CEO or manager who is board chair, founder, or owner (Banham and He 2010). Owner-managed firms are still sub-ject to agency problems due to a potential lack of external control mechanisms, and therefore face "self-control" problems due to incentives which lead owners to "harm themselves as well as those around them" (Schulze et al. 2001). Executive ownership together with good corporate governance mechanisms, such as separa-tion of board chair and CEO position, and appropriate board size increase commit-ment to corporate entrepreneurship (Zahra et al. 2000).

Governance processes

Social networking

Enterprises obtain resources through social networking (Szeto et al. 2006; Zhou et al. 2007; Bjørnåli and Gulbrandsen 2010; Stam et al. 2014). The VC network is particularly helpful in securing financial resources (Steier and Greenwood 1995). Although some early evidence shows that owner-managers' networks are relatively small and non-extensive and that the extent of owner-manager networking may be previously overstated (Curran et al. 1993), social networking has become a formal mechanism that demands legitimacy (Human and Provan 2000). Recent evidence shows that small firms with higher social capital perform better than those without as much social capital (Stam et al. 2014).

Strategic decision making

Successful entrepreneurial firms often plan strategically to achieve their growth and development goals, and these planning activities are increasingly sophisticated over time (Berry 1998). Board directors in VC-backed ventures play a more active role in strategy formation and evaluation than their director counterparts who lack larger ownership stakes (Fried et al. 1998). Concerning a board's involvement and strategy, leadership behaviors and processes play a greater role than structural leadership characteristics (Machold et al. 2011).

Outcomes of corporate governance

Innovation

Innovation is a heterogeneous concept and variously measured. Greater levels of board diversity and interlocking directorates are associated with greater levels of incremental innovation; in contrast, a greater education level leads to more radical innovations (Wincent et al. 2010). An early study identifies CEO characteristics such as innovativeness, attitude, and IT knowledge as key drivers of IT adoption in small businesses (Thong and Yap 1995).

Growth

Ability, need, and opportunity are three primary forces driving firm growth (Davidsson 1991). More specifically, small business growth is driven by the firm's entrepreneurial orientation and resources as well as environmental characteristics, and managers' personal values (Wiklund et al. 2009). Entrepreneurs' human capital and capability, resources from VCs, and advisory services performed by directors contribute to entrepreneurial firms' growth (e.g. Colombo and Grilli 2010; Huse and Zattoni 2008; Ahn 2014).

Internationalization

Small firms are pushed to go abroad due to the fast-changing environment at home (Andersson et al. 2009). Co-existing formal and informal governance mechanisms complement and supplement one another, thus increasing export intensity (Calabrò and Mussolino 2013).

Future research agenda: a focus on BOD-TMT interaction

Research questions

A large literature in management explores BODs and TMTs as these power groups significantly influence organizational functioning (Hambrick and Mason 1984). Researchers typically study each of these two groups' respective effects on organizational outcomes individually (Forbes and Milliken 1999), rather than answering calls to explore the joint effects of these two groups on different organizational outcomes (e.g. Pettigrew 1992). Future research should examine:

- How does the BOD interact with TMTs in an entrepreneurial firm?
- What is the outcome of the BOD-TMT interaction?
- How do group processes determine the effects of this interaction on organizational outcomes?

BODs and TMTs can be conceptualized as being parts of the dominant coalition of the firm (Hambrick and Mason 1984) or, in Finkelstein and Hambrick's (1996) terms, a "Supra TMT," i.e. a group of individuals – typically board directors and senior executives – who possess the decision-making power to affect organizational outcomes. Joint membership of BOD and TMT members in a supra TMT has been detected in some contexts (e.g. Norway) where researchers and popular media alike report about interactions in informal settings, i.e. social gathering and joint business trips (Huse 2007), or in more formalized situations, e.g. joint strategy and BOD meetings in which TMT members in different constellations attend (Ström 2015). Castro et al. (2009) and Umans and Smith (2013) argue that exploring the dynamics of the interaction between the two groups is important for understanding organizational function and survival, since the decisions inside supra TMTs are strategically important for the firm, affecting organizational outcomes.

One way forward in understanding BOD-TMT interactions within the supra TMT constellation is to explore the two domains in which this interaction takes place. BODs have two key roles: monitoring and resource provision (Hillman and Dalziel 2003) which differ in their hierarchical nature. Monitoring the interaction is a top-down process, while the resource provision domain allows more collaborative peer-to-peer interaction. Thus, we expect the nature and outcomes of interaction within supra TMTs to differ across the two domains. We further argue that the nature of these two domains will be reflected in organizational outcomes through intergroup processes (here and further the processes that take place between the

BOD and TMT members within the supra TMT constellation). Exploration of the group processes in general, and the executive team processes in particular, establishes that the most likely processes are communication, cohesion, and conflict (Umans 2012), and are the means through which executive groups (e.g. supra TMTs) influence team and organizational outcomes. In other words, depending on whether the group finds itself in a monitoring or a resource provision domain, intergroup processes will vary, ultimately reflected in organizational outcomes.

Future studies are expected to respond to calls to integrate research streams on BODs and TMTs (Pettigrew 1992; Finkelstein and Hambrick 1996) by exploring intergroup processes taking place between these two key organizational actors within two distinct interaction domains, i.e. monitoring and resource provision. Focusing on intergroup processes such as communication, cohesion, and conflict will help answer other researchers' calls to explore the black-box of executive processes (Pettigrew 1992; van Ees et al. 2009). These explorations of interactions between BODs and TMTs will provide a better understanding of how the upper echelons of organizations contribute to various organizational outcomes including both economic and strategic performance.

Theoretical perspective

We encourage future research to open this black box by analyzing the processes guiding BOD-TMT interaction within the two domains of monitoring and resource provision, and the effects on organizational outcomes. We illustrate our basic theoretical model in Figure 9.1.

Previous research discusses the duality associated with the two domains of interaction between the board and the TMT. On one hand, the board is expected to engage top down, evaluating TMT performance and strategic decisions. On the other hand, the board collaborates with the TMT on an equal basis, jointly formulating firm strategy. This duality has been problematized in the literature on board roles. While some studies argue for complementarity of these two types of interaction (Jonnergård and Stafsudd 2011), others question the board's ability to operate as both a collaborative partner and a vigilant monitor, suggesting these roles are mutually exclusive (Adams and Ferreira 2007). Recent studies propose that the

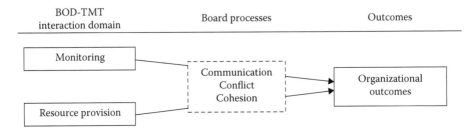

Figure 9.1   BOD-TMT interactions, board processes, and outcomes

board influence on managerial decision making does not function in a vacuum, but rather needs to be considered in terms of bundles of governance mechanisms, suggesting a configurational approach to board governance (Ward et al. 2009; García-Castro et al. 2013; Misangyi and Acharya 2014). One step towards resolving this debate is to gain a deeper understanding of processes, underlining the intergroup interaction between the board and TMT. The nature of these processes can shed light on the fundamental differences between the two roles of the board and the nature of interactions these two roles require within the above-described domains. This issue has not been discussed in detail in previous research.

Bases for interaction

Research on BODs and TMT interactions is frequently grounded in either agency theory or resource dependence theory; however, Hillman and Dalziel (2003) argue that integrating the two perspectives is critical to better understanding the BODs' contribution to firm performance. Umans and Smith (2013) identify three pillars on which interaction between BODs and TMTs rests: rapport over control, rapport over strategy, and rapport over performance.

According to agency theory, a board's underlying function is to monitor/control managers (Fama 1980; Eisenhardt 1989). Boards mainly exercise control through their power to appoint and discharge the CEO. The TMT also holds control through indirect power stemming from expertise, knowledge, and informational advantage. This resource pool enables the TMT to control daily operations which board directors are less able to directly observe. Boards also depend on the TMTs' firm-specific issue understanding. That is, the board can control strategy; however, the TMT can control information flow about operations. This argument suggests that the combined control of a firm depends on BOD-TMT interactions – based on rapport over control.

The second interaction pillar rests on the assumption that BODs and TMTs have direct, shared responsibility for firm decision-making processes (Zahra and Pearce 1989; Pearce and Zahra 1992). From a resource dependency perspective, BOD functions include providing services and setting strategy (Zahra and Pearce 1989; Pearce and Zahra 1992) and enabling access to resources such as capital (Mizruchi and Stearns 1988). The role of the TMT, on the other hand, is usually cast in terms of strategy implementation, including the execution of various processes (Fama and Jensen 1983). European studies in particular emphasize shared responsibility over decision-making processes, where strategy is formulated by the BOD (Huse 2007) and executed by the TMT (Ingley and Van der Walt 2001). Thus, strategy formulation creates interactions between the TMT and BOD (Hendry and Kiel 2004) and work on strategy in general, albeit from their different power positions in the organization.

The third interaction pillar comprises the common goals that BODs and TMTs share and strive to fulfill. Apart from their work on strategy, both groups seek to improve firm performance (Anderson et al. 2007). A large literature describes BOD contributions to firm performance (see Collin 2008 for a review). The BODs' control, experiences, and cognitive resources impact firm functioning and performance (Rindova 1999). While directors are usually compensated with a fixed sum of money unrelated to performance, there is also a labor market for directors (e.g. future director positions and other opportunities), creating incentives for directors to improve financial performance. Similarly, a vast body of research suggests that TMTs impact firm performance (see Umans 2009 for a review), and managers' desire to increase their value in the managerial labor market incentivizes the TMT to strive for high performance (Murphy 1985). Managerial compensation systems linked to firm performance create yet more TMT incentives (Jensen and Zimmerman 1985; Carpenter and Sanders 2002) to prioritize firm performance (Jensen and Murphy 1990). Apart from BOD and TMT labor market incentives, and the TMTs' incentive system, the very aim of the firms' financial performance orientation aligns BOD and TMT interests. Thus, interaction between BODs and TMTs is a product of rapport over performance.

Interaction through process

Studies of both BODs and TMTs have long acknowledged that understanding group processes is essential for understanding how these groups contribute to organizational outcomes (Forbes and Milliken 1999). According to Finkelstein and Hambrick (1996), communication, conflict, and strategic decision making are the most frequently explored group processes in BODs and TMTs – probably because these processes provide "[. . .] greater efficiency (e.g. reducing costs or increasing speed of decision making) or greater effectiveness (e.g. better quality of decisions)" (Knight et al. 1999, 448) in interactions among organizations' top leaders. Thus, we assume that communication, conflict, and strategic decision making emerge in interaction within the supra TMT. This assumption is somewhat supported by a few extant studies (e.g. Kor 2006; Anderson et al. 2007; Behfar et al. 2008) indicating that openness of communication, task-oriented conflict, and effectiveness of decision making between BODs and TMTs positively impact organizational outcomes.

The quality (O'Reilly et al. 1993), frequency (Smith et al. 1994), and openness (Lubatkin et al. 2006) of communication seemingly form an important base for effective and efficient interaction in groups at the top of organizations. For example, Anderson et al. (2007) argues that open communication among members of the BOD and TMT leads to a more positive work environment within the group through the development of respect and trust for one another. Moreover, Castro et al. (2009) highlight that ineffective communication between the two groups may negatively impact organizational outcomes.

Upper echelons research often discusses two dimensions of conflict: interpersonal and task related (De Dreu and Weingart 2003). Interpersonal conflicts in BODs and

TMTs lead to poor task performance (Forbes and Milliken 1999), which negatively impacts organizational outcomes (Certo et al. 2006). Conflict over tasks, on the other hand, seems to increase the effectiveness of BODs (Zona and Zattoni 2007) and TMTs (de Wit et al. 2012), leading to innovative solutions to the tasks at hand (De Dreu 2006) with positive effects on organizational outcomes (de Wit et al. 2012). The supra TMT may experience both types of conflict, given the different roles that TMTs and BODs play in firms. Pearce and Zahra (1992) claim that conflicts between the two groups occur due to differences in perceptions of how decision-making authority is divided. Kor (2006) argues that conflict often circles around the groups' respective takes on strategy as the BOD might have a long-term perspective whereas the TMT might assume a middle- or short-term perspective, which may ultimately affect decisions concerning organizational outcomes. Behfar et al. (2008) argue, however, that BODs that work proactively to create solidarity with the TMTs are often able to reduce conflict levels between the two groups, resulting in more efficient conflict resolution (Collin 2008) and effective supra TMT functioning (Knapp et al. 2011).

Strategic decision making is an important interaction process involving both the BOD and TMT (Zahra and Pearce 1989; Pearce and Zahra 1992). Effectiveness and efficiency in making strategic decisions are usually enhanced by other group processes, such as high quality and quantity of communication and task-oriented conflict within groups (Li and Hambrick 2005). Since the supra TMT consists of two subgroups (BOD and TMT), one can assume that the fault line dividing the supra TMT could affect the group's strategic decision-making processes (Lau and Murnighan 2005). For example, Rico et al. (2007) argue that group members' identification with the subgroup, rather than with the larger group, leads to less sharing of task-related information, potentially resulting in increased conflict and inefficient decision making. Umans (2012) argues that unity over values and goals in groups could reduce the strength of fault lines, increasing effectiveness in communication, conflict management, and decision making.

Interaction process and organizational outcomes

Previous research (e.g. Daily 1996; Kor 2006; García-Castro et al. 2013) touches upon the important role of interaction processes between TMTs and BODs for organizational outcomes. However, the majority of these studies explore interaction indirectly through BOD/TMT characteristics using contingency theory. This approach describes how BOD characteristics (e.g. independence) interact with TMT characteristics (e.g. tenure, experience) to produce outcomes such as R&D investment, based on the implicit assumption that these characteristics proxy differences in interaction processes. Another example is Umans and Smith's (2013) study of how the interaction of diversity in terms of visible characteristics of BODs and TMTs relates to firm performance. The few studies exploring the BOD/TMT interaction in relationship to organizational outcomes indicate some effect of interaction, but they are limited by "black-boxing" the interaction process taking place within the supra TMT.

We argue that it is not the roles per se that determine firm outcomes, but rather the interaction within each of these domains that influences organizational outcomes. By examining the interaction between the board and the TMT within the two domains – monitoring and resource provision – we can explore the board's engagement in each of the particular domains. Considering the degree of interaction can overcome the limitations associated with earlier studies assuming that boards, possessing certain characteristics, will ultimately use these in the decision-making process (Neville and Currie 2015).

Since the hierarchical nature of this interaction can be different in monitoring and resource provision domains, we propose that interaction effects result in different effects on shareholder value. On the one hand, shareholder value could be created through the reduction of the agency costs of managerial opportunism through interaction within the monitoring domain. On the other hand, interaction within the resource domain could enhance shareholder value through value creation, growth, and development of a corporation (Ponomareva 2016). Interaction within the monitoring domain focuses on cost reduction and may benefit short-term organizational outcomes, such as organizational efficiency and financial performance. The collaborative nature of interaction within the resource-provision domain, on the other hand, could result in non-economic outcomes, such as firm strategic performance, organizational ambidexterity, R&D activities, growth, and more long-term performance outcomes. Considering the varying effects of BOD-TMT interaction, this chapter explores the relationship between BOD and TMT interaction within the two outlined domains in relation to a variety of financial and non-financial organizational outcomes.

We then propose that the interaction is determined by group processes. More specifically, group conflict, cohesion, and communication within the supra TMT influence the effects of interaction differently within each of the two domains, ultimately reflecting in organizational outcomes. Depending on the quality of communication, level of conflict, and cohesions, the board and TMT may prioritize one domain of interaction over another to achieve superior organizational outcomes. In addition, we could theorize and empirically explore whether the interaction between BODs and TMTs in both domains could lead to superior performance outcomes.

Furthermore, different group processes may have varying effects on the impact of BOD-TMT interaction within each of the two domains. As argued earlier, board cohesion improves the performance effects of interaction within the resource provision domain and has no or a possibly negative influence on the performance effects of interaction within the monitoring domain. Similarly, effective communication can facilitate the interaction within the two domains; however, further increases in communication may eventually compromise the BODs' ability to monitor, thus decreasing the positive effects of BOD-TMT interaction within the monitoring domain. Lastly, group conflict may have a different influence on the performance effects of BOD-TMT interaction within the two domains, depending on the nature of this conflict. Overall by accounting for three processes within the supra TMT, we can gain a deeper understanding on how the interaction within each of the two domains influences varying organizational outcomes.

Concluding remarks

BODs and TMTs comprise the two central actors within a corporation (Monks and Minow 2012). Board members, meeting only a few times a year and having other board appointments as well as full-time job assignments, do not have comprehensive information about the firm in which they exercise their directorial duties. In contrast to the board members, managers are directly involved in firm daily operations, and therefore possess an information advantage over the board. In order to exercise their roles as monitors and resource providers, board members need to obtain information about the firm, which they can only acquire from TMTs (Umans and Smith 2013). Thus, the interaction between these two organizational actors becomes crucial for the effective functioning and the survival of a corporation.

The intergroup interaction between the BOD and the TMT revolves around the two main domains: interaction for the purpose of monitoring and interaction for the purpose of service provision. From an agency theory perspective, a board's underlying function is to monitor and control managers (Fama and Jensen 1983; Eisenhardt 1989). Boards primarily exercise this power by appointing and discharging the CEO and, in some instances, other TMT members. Based on this view, board independence is crucial for its ability to exercise vigilant monitoring over managerial decisions. The independent directors, who are less likely to be a subject of a strong internal pressure from powerful executives or to run the risk of retaliation, are expected to more objectively evaluate managerial decisions. However, in order to exercise efficient monitoring, directors need information from the managers. Managers need to report their activities to the board, presenting proposed courses of action and the analytical assessment of the firm's strategic environment. Consequently, this type of interaction is hierarchical where the board is the superior oversight body, responsible for decision control including ratification and approval of managerial decisions (Fama and Jensen 1983).

Moreover, the BOD-TMT interaction revolves around the board's resource provision role. From a resource dependency perspective, the board's function is to provide resources in terms of access to capital, networks, advice, and counsel to managers (Mizruchi and Stearns 1988; Zahra and Pearce 1989; Judge and Zeithaml 1992). Since the board and the management share the responsibility over strategy formulation (Huse 2007), the latter creates interactions between the TMT and the BOD. In order to maximize the value of its advice, the board requires information from the CEO as well as willingness from the executives to solicit strategic advice from the board. If managers are not eager to ask for the advice and counsel from the board members, the resource provision role of the board is jeopardized. As board members can constitute value links between the organization and its external environment through providing contacts and information, the TMT members depend on board resources and capital in seeking strategic opportunities for the development of the corporation. As the social ties between the board and the TMT can enhance the propensity of the TMT members to solicit advice from the board (Westphal 1999), the interaction between the board and the TMT is of a paramount importance for the fulfillment of the resource provision role. This type of interaction is expected to be more of a collaborative character, where the board and the TMT jointly work together formulating corporate strategy (Hendry and Kiel 2004).

BODs and TMTs are well-researched topics in the management and governance field. The interaction between the BOD and the TMT are with a few exceptions (e.g. Brunninge et al. 2007) less well-researched and thus future studies are expected to extend this nascent literature. The proposed focus of considering the interaction domains in their relationship to supra TMT processes is a new and unexplored topic which goes well in line with the recently developed trend in corporate governance that puts emphasis on a more behavior-focused view of corporate governance (van Ees et al. 2009). On a final note, all but two of the reviewed studies are based on multi-country studies. We encourage future researchers to pursue the comparative cross-country research (see e.g. Terjesen et al. 2016). This line of research might consider the emerging theory of "corporate governance deviance" which explores factors that affect a firm's decision to either follow or deviate from the typical governance template for firms in a particular country.

References

Adams, R. B., and D. Ferreira. (2007), 'A theory of friendly boards', *The Journal of Finance*, **62** (1), 217–50.

Ahn, M. J. (2014), 'Enhancing corporate governance in high-growth entrepreneurial firms', *International Journal of Innovation and Technology Management*, **11** (06), 1450038.

Anderson, D. W., S. J. Melanson, and J. Maly. (2007), 'The evolution of corporate governance: Power redistribution brings boards to life', *Corporate Governance: An International Review*, **15** (5), 780–97.

Andersson, S., J. Gabrielsson, and I. Wictor. (2009), 'International activities in small firms: Examining factors influencing the internationalization and export growth of small firms', *Canadian Journal of Administrative Sciences*, **21** (1), 22–34.

Banham, H., and Y. He. (2010), 'SME governance: Converging definitions and expanding expectations', *International Business & Economics Research Journal*, **9** (2), 77–82.

Behfar, K. J., R. S. Peterson, E. A. Mannix, and W. M. K. Trochim. (2008), 'The critical role of conflict resolution in teams: A close look at the links between conflict type, conflict management strategies, and team outcomes', *Journal of Applied Psychology*, **93** (1), 170–88.

Bell, R. G., I. Filatotchev, and R. V. Aguilera. (2014), 'Corporate governance and investors' perceptions of foreign IPO value: An institutional perspective', *Academy of Management Journal*, **57** (1), 301–20.

Berry, M. (1998), 'Strategic planning in small high tech companies', *Long Range Planning*, **31** (3), 455–66.

Bjørnåli, E. S., and M. Gulbrandsen. (2010), 'Exploring board formation and evolution of board composition in academic spin-offs', *The Journal of Technology Transfer*, **35** (1), 92–112.

Boone, A. L., L. Casares Field, J. M. Karpoff, and C. G. Raheja. (2007), 'The determinants of corporate board size and composition: An empirical analysis', *Journal of Financial Economics*, **85** (1), 66–101.

Boone, C., B. Brabander, and A. Witteloostuijn. (1996), 'CEO locus of control and small firm performance: An integrative framework and empirical test', *Journal of Management Studies*, **33** (5), 667–700.

Brunninge, O., M. Nordqvist, and J. Wiklund. (2007), 'Corporate governance and strategic change in SMEs: The effects of ownership, board composition and top management teams', *Small Business Economics*, **29** (3), 295–308.

Calabrò, A., and D. Mussolino. (2013), 'How do boards of directors contribute to family SME export intensity? The role of formal and informal governance mechanisms', *Journal of Management & Governance*, **17** (2), 363–403.

Carpenter, M. A., and W. G. Sanders. (2002), 'Top management team compensation: the missing link between CEO pay and firm performance?', *Strategic Management Journal*, **23** (4), 367–75.

Castro, C. B., M. D. De La Concha, J. V. Gravel, and M. M. V. Periñan. (2009), 'Does the team leverage the board's decisions?', *Corporate Governance: An International Review*, **17** (6), 744–61.

Certo, S. T., J. G. Covin, C. M. Daily, and D. R. Dalton. (2001), 'Wealth and the effects of founder management among IPO-stage new ventures', *Strategic Management Journal*, **22** (6–7), 641–58.

Certo, S. T., R. H. Lester, C. M. Dalton, and D. R. Dalton. (2006), 'Top management teams, strategy and financial performance: A meta-analytic examination', *Journal of Management Studies*, **43** (4), 813–39.

Charas, S., and S. Perelli. (2013), 'Threats to board stability: Understanding SME director behavior', *International Journal of Disclosure and Governance*, **10** (2), 175–91.

Collin, S.-O. (2008), 'The mastering of the corporation: An integrated view of corporate governance', unpublished manuscript, Department of Business Studies, Kristianstad University College, Sweden.

Colombo, M. G., and L. Grilli. (2010), 'On growth drivers of high-tech start-ups: Exploring the role of founders' human capital and venture capital', *Journal of Business Venturing*, **25** (6), 610–26.

Curran, J., R. Jarvis, R. A. Blackburn, and S. Black. (1993), 'Networks and small firms: Constructs, methodological strategies and some findings', *International Small Business Journal*, **11** (2), 13–25.

Daily, C. (1996), 'Chief executive officers, top management teams, and boards of directors: Congruent or countervailing forces?', *Journal of Management*, **22** (2), 185–208.

Daily, C. M., and D. R. Dalton. (1992), 'The relationship between governance structure and corporate performance in entrepreneurial firms', *Journal of Business Venturing*, **7** (5), 375–86.

Davidsson, P. (1991), 'Continued entrepreneurship: Ability, need, and opportunity as determinants of small firm growth', *Journal of Business Venturing*, **6** (6), 405–429.

De Dreu, C. K. W. (2006), 'When too little or too much hurts: Evidence for a curvilinear relationship between task conflict and innovation in teams', *Journal of Management*, **32** (1), 83–107.

De Dreu, C. K. W., and L. R. Weingart. (2003), 'Task versus relationship conflict, team performance, and team member satisfaction: A meta-analysis', *Journal of Applied Psychology*, **88** (4), 741–49.

van Ees, H., J. Gabrielsson, and M. Huse. (2009), 'Toward a behavioral theory of boards and corporate governance', *Corporate Governance: An International Review*, **17** (3), 307–19.

Eisenberg, T., S. Sundgren, and M. T. Wells. (1998), 'Larger board size and decreasing firm value in small firms', *Journal of Financial Economics*, **48** (1), 35–54.

Eisenhardt, K. M. (1989), 'Agency theory: An assessment and review', *The Academy of Management Review*, **14** (1), 57–74.

Fama, E. F. (1980), 'Agency problems and the theory of the firm', *Journal of Political Economy*, **88** (2), 288–307.

Fama, E. F., and M. C. Jensen. (1983), 'Separation of ownership and control', *The Journal of Law and Economics*, **26** (2), 301–25.

Finkelstein, S., and D. C. Hambrick. (1996), *Strategic Leadership: Top Executives and Their Effects on Organizations*. St. Paul, MN: West Publishing Company.

Finkelstein, S., D. C. Hambrick, and A. A. Cannella. (2009), 'Strategic leadership: Theory and research on executives, top management teams, and boards'. In *Theory and Research on Executives, Top Management Teams, and Boards*. Oxford: Oxford University Press.

Forbes, D. P., and F. J. Milliken. (1999), 'Cognition and corporate governance: Understanding boards of directors as strategic decision-making groups', *The Academy of Management Review*, **24** (3), 489–505.

Fried, V. H., G. D. Bruton, and R. D. Hisrich. (1998), 'Strategy and the board of directors in venture capital-backed firms', *Journal of Business Venturing*, **13** (6), 493–503.

Gabrielsson, J. (2017), 'Corporate governance and entrepreneurship: Current states and future directions'. In *Handbook of Research on Corporate Governance and Entrepreneurship*, 3–26. Cheltenham, UK and Northampton, MA, USA: Edward Elgar.

García-Castro, R., R. V. Aguilera, and M. A. Ariño. (2013), 'Bundles of firm corporate governance practices: A fuzzy set analysis', *Corporate Governance: An International Review*, **21** (4), 390–407.

Hambrick, D. C., and P. A. Mason. (1984), 'Upper echelons: The organization as a reflection of its top managers', *Academy of Management Review*, **9** (2), 193–206.

Hansen, B., and R. T. Hamilton. (2011), 'Factors distinguishing small firm growers and non-growers', *International Small Business Journal*, **29** (3), 278–94.

Hellmann, T., and M. Puri. (2002), 'Venture capital and the professionalization of start-up firms: Empirical evidence', *The Journal of Finance*, **57** (1), 169–97.

Hendry, K., and G. C. Kiel. (2004), 'The role of the board in firm strategy: Integrating agency and organisational control perspectives', *Corporate Governance*, **12** (4), 500–20.

Hillman, A. J., and T. Dalziel. (2003), 'Boards of directors and firm performance: Integrating agency and resource dependence perspectives', *Academy of Management Review*, **28** (3), 383–96.

Human, S. E., and K. G. Provan. (2000), 'Legitimacy building in the evolution of small-firm multilateral networks: A comparative study of success and demise', *Administrative Science Quarterly*, **45** (2), 327–65.

Huse, M. (2007), *Boards, Governance and Value Creation*. Cambridge: Cambridge University Press.

Huse, M., and A. Zattoni. (2008), 'Trust, firm life cycle, and actual board behavior: Evidence from "one of the lads" in the board of three small firms', *International Studies of Management and Organization*, **38** (3), 71–97.

Ingley, C. B., and N. T. Van der Walt. (2001), 'The strategic board: The changing role of directors in developing and maintaining corporate capability', *Corporate Governance*, **9** (3), 174–85.

Jensen, M. C., and K. J. Murphy. (1990), 'Performance pay and top-management incentives', *Journal of Political Economy*, **98** (2), 225–64.

Jensen, M. C., and J. L. Zimmerman. (1985), 'Management compensation and the managerial labor market', *Journal of Accounting and Economics*, **7** (1–3), 3–9.

Jonnergård, K., and A. Stafsudd. (2011), 'The making of active boards in Swedish public companies', *Journal of Management & Governance*, **15** (1), 123–55.

Judge, W. Q., and C. P. Zeithaml. (1992), 'Institutional and strategic choice perspectives on board involvement in the strategic decision process', *Academy of Management Journal*, **35** (4), 766–94.

Knapp, J. R., T. Dalziel, and M. W. Lewis. (2011), 'Governing top managers: Board control, social categorization, and their unintended influence on discretionary behaviors', *Corporate Governance: An International Review*, (4), 295–310.

Knight, D., C. L. Pearce, K. G. Smith, J. D. Olian, H. P. Sims, K. A. Smith, and P. Flood. (1999), 'Top management team diversity, group process, and strategic consensus', *Strategic Management Journal*, **20** (5), 445–65.

Kor, Y. Y. (2006), 'Direct and interaction effects of top management team and board compositions on R&D investment strategy', *Strategic Management Journal*, **27** (11), 1081–99.

Kor, Y. Y., and J. T. Mahoney. (2005), 'How dynamics, management, and governance of resource deployments influence firm-level performance', *Strategic Management Journal*, **26** (5), 489–96.

Lau, D. C., and J. K. Murnighan. (2005), 'Interactions within groups and subgroups: The effects of demographic faultlines', *Academy of Management Journal*, **48** (4), 645–59.

Li, H., S. A. Terjesen, and T. Umans. (2019), 'Corporate governance in entrepreneurial firms: A systematic review and research agenda', *Small Business Economics*, forthcoming. https://link.springer.com/article/10.1007/s11187-018-0118-1

Li, J., and D. C. Hambrick. (2005), 'Factional groups: A new vantage on demographic faultlines, conflict, and disintegration in work teams', *Academy of Management Journal*, **48** (5), 794–813.

Lubatkin, M. H., Z. Simsek, Y. Ling, and J. F. Veiga. (2006), 'Ambidexterity and performance in small-to medium-sized firms: The pivotal role of top management team behavioral integration', *Journal of Management*, **32** (5), 646–72.

Machold, S., M. Huse, A. Minichilli, and M. Nordqvist. (2011), 'Board leadership and strategy involvement in small firms: A team production approach', *Corporate Governance: An International Review*, **19** (4), 368–83.

Misangyi, V. F., and A. G. Acharya. (2014), 'Substitutes or complements? A configurational examination of corporate governance mechanisms', *Academy of Management Journal*, **57** (6), 1681–705.

Mizruchi, M. S., and L. B. Stearns. (1988), 'A longitudinal study of the formation of interlocking directorates', *Administrative Science Quarterly*, **33** (2), 194–210.

Monks, R. A. G., and N. Minow. (2012), *Corporate Governance*. Hoboken, NJ: John Wiley.

Murphy, K. J. (1985), 'Corporate performance and managerial remuneration', *Journal of Accounting and Economics*, **7** (1–3), 11–42.

Neville, F., and R. Currie. (2015), 'Toward a psychological contract framework of director effectiveness: The role of CEO expectations', *Academy of Management Proceedings*, **2015** (1), 15475.

O'Reilly, C. A., R. C. Snyder, and J. N. Boothe. (1993), 'Effects of executive team demography on organizational change'. In *Organizational Change and Redesign*, 147–75. Oxford: Oxford University Press.

Pearce, J. A., and S. A. Zahra. (1992), 'Board composition from a strategic contingency perspective', *Journal of Management Studies*, **29** (4), 411–38.

Pettigrew, A. M. (1992), 'The character and significance of strategy process research', *Strategic Management Journal*, **13** (S2), 5–16.

Pollock, T. G., G. Chen, E. M. Jackson, and D. C. Hambrick. (2010), 'How much prestige is enough? Assessing the value of multiple types of high-status affiliates for young firms', *Journal of Business Venturing*, **25** (1), 6–23.

Ponomareva, Y. (2016), 'Costs and benefits of delegation: Managerial discretion as a bridge between strategic management and corporate governance', Linnaeus University, Sweden.

Rico, R., E. Molleman, M. Sánchez-Manzanares, and G. S. Van der Vegt. (2007), 'The effects of diversity faultlines and team task autonomy on decision quality and social integration', *Journal of Management*, **33** (1), 111–32.

Rindova, V. P. (1999), 'What corporate boards have to do with strategy: A cognitive perspective', *Journal of Management Studies*, **36** (7), 953–75.

Sapienza, H. J., S. Manigart, and W. Vermeir. (1996), 'Venture capitalist governance and value added in four countries', *Journal of Business Venturing*, **11** (6), 439–69.

Schulze, W. S., M. H. Lubatkin, R. N. Dino, and A. K. Buchholtz. (2001), 'Agency relationships in family firms: Theory and evidence', *Organization Science*, **12** (2), 99–116.

Sciascia, S., P. Mazzola, J. H. Astrachan, and T. M. Pieper. (2013), 'Family involvement in the board of directors: Effects on sales internationalization', *Journal of Small Business Management*, **51** (1), 83–99.

Smith, K. G., K. A. Smith, J. D. Olian, H. P. Sims, D. P. O'Bannon, and J. A. Scully. (1994), 'Top management team demography and process: The role of social integration and communication', *Administrative Science Quarterly*, **39** (3), 412–38.

Stam, W., S. Arzlanian, and T. Elfring. (2014), 'Social capital of entrepreneurs and small firm performance: A meta-analysis of contextual and methodological moderators', *Journal of Business Venturing*, **29** (1), 152–73.

Steier, L., and R. Greenwood. (1995), 'Venture capitalist relationships in the deal structuring and post investment stages of new firm creation', *Journal of Management Studies*, **32** (3), 337–57.

Ström, P. (2015), Personal interview. Flyinge, Sweden.

Szeto, R., P. C. Wright, and E. Cheng. (2006), 'Business networking in the Chinese context', *Management Research News*, **29** (7), 425–38.

Terjesen, S., J. Hessels, and D. Li. (2016), 'Comparative International entrepreneurship research: A review and research agenda', *Journal of Management*, **42** (2), 299–344.

Thong, J. Y. L., and C. S. Yap. (1995), 'CEO characteristics, organizational characteristics and information technology adoption in small businesses', *Omega*, **23** (4), 429–42.

Umans, T. (2009), 'Research angles on cultural diversity in top management teams', *Problems & Perspectives in Management*, **7** (1), 90–105.

Umans, T. (2012), 'The bottom line of cultural diversity at the top: The top management team's cultural diversity and its influence on organisational outcomes', Lund University, Sweden.

Umans, T., and E. Smith. (2013), 'Isolated islands in the upper apex of organisations: In search of interaction netween the board of directors and the top management team', *Corporate Ownership and Control*, **10** (2), 80–90.

Ward, A. J., J. A. Brown, and D. Rodriguez. (2009), 'Governance bundles, firm performance, and the substitutability and complementarity of governance mechanisms', *Corporate Governance: An International Review*, **17** (5), 646–60.

Westhead, P., M. Wright, and D. Ucbasaran. (2001), 'The internationalization of new and small firms', *Journal of Business Venturing*, **16** (4), 333–58.

Westphal, J. D. (1999), 'Collaboration in the boardroom: Behavioral and performance consequences of CEO-board social ties', *Academy of Management Journal*, **42** (1), 7–24.

Wiklund, J., H. Patzelt, and D. A. Shepherd. (2009), 'Building an integrative model of small business growth', *Small Business Economics*, **32** (4), 351–74.

Wincent, J., S. Anokhin, and D. Örtqvist. (2010), 'Does network board capital matter? A study of innovative performance in strategic SME networks', *Journal of Business Research*, **63** (3), 265–75.

Wirtz, P. (2011), 'The cognitive dimension of corporate governance in fast growing entrepreneurial firms', *European Management Journal*, **29** (6), 431–47.

de Wit, F. R. C., L. L. Greer, and K. A. Jehn. (2012), 'The paradox of intragroup conflict: A meta-analysis', *Journal of Applied Psychology*, **97** (2), 360–90.

Zahra, S. A., and J. A. Pearce. (1989), 'Boards of directors and corporate financial performance: A review and integrative model', *Journal of Management*, **15** (2), 291–334.

Zahra, S. A., D. O. Neubaum, and M. Huse. (2000), 'Entrepreneurship in medium-size companies: Exploring the effects of ownership and governance systems', *Journal of Management*, **26** (5), 947–76.

Zhou, L., W. P. Wu, and X. Luo. (2007), 'Internationalization and the performance of born-global SMEs: The mediating role of social networks', *Journal of International Business Studies*, **38** (4), 673–90.

Zona, F., and A. Zattoni. (2007), 'Beyond the black box of demography: Board processes and task effectiveness within Italian firms', *Corporate Governance: An International Review*, **15** (5), 852–64.

Appendix 1   Most-cited empirical studies

Studies	Citations	Qualitative/ quantitative	Methods	Data geography
2010–2017				
Colombo and Grilli (2010)	348	Quantitative	Archival	Italy
Stam et al. (2014)	287	Quantitative	Meta-analysis	Multi-national
Pollock et al. (2010)	136	Quantitative	Archival	US
Bell et al. (2014)	125	Quantitative	Archival	US
Wincent et al. (2010)	125	Quantitative	Survey	Sweden
Hansen and Hamilton (2011)	115	Qualitative	Cases	New Zealand
Calabrò and Mussolino (2013)	95	Quantitative	Survey	Norway
Machold et al. (2011)	92	Quantitative	Survey	Norway
Bjørnåli and Gulbrandsen (2010)	63	Qualitative	Cases	US Norway
Sciascia et al. (2013)	49	Quantitative	Survey	US
2000–2009				
Hellmann and Puri (2002)	2073	Quantitative	Survey	US
Schulze et al. (2001)	2056	Quantitative	Survey	US
A. L. Boone et al. (2007)	1402	Quantitative	Archival	US
Westhead et al. (2001)	1109	Quantitative	Survey	UK
Zahra et al. (2000)	759	Quantitative	Survey	US
Human and Provan (2000)	725	Qualitative	Cases	US
Wiklund et al. (2009)	506	Quantitative	Survey	Sweden
Kor and Mahoney (2005)	419	Quantitative	Archival	US
Certo et al. (2001)	395	Quantitative	Survey	US
Andersson et al. (2009)	380	Quantitative	Survey	Sweden
1990–1999				
Eisenberg et al. (1998)	2252	Quantitative	Archival	Finland
Sapienza et al. (1996)	922	Quantitative	Survey	Multi-national
Davidsson (1991)	918	Quantitative	Survey	Sweden
Thong and Yap (1995)	868	Quantitative	Survey	Singapore
Daily and Dalton (1992)	547	Quantitative	Archival	US
Curran et al. (1993)	369	Qualitative	Interview	UK
Berry (1998)	326	Qualitative	Survey	UK
Fried et al. (1998)	302	Quantitative	Survey	US
C. Boone et al. (1996)	251	Quantitative	Survey	UK
Steier and Greenwood (1995)	232	Qualitative	Case	UK

Appendix 2 Summary of previous studies

Research questions	Findings	Theoretical perspective	Topics
2010–2017			
How do founders' human capital and VCs affect the growth of new technology-based firms (NTNFs)?	Founders' skills are associated with the capabilities of non–VC-backed firms; such association is not obvious in VC-backed firms, pointing to VCs' "coach" function (Colombo and Grilli 2010).	Competence-based View	Venture Capitalists Entrepreneurs
Do entrepreneurs' social networks affect firms' performance?	Small firms with higher social capital perform better than those with less social capital (Stam et al. 2014).	Social Capital Theory Actor Network Theory	Entrepreneurs Social Networks
What are the effects of affiliations with various types of prestigious parties on the success of young firms?	Prestigious executives, directors, VC firms, and underwriters convey different positive signals of IPO worth (Pollock et al. 2010).	Signaling Theory	Venture Capitalists Outside Directors Entrepreneurs Social Networks
How stock market responds to different constellations of firm-level corporate governance mechanisms in IPOs?	Some different combinations of corporate governance mechanisms (e.g. independent directors, VC ownership, and CEO ownership) can lead to the same level of investor valuation of firms. The strength of minority shareholder protection in a foreign IPO affects the number of governance mechanisms required to achieve high-value perceptions among US investors (Bell et al. 2014).	Institutional Theory	Venture Capitalists Outside Directors Entrepreneurs Social Networks
How does network board capital (i.e. human capital and relational capital) affect innovative performance?	Board diversity and interlocking directorates affect incremental innovation, whereas education level affects radical innovation (Wincent et al. 2010).	Resource Dependence Theory	Innovation

Research question	Finding	Theory	Keywords
Why do some firms grow while others do not?	Four factors help firms grow: opportunistic perceptions of external environment, controlled ambition of the owner-manager to grow, business culture of innovation and flexibility, and use of extensive private business networks (Hansen and Hamilton 2011).	Stage Model of Growth	Growth
How do family-owned SMEs internationalize their business through exports?	Co-existing formal and informal governance mechanisms complement and supplement each other, thus positively affecting export intensity (Calabrò and Mussolino 2013).	Institutional Theory	Informal Mechanisms / Internationalization
How is board leadership associated with strategic involvement?	Leadership behaviors and processes have a greater impact on boards' strategy involvement than structural leadership characteristics alone (Machold et al. 2011).	Team Production Theory	Outside Directors / Strategic Decision Making
How do boards change over time?	Board composition convergences over time in subsequent board changes, which are mainly driven by the board chair's social networks (Bjørnåli and Gulbrandsen 2010).	Resource Dependence Theory	Board Composition / Outside Directors
How does family involvement in the board affect a firm's internationalization?	Family involvement in the board of directors and sales internationalization of the company have a J-shaped, non-linear relationship (Sciascia et al. 2013).	Stewardship Perspective	Family Directors / Internationalization
2000–2009			
How do VCs influence the development of new firms?	VCs take a variety of professionalization measures, such as HR policies, the adoption of stock option plans, and hiring of a marketing VP and outside CEO (Hellmann and Puri 2002).	Financial Intermediation Theory	Venture Capitalists
Does owner management necessarily eliminate the agency costs of ownership?	Private ownership and owner management not only reduce the effectiveness of external control mechanisms, but also expose firms to a "self-control" problem created by incentives that cause owners to take actions which "harm themselves as well as those around them" (Schulze et al. 2001).	Agency Theory	Entrepreneurs
How is board size affected over time?	Board size and independence increase as firms grow and diversify over time (Boone et al. 2007).	Agency Theory	Outside Directors / Growth

Research questions	Findings	Theoretical perspective	Topics
2000–2009			
Can the characteristics of principal founders, businesses, and the external environment explain whether a firm is still an exporter or a non-exporter at a later date?	Characteristics of principal founders, businesses, and the external environment that are significantly associated with the propensity to export sales abroad are not the same as those significantly associated with selected size and performance measures (Westhead et al. 2001).	Resource-based View	Entrepreneurs Internationalization
How do ownership and governance affect corporate entrepreneurship (CE)?	Executive ownership, separation of board chair and CEO position, and medium-sized board increase commitment to corporate entrepreneurship (Zahra et al. 2000).	Agency Theory	Entrepreneurs Board Composition
How do SME networks build legitimacy?	SME networks can establish legitimacy in three distinct dimensions: the network as form, the network as entity, and the network as interaction (Human and Provan 2000).	Institutional Theory	Social Networks
What are the impacts of entrepreneurial orientation, environmental characteristics, firm resources, and managers' personal attitudes on growth?	Entrepreneurial orientation, environmental characteristics, firm resources, and managers' personal attitudes directly and/or indirectly influence the growth of small businesses (Wiklund et al. 2009).	Resource-based View	Entrepreneurs Growth
How do firms develop and maintain dynamic capabilities?	A history of increased investments in marketing is an enduring source of competitive advantage; institutional ownership is positively associated with economic returns from marketing deployments as institutional owners scrutinize these deployments and send positive signals to the market about the firm (Kor and Mahoney 2005).	Resource-based View Agency Theory	Institutional Investor Strategic Decision Making
How does founder management affect IPO underpricing?	Founder management positively impacts IPO underpricing (Certo et al. 2001).	Agency Theory	Entrepreneurs
What factors lead small firms to go international?	Small firms are pushed to go abroad due to the fast-changing environment at home (Andersson et al. 2009).	Stage Theory of Internationalization	Internationalization

1990–1999

Research question	Key finding	Theory	Topic
Does board size affect financial performance?	We find a significant negative correlation between board size and profitability in a sample of small and midsize Finnish firms (Eisenberg et al. 1998).	Agency Theory	Outside Directors
Can VCs add value beyond the money they provide to their portfolio companies?	VCs add more value than just financial support for their portfolio companies, such as additional advisory support and mentorship (Sapienza et al. 1996).	Agency Theory / Resource Dependence Theory	Venture Capitalists
What determines entrepreneurship firm growth?	All of the specific low-level explanatory variables that have previously been used can be regarded as aspects of any of three major determinants: ability, need, and opportunity (Davidsson 1991).	Psychological Economics	Growth
Do individual or organizational characteristics have a bigger impact on technology adaptation for small firms?	CEO characteristics affect IT adoption in small businesses (Thong and Yap 1995).	Innovation Theory	Innovation
How do CEOs and BODs affect the growth and productivity of medium-sized businesses?	CEOs of successful entrepreneurial firms do not demonstrate a tendency to adopt inappropriate governance structures (Daily et al. 2003).	Agency Theory	Entrepreneurs / Growth
How does networking affect the success of small businesses?	Owner-managers' networks are relatively small and non-extensive; the extent of networking of owner-managers was previously overstated (Curran et al. 1993).	Strategic Management Theory / Business Policy Theory / Social Network Theory	Entrepreneurs / Social Networks
Do managers of small firms in the turbulent industrial environment bother to plan for the longer term?	Successful small high-tech firms plan strategically to achieve long-term growth and development; their planning processes become more sophisticated as they grow (Berry 1998).	N/A	Strategic Decision Making

Research questions	Findings	Theoretical perspective	Topics
1990–1999			
How do boards of VC-backed companies differ from boards of other types of firms?	Boards of directors in VC-backed companies are more involved in strategy formation and evaluation than boards where members do not have large ownership stakes (Fried et al. 1998).	Agency Theory Institutional Theory	Venture Capitalists Strategy
How is CEO locus of control related to organizational performance?	Our results demonstrate that an integrative approach (that includes strategic choice and firm performance) increases our insight into the impact of CEO locus of control by revealing why some CEOs achieve higher organizational performance than others (Boone et al. 1996).	Social Learning Theory Strategy	Entrepreneurs
How do entrepreneurs who receive co-investing differ from those who receive staged financing?	Penetrating the VC network is a significant first step in securing financial resources and, intriguingly, relationships supersede business plans in securing these resources; para-doxically, VCs establish milestones and tight time-lines yet inadvertently contribute to many of the delays experienced by a start-up firm (Steier and Greenwood 1995).	Social Network Theory	Venture Capitalists Entrepreneurs

10 Research opportunities considering student entrepreneurship in university ecosystems

Simon Mosey and Paul Kirkham

Introduction

Universities globally are increasing their support for student entrepreneurship through curricular and extra-curricular programmes. Within the curriculum there is a shift towards experiential education as students work on contemporary industrial and societal challenges in the classroom. This is complemented by extra-curricular activities where students and alumni are encouraged to address such challenges through venture creation. University support for student entrepreneurship is diverse and far reaching and includes hackathons, germinators, incubators, seed and angel funding, entrepreneurs in residence and growth programmes.

Research considering the impact of such interventions offers great promise. For the first time, researchers have relatively straightforward access to the antecedents of venture creation in real time. There is potential to consider the earliest stages of venture creation across a vast natural experiment where the factors associated with venture performance can be captured and controlled for. Such an empirical bonanza encourages novel theoretical approaches. We highlight the possibilities for deploying theories from disparate disciplines across and between different levels of analysis.

For instance, we advocate taking an entrepreneurial ecosystem approach to help explain the creation, development and growth of new systems of entrepreneurship within university regions. We also revitalise the, more traditional, individual level of analysis by utilising diverse theoretical and methodological approaches, such as a sense-making and visual mapping and show how this could yield new insights into the antecedents of student entrepreneurship.

We conclude that student entrepreneurship as a domain can yield exciting new contributions to the study of entrepreneurship and management through the use of novel methodological, theoretical and multi-level investigations.

Why study student entrepreneurship?

The very first business schools were set up as collaborations between business people and economists. The oldest, École supérieure de commerce de Paris (ESPC), was co-founded by the economist Jean-Baptiste Say and the trader Vital Roux in 1819. Their original curriculum was based on a combined theoretical and practical approach to business education. Since that time business schools have developed and evolved in a variety of directions and many have received critiques of their practice including an overemphasis on theory at the expense of practice, a retreat into single disciplinary siloes and a lack of critical consideration of the role of business within society (Martin, 2013; Starkey et al., 2004; Starkey and Tempest, 2009). However, some business schools have responded to this critique with an ideological return to the original purpose of business schools such as ESPC. Select business schools across the world are re-engaging with business people with a new sense of common purpose – to support and encourage student entrepreneurship (Wright et al., 2017).

Student entrepreneurship is defined as venture creation by students or recent alumni and is estimated to contribute up to 20 times more economic impact than venture creation based upon university intellectual property (Wright et al., 2017). Yet, research considering student venture creation has lagged behind that of academic venture creation due to a lack of formal data capture by universities and policy makers and a lack of appreciation of the economic and social impact of the phenomena amongst researchers. This is now changing – fast.

Student entrepreneurship appears within the strategic objectives of an ever-growing number of universities; they gather data on it and proudly publish the successes of their entrepreneurial alumni. Yet the practices that encourage or constrain this activity are poorly understood. This may explain why there are a multitude of support structures, policies and practices in evidence with contradictory views upon their relative efficacy (Wright, 2014). Regardless of the approach taken, the most common academic department involved in student entrepreneurship is the business school, with Katz (2003) reporting over 2,200 courses in entrepreneurship being taught worldwide. We propose therefore that academics within the business school are best placed to study this phenomenon from a data access perspective. Moreover, it can be argued that within the business school, there exists a plurality of theoretical traditions that, when combined with this empirical access, could yield valuable new insights into the antecedents and consequences of student entrepreneurship.

Wright et al. (2017) provide a useful framework to describe the different factors that may support or inhibit student entrepreneurship (Figure 10.1).

They take an ecosystem perspective towards student entrepreneurship highlighting the interrelationship between university mechanisms to facilitate entrepreneurship, entrepreneurship education, accelerators and incubators, regional support

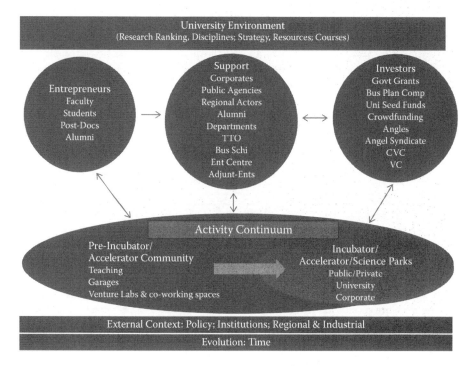

Figure 10.1   An eco-system for student entrepreneurship (adapted from Wright et al., 2017)

actors and investors, the specific nature of the university and local context and how these evolve over time. Autio et al. (2017) advocate the value of taking an entrepreneurial ecosystems approach. They argue that ecosystems are distinct from the more commonly studied innovation systems in their organisation around entrepreneurial opportunity discovery and pursuit and in the existence of shared goals. They propose that understanding and explaining the performance of entrepreneurial ecosystems requires consideration of system-level critical factors that cannot be meaningfully observed at an individual or institutional level of analysis. We therefore consider the different components of the student entrepreneurial ecosystem and consider the empirical and theoretical opportunities therein for academics based in the business school to exploit.

Empirical and theoretical opportunities to study student entrepreneurship

University environment and external context

Considering the entrepreneurial ecosystem of student start-ups in Figure 10.1, we can isolate different areas that could be usefully examined through the deployment of novel theoretical approaches. For instance, considering the university environment, with the variety of research rankings, disciplines of study, strategic approaches, resources and courses offered. Fritsch (2001) observes that the traditional approach to evaluate the impact of the university environment upon innovation is through the relationship between the environment and university intellectual property and how that relates to innovation performance in recipient organisations. He advocates a need to also consider the influence of organisational and institutional differences between universities and how they manifest in different knowledge transfer outcomes such as collaborative research, consultancy and training. Hewitt-Dundas (2012) takes such an approach by categorising UK universities as either high- or low-research intensity. However, rather than finding the expected correlation between research rankings and knowledge transfer performance she finds a stronger correlation between strategic approach and the type of knowledge transfer activities universities engaged in. She concludes that the culture and aims of the university appear more influential towards knowledge transfer practices than the resources available. This is a contemporary echo of Minztberg's assertions on the relative efficacy of culture over strategy in general management (Mintzberg, 2004). For instance, Hewitt-Dundas (2012) found that universities' resources deployed within technology transfer offices did not directly correlate to spin-out performance, even when controlling for other resource effects. Taking an analogous approach towards the effect of university environment upon student entrepreneurship performance could also yield counterintuitive findings. At present it remains unclear whether there is a relationship between resource endowments in student enterprise centres and student venture creation. It may be the case that this relationship is moderated by, or indeed dictated by, the culture and strategic aims of the university.

Considering the potential influence of external context upon student entrepreneurship, Wright et al. (2017) suggest evaluating the relative influence of regional institutions and regional policies. Fini et al. (2011) provide a fascinating new approach for such an enquiry when seeking to disentangle the influence of universities and regional institutions and policies upon university spin-off performance. They utilise the natural experiment provided by the different regions across Italy and examine how variance in university capabilities to build spin-out companies is complimented by or substituted by regional institutions and policies. Using a multi-level and temporal analysis they find that regions and universities appear to have co-evolved where the university develops substitutes for deficiencies in regional support for USOs and vice versa. This approach could be gainfully employed to explore variances in regional support for student entrepreneurship. Mosey et al. (2016) highlight the utility of the European context for conducting such multi-level studies. As Europe has nation states with defined regions where policy and institutional support for student entrepreneurship vary significantly then this provides numerous natural experiments within which to tease out the relative efficacy of different approaches, whilst controlling for national policies.

Student entrepreneurship activity with support actors and investors

After considering the university environment and the external context, Wright et al. (2017) highlight the need to consider interactions between the activity continuum of student entrepreneurship and support actors and investors. This area has a rich tradition of research which tends to be divided into two distinct areas. The most prevalent is research considering the pre-incubator/accelerator community where studies of the efficacy of entrepreneurship education dominate. Nabi et al. (2017) conducted a systematic review of work in the field and noted the limitation that most work concentrated upon short-term and subjective outcomes such as changes in students' entrepreneurial intentions or self-perceived entrepreneurial efficacy. This limitation is compounded by the few studies seeking to explore the relationship between entrepreneurial intentions and entrepreneurial actions reporting contradictory findings. A plausible explanation for such confusion is because the transition from intention to action is non-linear and therefore difficult to capture using cross-sectional analysis (Bhave, 1994). Nabi et al. (2017) suggest that studies should therefore re-focus upon different impact indicators related to emotion and mind-set and, in this way, unpick the different contextual factors that may influence the transition from intent to action.

Munoz et al. (2011) took a novel approach in this regard when they looked at the effect of an experiential entrepreneurial education course upon students whilst controlling for gender, nationality, family background and entrepreneurial intent. They found that those students whose mind-set had changed were also capable of identifying more and better-quality business ideas. Two aspects of this study could be usefully deployed in other contexts. The first was the method they used to capture changes in mind-set. Here, before they engaged in the course each student was asked to draw "what you think entrepreneurs do and how they do it". They were then asked to repeat the exercise after the course, during which they had direct experience of identifying business opportunities in conjunction with local entrepreneurs. This methodology draws upon the seminal work of Zuboff (1988), who argues that capturing visual data helps researchers to isolate information that students cannot communicate verbally as it is tacit in nature (Kearney and Hyle, 2004). Ambrosini and Bowman (2001) propose that such techniques are an invaluable way to capture the tacit aspects of skills development. Asking participants to draw allows them to represent their thoughts more freely as in a mind map, a technique commonly used to help learning (Clarkson, 2008). Students were able to draw concepts and images they associated with entrepreneurial activity and depict the interrelationship between them, which proved invaluable in ascertaining whether students' entrepreneurial mind-set had changed as a result of their educational experiences. Two examples of such drawings are displayed in Figures 10.2 and 10.3, which show the drawings of Christopher, a student who did not develop his entrepreneurial skills during the course. Here it is clear that there is also a corresponding lack of change in his representation of the practice of entrepreneurship.

By contrast, Figures 10.4 and 10.5 show the drawings of Michael, a student who significantly increased his skills of identifying new business opportunities through taking the course. Here we can see a corresponding change in his understanding of the practice of entrepreneurship through the changes in his representation of entrepreneurship.

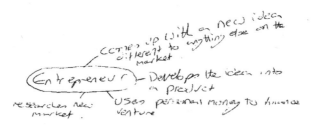

Figure 10.2   Christopher, first interview. Student who did not develop his entrepreneurial skills during the course

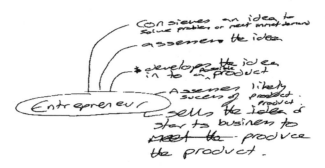

Figure 10.3   Christopher, second interview. Student who did not develop his entrepreneurial skills during the course

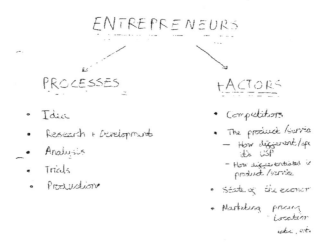

Figure 10.4   Michael, first interview. Student who developed his entrepreneurial skills during the course

We propose that such visualisation techniques could be gainfully employed to reveal new insights into how students' mind-sets towards entrepreneurship may be affected by other activities such as hackathons, entrepreneurship garages and co-working spaces.

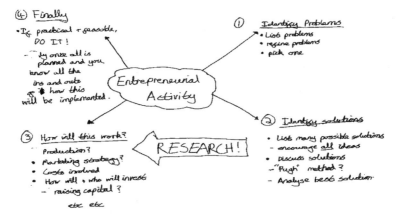

Figure 10.5   Michael, second interview. Student who developed his entrepreneurial skills during the course

The transition from student intent to entrepreneurial action

A common critique of the prior art in entrepreneurship education is the opacity of the transition from changes in mind-set towards entrepreneurial action, illustrated by the arrow in the centre of Figure 10.1. Nabi et al. (2017) echo Wright et al. (2017) in calling for more research exploring those individuals who support the aspiring student entrepreneurs through this transition, such as academics, entrepreneurs in residence and potential investors. They also propose that possible moderating factors such as culture, gender and identity could explain the contradictory findings across different national and cultural contexts.

One potential route through this opacity is the theoretical approach of sense-making. Originating within the organizational behaviour literature (McAdam and Marlow, 2011), sense-making occurs when a student turns their educational and networking experiences into words and salient categories they can comprehend and then use for entrepreneurial action (Weick et al., 2005). Sense-making is apposite for the early stages of entrepreneurship as it is triggered when there are discrepancies between expectations and reality. Such discrepancies can vary greatly, and when the discrepancy between what a student expects and what they experience is great enough, and important enough, to cause them to reflect upon what is going on and what their actions should be then sense-making is triggered (Maitlis and Christianson, 2014). When students make sense, particularly with others such as local entrepreneurs or educators, it can be thought of as "a matter of knowledge and technique applied to the world" (Weick et al., 2005: 412).

Sense-making theory highlights three processual aspects where students may notice or perceive cues, create interpretations and then take action. Within the organisational behaviour literature, sense-making has proven an insightful explanatory framework showing how leaders and managers make sense of significant organisational change (e.g. Gioia and Chittipeddi, 1991), organizational learning and innovation (Drazin et al., 1999). These three areas of research are relevant because they show that sense-making, which is often thought of as a reconciling mechanism during crises (Weick, 1993), also helps to explain processes that require disruption (Maitlis and Christianson, 2014). This makes sense-making a particularly insightful approach with which to explore the transitions from intent to action for students, especially those that ultimately involve disruption of the status quo (Dimov, 2007).

Hoyte et al. (2016) showed the promise of this approach when they considered the sense-making approaches of student entrepreneurs based within a university incubator in the UK. Using a qualitative longitudinal case study approach, they reveal a typology of key sense-givers that the entrepreneurs draw upon to co-construct the idea and enact it into an entrepreneurial opportunity (Figure 10.6). These include family and friends, work colleagues, stakeholder partners such as entrepreneurs in residence and potential customers. Such an approach shows great potential to contribute to the field of entrepreneurship by providing a theoretical language to describe how student venture ideas are translated into entrepreneurial opportunities. It identifies the critical role of specific sense-givers in legitimatising entrepreneurial activities and shows how a sense-making approach helps to reconcile

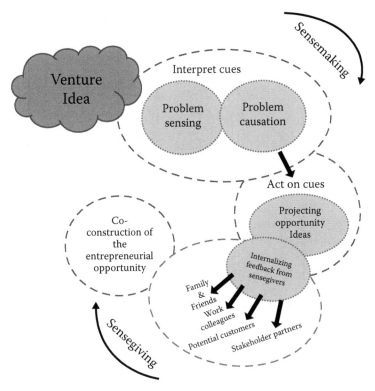

Figure 10.6   Translating student venture ideas into entrepreneurial opportunities: the role of sense-making and sense-giving (adapted from Hoyte et al., 2016)

contemporary debates surrounding the discovery or creation of entrepreneurial opportunities.

Student entrepreneurship ecosystem development and growth

Returning to the level of the ecosystem, a key question remains regarding how the goals of the system are coordinated across the different stakeholders for mutual benefit and ecosystem growth (Autio et al., 2017). One possible answer to the coordination conundrum is through the use of "grand challenges". The concept of grand challenges was first expounded by Hilbert over one hundred years ago.[1] Perhaps the most widely adopted grand challenges today are those adopted by 193 member states of the UN in 2015. These consist of 17 sustainable development goals (SDGs) "to end poverty, protect the planet and ensure that all people enjoy peace and prosperity".[2] George et al. (2016: 1880) insist that grand challenges "by their very nature, require coordinated and sustained effort from multiple and diverse stakeholders toward a clearly articulated problem or goal". And that: "The elegance of the SDGs are in the articulation that human progress stems from achieving these clear targets through collective, collaborative, and coordinated effort."

They define grand challenges as: "Specific critical barrier(s) that, if removed, would help solve an important social problem with a high likelihood of global impact through widespread implementation", and argue that ". . . tackling GCs could be fundamentally characterised as a managerial (organisational) and scientific problem" (George et al., 2016: 1881).

However, the insistence on top-down coordination is not uncontested. For example, in many ways the mobile phone has become the enabling technology of the developing world. And yet the idea of providing near-universal access to the internet through an affordable hand-held device was not one of the UN's millennium goals. Traditional economists may see an invisible hand at work that defies coordination and control, but an alternative view is that such paradigm shifts occur when multiple factors are aligned. And so, we believe it is possible, perhaps also desirable, for smaller players, such as those found within student entrepreneurial ecosystems, to respond to grand challenges piecemeal. In practical pedagogical terms this approach encourages and recognises entrepreneurial talent among those students who do not readily identify with the reified stereotypical image of the entrepreneur (Hebert and Link, 2006) and may therefore provide that crucial coordination mechanism between student, university, local policy makers and local businesses.

To investigate this phenomenon, Avram and Carter (2018) have deployed constructs from organisational psychology to explore whether students working on

---

1 The term "grand challenge" begins with the efforts of Dr David Hilbert, a German mathematician later recognised as one of the most influential twentieth-century mathematicians, who, in 1900, at the International Congress of Mathematicians in Paris, listed a set of 23 problems that were collectively termed as "grand challenges".

2 See https://www.sciencedirect.com/science/article/pii/S0263237314000425?via%3Dihub

grand challenges help to coordinate their activities within a nascent entrepreneurial ecosystem. They theorise that "collective intelligence" plays a key role in predicting entrepreneurial team performance across tasks and seek to explore early entrepreneurial activity by including team characteristics and processes. Using data from digital learning platforms, they were able to analyse a unique data set of student-generated ideas and solutions to grand challenges and found a complex picture of performance at the intersection of psychological, cognitive and behavioural factors. Their findings suggest that working on grand challenges helped to enhance team members' perceptions of psychological safety and functionality. They concluded that team members' personality characteristics – such as openness to experience and extraversion – to be moderating factors conducive to enhanced entrepreneurial team performance.

Such insights into the micro foundations of entrepreneurial ecosystems provide intriguing potential explanations for unexpected findings from larger-scale macro studies. Ratzinger et al. (2017) used a novel data set by drawing from information on more than 220,000 start-ups on the crowdsourced platform Crunchbase. They showed that such a data set can be as robust and reliable as traditional survey data by conducting statistical comparisons with GEM data and gender studies (Coleman and Robb, 2009) and it offers the added advantage of a global population within which to consider student entrepreneurship.

They sought to investigate the impact of higher education upon a founding team's probability of securing equity investment and subsequent exit for their digital ventures. Across this unique global data set, they found confirmatory evidence that teams with a founder with technical higher education are more likely to secure equity investment and exit for their ventures than those that do not. However, they uncovered some counterintuitive findings that suggest rich seams of future enquiry.

They found that teams with a founder with doctoral level business education had a higher probability of securing equity investment, whilst undergraduate business education had no significant effect, suggesting that increased human capital within business education provides performance benefits.

By contrast, they found that teams with a founder who had an undergraduate education in the arts and humanities were also more likely to secure equity investment and exit. This suggests that the experience of studying subjects other than business or STEM has utility for student entrepreneurship that clearly requires further study.

Finally, they found that teams with a founder with postgraduate or doctoral education in the arts and humanities had no significant effect upon securing equity investment and exit. This suggests the possibility of an inverted u-shape relationship between the human capital gained through arts and humanities study and subsequent entrepreneurial performance, which could be explored further by using the organisational psychology constructs introduced by Avram and Carter (2018).

This leaves us with the tantalising possibility that student entrepreneurial ecosystems working on grand challenges may be the coordinating mechanism by which C.P. Snow's two cultures of the humanities and sciences can be reconciled (Snow, 1963). And that we, as business school academics, have a ringside seat from which to observe, categorise and hopefully contribute towards this exciting phenomenon.

Conclusions

As academics in the business school we have a fantastic opportunity to evaluate and help shape a contemporary mission of universities globally – to encourage the creation and development of student entrepreneurship.

Empirically, student entrepreneurship represents a growing and relatively accessible phenomena that, somewhat unusually, has the unequivocal support of university leaders, academics, and national and regional policy makers, not to mention the students themselves.

Theoretically, student entrepreneurship presents an ideal opportunity to experiment with frameworks and constructs from long-established fields such as organisational behaviour and psychology to add richness to the theoretical language we use within entrepreneurship and management more generally.

Student entrepreneurship has the potential to take universities back to their original role of engines of local economic development. Taking an ecosystem approach shows how this role may manifest through the complex and non-linear interaction of environmental, institutional, social and individual factors. Although the direction of causality remains unclear, it seems apparent that the iteration between universities, student entrepreneurs and regional actors, if appropriately coordinated, leads to significant economic impact.

It is now up to us to explore, codify and explain this phenomenon.

References

Ambrosini, V., and Bowman, C. (2001) Tacit knowledge: Some suggestions for operationalization. *Journal of Management Studies*, **38** (6), 811–29.

Autio, E., Nambisan, S., Thomas, L.W., Wright, M. (2017) Digital affordances, spatial affordances, and the genesis of entrepreneurial ecosystems. *Strategic Entrepreneurship Journal*, **12**, 72–95.

Avram, G., and Carter, C. (2018) Understanding the relationship between collective intelligence and entrepreneurial team performance through online creative problem-solving. Babson Entrepreneurship Conference, Boston. MA.

Bhave, M.P. (1994) A process model of entrepreneurial venture creation. *Journal of Business Venturing*, **9**, 223–42.

Clarkson, G.P. (2008) Causal cognitive map. In R. Thorpe, and R. Holt (eds), *The SAGE Dictionary of Qualitative Management Research*, 40–42. London: SAGE Publications.

Coleman, S., and Robb, A. (2009) A comparison of new firm financing by gender: Evidence from the Kauffman Firm Survey data. *Small Business Economics*, **33** (4), 397–411.

Dimov, D. (2007) Beyond the single-person, single-insight attribution in understanding entrepreneurial opportunities. *Entrepreneurship Theory and Practice*, **31** (5), 713–31.

Drazin, R., Glynn, M.A. and Kazanjian, R.K. (1999) Multilevel theorizing about creativity in organizations: A sensemaking perspective. *Academy of Management Review*, **24** (2), 286–307.

Fini, R., Grimaldi, R., Santoni, S., and Sobrero, M. (2011) Complements or substitutes? The role of universities and local context in supporting the creation of academic spin-offs. *Research Policy*, **40**, 1113–27.

Fristch, M. (2001) Cooperation in regional innovation systems. *Regional Studies*, **35**, 297–307.

George, G., Howard Grenville, J., Joshi, A., and Tihanyi, L. (2016) Understanding and tackling societal grand challenges through management research. *Academy of Management Journal*, **59** (6), 1880–95.

Gioia, D.A., and Chittipeddi, K. (1991) Sensemaking and sensegiving in strategic change initiation. *Strategic Management Journal*, **12** (6), 433–48.

Hebert, R.F., and Link, A.N. (2006) Historical perspectives on the Entrepreneur. *Foundations and Trends in Entrepreneurship*, **2** (4), 261–408.

Hewitt-Dundas, N. (2012) Research intensity and knowledge transfer activity in UK universities. *Research Policy*, **41**, 262–75.

Hoyte, C., Noke, H., and Mosey, S. (2016). Translating venture ideas into entrepreneurial opportunities: The role of sensemaking & sensegiving. Academy of Management Conference, Anaheim, CA.

Katz, J.A. (2003) A chronology and intellectual trajectory of American entrepreneurship education. *Journal of Business Venturing*, **18**, 283–300.

Kearney, K.S., and Hyle, A.E. (2004) Drawing out emotions: The use of participant-produced drawings in qualitative inquiry. *Qualitative Research*, **4** (3), 361–82.

Maitlis, S., and Christianson, M. (2014) Sensemaking in organizations: Taking stock and moving forward. *The Academy of Management Annals*, **8** (1), 57–125.

Martin, R. (2013) The future of business and the role of business education. Academy of Management Conference, Orlando, 2013.

McAdam, M., and Marlow, S. (2011) Sense and sensibility: The role of business incubator client advisors in assisting high-technology entrepreneurs to make sense of investment readiness status. *Entrepreneurship & Regional Development*, **23** (7–8), 449–68.

Mintzberg, H. (2004) *Managers Not MBAs. A Hard Look at the Soft Practice of Managing and Management Development*. San Francisco, CA: Berrett-Koehler Publishers, Inc.

Mosey, S., Guerreo, M., and Greenman, A. (2016) Technology entrepreneurship research opportunities: Insights from across Europe. *Journal of Technology Transfer*. DOI 10.1007/s10961-015-9462-3.

Munoz, C., Mosey, S., and Binks, M. (2011) Developing opportunity-identification capabilities in the classroom visual evidence for changing mental frames. *Academy of Management Learning and Education*, **10** (2), 277–95.

Nabi, G., Linan, F., Fayolle, A., Krueger, N., and Walmsley, A. (2017) The impact of entrepreneurship education in higher education: A systematic review and research agenda. *Academy of Management Learning and Education*, **16**, 277–99.

Ratzinger, D., Amess, K., Greenman, A., and Mosey, S. (2017) The impact of digital start-up founders higher education on reaching equity investment milestones. *Journal of Technology Transfer*, **42**, 1–19.

Snow, C.P. (1963) *The Two Cultures: A Second Look*. Cambridge: Cambridge University Press.

Starkey, K. and Tempest, S. (2009) The winter of our discontent: The design challenge for business schools. *Academy of Management Learning and Education*, **8**, 576–86.

Starkey, K., Hatchuel, A., and Tempest, S. (2004) Rethinking the business school. *Journal of Management Studies*, **41**, 1521–32.

Weick, K.E. (1993) The collapse of sense-making in organizations: The Mann Gulch disaster. *Administrative Science Quarterly*, **38** (4), 628–52.

Weick, K.E., Sutcliffe, K.M., and Obstfeld, D. (2005) Organizing and the process of sensemaking. *Organization Science*, **16** (4), 409–21.

Wright, M. (2014) Academic entrepreneurship, technology transfer and society: Where next? *Journal of Technology Transfer*, **39**, 322–34.

Wright, M., Siegel, D.S., and Mustar, P. (2017) An emerging ecosystem for student start-ups. *Journal of Technology Transfer*, **42**, 909–22.

Zuboff, S. (1988) *In the Age of the Smart Machine, The Future of Work and Power*. New York: Basic Books.

11 Entrepreneurial leadership in the academic community: a suggested research agenda

Rati Ram, Devrim Göktepe-Hultén, and Rajeev K. Goel

1 Introduction

The landmark Bayh-Dole Act of 1980 that enabled universities, small businesses, or non-profit institutions to patent government-funded innovations can be seen a major policy shift that brought academic entrepreneurship to the forefront. Over time, other nations, primarily in Europe, have also enacted similar measures to promote academic entrepreneurship.

On the research front, Shane (2004), Lacetera (2009), Harrison et al. (2015) and Dean and Ford (2017), besides other scholars, have noted the emerging field of entrepreneurial leadership, and have discussed several theoretical and empirical aspects related to the concept (see Grimaldi et al. (2011), Bozeman et al. (2013) and Siegel and Wright (2015) for reviews of the related literature). In particular, Harrison et al. (2015, pp. 700–701) have articulated a research agenda for gendered analysis of entrepreneurial leadership and have proposed three themes around which the future research on entrepreneurial leadership can be organized. Dean and Ford (2017, p. 183) define "the female entrepreneur as the leader of a business that is wholly or majority female-owned and managed." Based on a small-scale empirical study of female business owners, they note "the fluidity and variability of the entrepreneurial concept" and find "multiple subjectivities of entrepreneurs." They also find (a) the entrepreneurial leader as "living the passion," (b) the entrepreneurial leader wanting to make a difference in people's lives, and (c) the valorizing of masculinity in leadership practice inhibits performance.

After the foregoing introduction to the research on entrepreneurial leadership, we now articulate some major differences between entrepreneurs in the academe and the general class of entrepreneurs.

2 Distinctive characteristics of entrepreneurship in the academe

Our work deals primarily with entrepreneurial leadership in the academic context, and thus it is useful to first state how an academic entrepreneur differs from a non-academic or "general" entrepreneur. We make short statements about twelve differences, some of which have been noted by Goel et al. (2017, pp. 77–78) and Goel and Rich (2005). First, unlike a typical entrepreneur, the main activity of an academic entrepreneur is not to start or own a business, but to teach and do research so as to generate useful new knowledge (Goel and Grimpe (2012), for instance, consider the distinction between research-driven academic entrepreneurs and overall academic entrepreneurs). Second, unlike the typical case, an academic entrepreneur is not self-employed. As a rule, he or she is employed by a university or research institution. Third, these entrepreneurs do not seek financing through the usual business channels. Most of their funding comes from public or private institutions that support scientific research. In the United States, most of their funding comes from the National Science Foundation, National Institutes of Health, and other similar public or private funding agencies. Fourth, their assets are often owned by the institution that employs them, and unlike the usual entrepreneur, they have no tangible assets. Fifth, therefore, unlike the usual entrepreneur, they are usually not associated with activities related to the establishment, management, growth and death of independent firms. Sixth, they have much higher education levels than a typical entrepreneur. Seventh, their entrepreneurial activities typically consist of (a) seeking patents for their innovations and inventions, (b) commercializing their research through spin-offs, and (c) collaboration with business enterprises which may include entrepreneurial leaders. Eighth, due to the high education levels of academic entrepreneurs, their activities occur at a high technological level and are often an important source of technology production and transfer. Ninth, in most cases, they do not have a host of subordinates to supervise, and their leadership role is typically limited to scientific research and discovery, the application of the discoveries to generate useful products and patents, and to provide direct or indirect leadership in consulting or collaborative positions. Although they might have several lab assistants, research assistants and fellows, their relations with these subordinates or collaborators are often of a relatively limited duration and are somewhat different from the relation of a typical entrepreneurial leader with his or her workers or subordinates. Tenth, their measures of success do not usually include "breaking the glass ceiling (or wall)," but recognition in the scientific or research communities. Eleventh, academic research and related entrepreneurship is often conducted in teams, with differences across academic disciplines (e.g., research in hard sciences involving elaborate laboratory testing is typically not possible by single researchers). What makes academic collaborations and networks different from their non-academic counterparts is that academics have greater freedom in choosing the composition of their teams (see Goel and Rich (2005), Goel and Grimpe (2013), Goel et al. (2015a)). This flexibility has implications for free-riding and longevity of teams. This ability to choose teams would be greater for academic leaders (e.g., research group leaders, directors) and this aspect has been considered by Goel and Göktepe-Hultén (2018). Finally, they usually have an international perspective on a considerably wider scale than a typical entrepreneurial leader.

We now mention briefly some strands of scholarship in the area of entrepreneurial leadership, which will provide a setting for our suggested research agenda.

3   Strands of scholarship on entrepreneurial leadership

Harrison et al. (2015, p. 693) observe that the recent expansion in the literature on entrepreneurial leadership has not been matched with the development of theoretical frameworks, theory building and conceptual analyses, including the analysis of gender. They similarly note that within the emerging domain of entrepreneurial leadership research, gender issues have rarely been acknowledged. They list (p. 695) the evolving definitions of entrepreneurial leadership and end with that of Renko et al. (2015) to state that entrepreneurial leadership entails influencing and directing the performance of group members toward the achievement of organizational goals that involve recognizing and exploring entrepreneurial opportunities. They also do a typology of the literature on entrepreneurial leadership (p. 696), take a look at the main ingredients of that literature, list themes in the treatment of gender in management theory and their application in entrepreneurial leadership (pp. 700-701), and list 16 illustrative research questions that constitute a part of their research agenda for a gendered analysis of entrepreneurial leadership. It is interesting that while they state (p. 693) that "gender issues have been rarely acknowledged" in entrepreneurial leadership research, most papers in the special issue of *Journal of Small Business Management* (July 2015), including their own paper (Harrison et al. 2015), deal with gender issues or women's perspectives on entrepreneurial leadership. In fact, Henry et al. (2015, p. 581) state that the papers in the special issue highlight the diversity and complexity of women's entrepreneurial leadership and demonstrate that it is both "economically and contextually embedded."

Dean and Ford (2017) describe the "dominant hegemonic masculine entrepreneurship model" and, based on their small-scale empirical research, observe "the fluidity and variability of the entrepreneurial leadership construct." They note the multiple subjectivities of (women) entrepreneurs who live their passion, aspire to make a difference in people's lives, and the gap between their lived entrepreneurial leadership accounts and what they perceive as the authentic entrepreneurship leader being a source of tension that inhibited the performance of the participants.

Yousafzai et al. (2015) define women's entrepreneurial leadership (WEL) as "the ability of women to manage resources strategically in order to emphasize both opportunity-seeking and initiating, developing and managing entrepreneurial activity." They use a sample of 92 countries at different phases of economic development to study "the relationship between the regulatory, normative and cognitive pillars of institutional theory and women's entrepreneurial leadership." Their framework conceptualizes the contextual embeddedness of entrepreneurship and institutional theory. They found that regulatory institutions, entrepreneurial cognitions and entrepreneurial norms have a direct and an indirect effect on women's entrepreneurial leadership.

Lewis (2015) explored how entrepreneurial leadership is enacted by a female entrepreneur over time and how being a leader is integrated into entrepreneurial identity development via a gendered identity work. The empirical foundation of the paper was a longitudinal case study of a New Zealand female entrepreneur based on data spanning the period 2005–2014.

Aiming to contribute toward an understanding of entrepreneurship at the conceptual level, Galloway et al. (2015) argue that performativity, as described in feminist theory, can contribute to how we interpret entrepreneurship and that this might inform both the entrepreneurship and the leadership literatures to afford us a better understanding of what we might mean by "entrepreneurial leadership."

Henry et al. (2015, p. 582) considered some of the earlier literature that contributed to the general entrepreneurship discourse. They then (pp. 582–3) summarized some later studies that expanded the geographical scope, focus and, to some extent, the methodological approach adopted in women's entrepreneurial leadership research. In particular, they referred to Hamilton's (2014) study that contributed to the female entrepreneurial leadership theory "by arguing that epistemological shifts invoke the ontological dimension of narrative as well as contemporary theories of gender to understand entrepreneurial identity."

Vassiliki et al. (2015) investigate the role of competencies in shaping the leadership styles of female entrepreneurs in England and Wales and construct a detailed leadership profile of successful women entrepreneurial leaders.

Goel et al. (2015b) use survey data from a large German public research organization to study entrepreneurship propensities of academic researchers across gender. Results show significant gender differences in the association of several factors with propensities to start businesses. In particular, prior record of researchers' patenting and institutional leadership promote entrepreneurship among male researchers, but not female researchers. Also, unlike the male scientists, doctoral degrees and preference for open access of research results do not significantly influence the entrepreneurial tendencies of female researchers.

Although not directly related to entrepreneurial leadership, Greene and Brush (2018) provide an introduction to the volume *A Research Agenda for Women and Entrepreneurship* and outline the elements of women's entrepreneurial identity in terms of aspirations, behaviors and confidence. The goal of the volume is to use a concept of identity to explore ideas related to entrepreneurial identity for women and their businesses. While the focus of the collection is on women entrepreneurs' identity, that is done through a study of aspirations, behaviors and confidence which are related to the entrepreneur's identity. The suggested research agenda thus advocates an exploration of women's entrepreneurial identity as reflected in their aspirations, behaviors and confidence.

Having taken a quick look at the strands of scholarship on entrepreneurial leadership, we now consider the applicability of the general entrepreneurial leadership construct to the academic setting.

4   Application of the entrepreneurial leadership construct to entrepreneurs in the academe

Since the primary focus of this study is on entrepreneurial leadership in the academe, it is first important to consider whether the paradigm of entrepreneurial leadership needs some modification relative to academic entrepreneurs. The distinctive features of academic entrepreneurs were summarized in section 2. To recapitulate the most significant distinctive features: (a) they do not work with subordinates in the usual labor market sense, (b) their funding sources are well defined and typically different from the conventional business funding sources, (c) they are usually not self-employed, (d) their education levels are much higher than those of typical entrepreneurs, (e) they do not start or own a business, and their primary activities are teaching and research, (f) they do not produce a conventional output for sale, but do research to generate new technology, patents, spinoffs, consultation and collaboration, (g) their leadership role is largely limited to research, technology production and dissemination, and getting funding through grants, and (h) their success is not measured by the height of the "glass ceiling" they break, but by peer recognition of their scholarship and research output.

The foregoing listing suggests that the general concept of entrepreneurial leadership is likely to need a major modification in its application to the academic entrepreneur, and it is indeed possible that the concept has no useful application in the academe. For this purpose, we first look at the definition proposed by Renko et al. (2015) which states that entrepreneurial leadership entails "influencing and directing the performance of group members toward the achievement of organizational goals that involve recognizing and exploring entrepreneurial opportunities." The applicability of this concept to academic entrepreneurs seems weak since (a) they do not have "group members" in the usual sense, (b) their "organizational goals" are not closely related with their entrepreneurial activities, and (c) while they do perhaps recognize and explore entrepreneurial opportunities, they do so at an individual level and not in terms of the leader of a group. Similarly, we may consider the definition proposed by Yousafzai et al. (2015) as "the ability of women to manage resources strategically in order to emphasize both opportunity-seeking and initiating, developing and managing entrepreneurial activity." The applicability of this rather generic definition to women academic entrepreneurship also seems meager. Similarly, one may consider any other definition included in the list by Harrison et al. (2015, p. 695) and it would seem that these definitions have minimal applicability to entrepreneurial leaders in the academic community.

One can also consider the research agenda summarized by Harrison et al. (2015, pp. 700-701) in the form of illustrative research questions to see how far these may be applicable to an academic entrepreneurial leader. Table 11.1 lists the questions proposed by Harrison et al. (2015) and indicates our perception of the applicability of these to academic entrepreneurial leaders. It will perhaps be noticed that most of the research questions have a limited usefulness in their application to the

Table 11.1 List of questions in the research agenda on entrepreneurial leadership proposed by Harrison et al. (2015, pp. 700-701) and their possible applicability to academic entrepreneurs

1. **How do we give women entrepreneurial leaders voice?**
   The applicability of this question to academic entrepreneurial leaders is minor, if any. Female (and male) academic entrepreneurs are usually highly articulate.

2. **How do women entrepreneurial leaders develop and represent themselves as leaders?**
   Applicability of this question to women entrepreneurs in the academe seems little. Their leadership is primarily defined by the recognition received from their peers.

3. **In what ways do women entrepreneurial leaders jointly negotiate and navigate different markers of identity?**
   The identity of women entrepreneurial leaders in the academe is well defined by their academic standing and status.

4. **Relationship between entrepreneurial leadership and the wider structural and institutional fabric of the society in which it is embedded.**
   The characteristics of women entrepreneurial leaders in the academe are, in general, not as dependent on the structural and institutional fabric of the society as of the typical women entrepreneurial leaders who manage independent businesses.

5. **What are the implications of (in)visibility for the construction and practice of entrepreneurial leadership?**
   Women entrepreneurial leaders in the academe are not as (in)visible as women in business leadership.

6. **Implications of "glass walls" and "glass ceilings"**
   The applicability of these expressive concepts to the academe seems minor. Their success is measured largely in terms of peer recognition and successful funding and research output, and not in terms of breaking glass ceilings or walls.

7. **Implications of "gender fatigue"**
   This concept also applies only on a minor scale to women's entrepreneurial leadership in the academic community. The widely accepted leadership ideals seem to apply minimally to the academic entrepreneurial leadership.

8. **Leadership models other than that of "heroic individual leader"**
   The "heroic individual leader" model does not seem to apply, or applies minimally, to entrepreneurial leadership in the academe.

9. **How should gender research in entrepreneurial leadership reflect on both masculinity and femininity?**
   It is difficult to see the applicability of this question to the academic community. In the more general discourse, there should be consideration of both masculinity and femininity.

10. **How should entrepreneurial leadership research address the analysis of gender with ethnicity in a framework that transcends neo-liberal governance regimes?**
    This is a good question but appears to have little applicability to women entrepreneurial leaders in the academe since their sphere of action is so different from that of a typical

Table 11.1   (continued)

---

entrepreneur. In general, their entrepreneurial performance and its recognition directly depends only to a minor extent on gender or ethnicity in a neo-liberal or progressive regime.

11. **Implications of the narrow and broad contextual nature of the entrepreneurial process**
The broad contextual embeddedness of academic entrepreneurship appears minor. Even the narrow contextual relevance of much of scientific research and its production application is likely to be much more limited in the academe than in the business world at large.

12. **Critique of the other "function" as a process through which women are controlled by cultures and states**
We leave it to other better-informed scholars to consider this relative to academic entrepreneurial leadership.

13. **Implications of the way in which masculine signifiers are represented in ideas about the place of women in society**
We do not think these signifiers have an impact on entrepreneurial leadership in the academic community or the research on it.

14. **Tension between the global and the local for the new ways of "doing gender in entrepreneurial leadership"**
Such tension should not affect the entrepreneurial activities of the academic scientists who do most of their production in the western mode.

15. **Impact of the gendered "geographies of space and place" on the choices and identity positions of entrepreneurial leaders**
The unevenness may affect academic entrepreneurial leadership at the macro level but seems unlikely to affect the entrepreneurial leadership of women (or men) in a given micro unit such as a university or a research institution.

16. **Geographies of power as domains within which gendered entrepreneurial leadership is practiced and observed**
This aspect may affect women's (as well as men's) entrepreneurial leadership at an aggregate or macro level but appears unlikely to affect an individual entrepreneur in a university or research organization.

---

entrepreneurial leadership performance of women in the academic context. Most of the questions apply usefully to women's entrepreneurial leadership activities in the standard business context. However, we include this as a major item in our suggested agenda for future research.

Furthermore, one can consider the paradigm suggested by Dean and Ford (2017) and others that there is "the dominant hegemonic masculine entrepreneurial leadership model" that holds "a strong assumption that the entrepreneur is a heroic rational man" and that there is "valorizing of masculinity in leadership practice."

It seems unlikely that such a paradigm can be reasonably suggested for the academic entrepreneurial leadership of women. At any rate, this is one aspect that our research agenda can usefully include.

We would like to note that discussion of the characteristics of entrepreneurial leadership in the academic context is not a minor matter. Entrepreneurship in the academe is a major activity that consists of producing useful scientific research output and applying that research to produce valuable output in the form of patents, spinoffs, collaboration with business enterprises and consulting. Although sometimes not so recognized, much of production and transfer of new technology occurs through entrepreneurial scientists and leaders in the academic communities. For example, Goel et al. (2017, p. 78) noted that academic entrepreneurial activities usually occur at a high technological level and are an important source of technology transfer. Another important related aspect that has received relatively little formal attention in the literature concerns the changes in research productivity of academic leaders during their careers (see some related insights in Goel and Göktepe-Hultén (2019)). Therefore, consideration of the applicability of the predominant paradigms, and the suggested research agendas, relative to the academic entrepreneur should be of considerable significance.

Having noted the difficulties of applying the standard paradigms and research issues to the academic entrepreneur, we now briefly articulate the major components of the research agenda that we suggest.

5   A research agenda for entrepreneurial leadership in the academic community

The research agenda suggested by us largely follows from the foregoing discussion and mainly addresses the extent of applicability to the academic entrepreneurs of (a) the dominant paradigms relative to entrepreneurial leadership and (b) questions posed in the research agenda proposed by Harrison et al. (2015). To the extent that the paradigms and the suggested research issues are not usefully applicable to academic entrepreneurs, the research agenda would include the consideration of appropriate modifications and substitutions. As already noted, the primary motivation for the research agenda suggested by us is the observation of many major differences between the nature of entrepreneurial leadership in the business sector and the academic institutions that are a source of much technological change and innovation.

Table 11.2 provides a summary of the research agenda proposed by us. It is largely self-explanatory and follows the discussion in the preceding paragraphs. It urges consideration of the applicability to the academic entrepreneurs of (a) the dominant paradigms in the literature on entrepreneurial leadership, (b) definitions of entrepreneurial leadership, (c) some of the empirical findings about the driving motivations of entrepreneurial leaders, and (d) the extensive research agenda proposed by Harrison et al. (2015) in regard to entrepreneurial leadership.

Table 11.2   A suggested agenda for research on entrepreneurial leadership in the academic community

---

1.   Applicability of the dominant paradigms about the characteristics of an entrepreneurial leader
     1.1   Is there a dominant "hegemonic masculine entrepreneurial leadership" model? If so, does it apply to academic entrepreneurial leadership?
     1.2   Is there a general assumption of the entrepreneur being a heroic, rational man? If so, does it apply to the academic entrepreneurship?
     1.3   Is there "valorization of masculinity in leadership practice"? If so, would that apply to the academic context?

2.   Does the definition of a female entrepreneur suggested by Dean and Ford (2017, p. 183) apply to an academic entrepreneur? If not, what might be a better definition?

3.   Does the definition of entrepreneurial leadership suggested by Renko et al. (2015) described by Harrison et al. (2015, p. 695) apply to an entrepreneurial leader in the academic community? If not, what might be an appropriate modification?

4.   What would be the extent of applicability to the academic entrepreneur of other definitions of entrepreneurial leadership listed by Harrison et al. (2015, p. 695)?

5.   Based largely on the papers included in the special issue, Henry et al. (2015, p. 581) "highlight the diversity and complexity of women's entrepreneurial leadership, and demonstrate that it is both economically and contextually embedded." What would be the applicability of a statement of that kind to female (or male) entrepreneurial leaders in the academe?

6.   The small-scale empirical study of Dean and Ford (2017) indicates that two themes articulated by their research participants relative to entrepreneurial leadership include (a) "living the passion," and (b) making a difference in the lives of people. It would be of interest to explore whether some entrepreneurial leaders in the academe have similar guiding entrepreneurial themes.

7.   By way of a significant research undertaking, the applicability to the academic entrepreneurial leadership of the 16 research questions suggested by Harrison et al. (2015) may be explored.

It may be noted that, consistent with the strands of literature considered by us, we do not include entrepreneurial leadership research issues relative to men. These issues may be as important as those articulated in the literature that we looked at. There is perhaps as much variance in the degree of success of entrepreneurial leadership among men as between men and women. From a social perspective, both seem important.

6   Concluding thoughts

This study is based on a combination of five thoughts. Some similar recommendations have also been espoused by other scholars following their literature analyses (see Bozeman et al. (2013), Siegel and Wright (2015)). First, the emerging field of entrepreneurial leadership is significant and merits attention. Second, several dominant paradigms have been stated or perceived in regard to the characteristics of an entrepreneurial leader, and these need to be critically appraised. Third, entrepreneurial leadership in the academic community has many characteristics that are very different from those in the general population of entrepreneurial leaders. Fourth, academic entrepreneurship is an important dimension of the totality of entrepreneurial leadership. Fifth, therefore, it is of some importance that the applicability to the academic entrepreneurship of the relevant paradigms, definitions, empirical evidence and research agenda perceived or proposed in the literature on women's entrepreneurial leadership be given careful consideration. Based on these thoughts, we have suggested a research agenda relative to women's entrepreneurial leadership in the academic community and hope it will lead to productive research.

References

Bozeman, B., D. Fay and C.P. Slade, 2013, "Research collaboration in universities and academic entrepreneurship: The-state-of-the-art," *The Journal of Technology Transfer*, **38** (1), 1–67.

Dean, H. and J. Ford, 2017, "Discourses of entrepreneurial leadership: Exposing myths and exploring new approaches," *International Small Business Journal*, **35** (2), 178–96.

Galloway, L., I. Kapasi and K. Sang, 2015, "Entrepreneurship, leadership, and the value of feminist approaches to understanding them," *Journal of Small Business Management*, **53** (3), 683–92.

Goel, R.K. and D. Göktepe-Hultén, 2018, "Academic leadership and commercial activities at research institutes: German evidence," *Managerial and Decision Economics*, **39** (5), 601–9.

Goel, R.K. and D. Göktepe-Hultén, 2019, "Drivers of innovation productivity of academic researchers through career advancement," *The Journal of Technology Transfer*, forthcoming.

Goel, R.K. and C. Grimpe, 2012, "Are all academic entrepreneurs created alike? Evidence from Germany," *Economics of Innovation and New Technology*, **21** (3), 247–66.

Goel, R.K. and C. Grimpe, 2013, "Active versus passive academic networking: Evidence from micro-level data," *The Journal of Technology Transfer*, **38** (2), 116–34.

Goel, R.K. and D.P. Rich, 2005, "Organization of markets for science and technology," *Journal of Institutional and Theoretical Economics*, **161** (1), 1–17.

Goel, R.K., D. Göktepe-Hultén and R. Ram, 2015a, "Academic networks and the diffusion of knowledge," in C. Antonelli and A.N. Link (eds.), *Routledge Handbook of the Economics of Knowledge*, New York: Routledge, pp. 79–98.

Goel, R.K., D. Göktepe-Hultén and R. Ram, 2015b, "Academics' entrepreneurship propensities and gender differences," *The Journal of Technology Transfer*, **40** (1), 161–77.

Goel, R.K., D. Göktepe-Hultén and R. Ram, 2017, "Gender and entrepreneurship: Selected stylized propositions, a simple empirical illustration, and some comparisons," in A.N. Link (ed.), *Gender and Entrepreneurial Activity*, Cheltenham, UK and Northampton, MA, USA: Edward Elgar Publishing, pp. 69–91.

Greene, P.G. and C.G. Brush, 2018, "Introduction: The ABCs of women's entrepreneurial identity—aspirations, behaviors and confidence," in P.G. Greene and C.G. Brush (eds.), *A Research Agenda for Women and Entrepreneurship: Identity Through Aspirations, Behaviors and Confidence*, Cheltenham, UK and Northampton, MA, USA: Edward Elgar Publishing, pp. 1–24.

Grimaldi, R., M. Kenny, D.S. Siegel and M. Wright, 2011, "30 years after Bayh–Dole: Reassessing academic entrepreneurship," *Research Policy*, **40** (8), 1045–57.

Hamilton, E., 2014, "Entrepreneurial narrative identity and gender: A double epistemological shift," *Journal of Small Business Management*, **52** (4), 703–12.

Harrison, R., C. Leitch and M. McAdam, 2015, "Breaking glass: Toward a gendered analysis of entrepreneurial leadership," *Journal of Small Business Management*, **53** (3), 693–713.

Henry, C., L. Foss, A. Fayolle, E. Walker and S. Duffy, 2015, "Entrepreneurial leadership and gender: Exploring theory and practice in global contexts," *Journal of Small Business Management*, **53** (3), 581–6.

Lacetera, N., 2009, "Academic entrepreneurship," *Managerial and Decision Economics*, **30** (7), 443–64.

Lewis, K.V., 2015, "Enacting entrepreneurship and leadership: A longitudinal exploration of gendered identity work," *Journal of Small Business Management*, **53** (3), 662–82.

Renko, M., A. El Tarabishy, A.L. Carsrud and M. Brannback, 2015, "Understanding and measuring entrepreneurial leadership style," *Journal of Small Business Management*, **53** (1), 54–74.

Shane, S., 2004, *Academic Entrepreneurship: University Spinoffs and Wealth Creation*, Cheltenham, UK and Northampton, MA, USA: Edward Elgar Publishing.

Siegel, D.S. and M. Wright, 2015, "Academic entrepreneurship: Time for a rethink?" British Journal of Management, **26** (4), 582–95.

Vassiliki, B., S. Jones, S. Mitchelmore and K. Nikolopoulos, 2015, "The role of competencies in shaping the leadership style of female entrepreneurs: The case of North West of England, Yorkshire, and North Wales," *Journal of Small Business Management*, **53** (3), 627–44.

Yousafzai, S.Y., S. Saeed and M. Muffatto, 2015, "Institutional theory and contextual embeddedness of women's entrepreneurial leadership: Evidence from 92 countries," *Journal of Small Business Management*, **53** (3), 587–604.

12 The power of words and images: towards talking about and seeing entrepreneurship and innovation differently

Friederike Welter

1. Out of tune with the real world of entrepreneurs?

Recently, I was invited to visit the company site of an automotive supplier – a brilliant example of Simon's (1992) hidden champions: a family-held, mid-sized company, located in a small town in one of the more picturesque regions in Germany and operating worldwide in its particular, niche market. The entrepreneur took me on an extended company tour, demonstrating not only his familiarity with all technical processes, but also his knowledge of each employee, down to the youngest trainee, by name and chatting with them. He proudly showed off the gleaming research lab and the newly established modern automotive training centre, which had been set up together with engineering researchers from the nearby university and which he saw as the next step to further develop and grow his business. High-tech, growth-oriented and innovative entrepreneurship at its best, wouldn't you agree?

Let's switch scenes: Saturdays, I like to go to the farmers' market in the small town I live in, with its typical colourful, small market scenes: local farmers offering a wide range of regionally grown products. One of my favourite places to stop by is a local honey producer. Each spring she comes back to the market with different product variants, either adding new ingredients or selling new variants of honey. She also offers educational visits to her apiary for schools to teach them about the importance of honey bees for our environment. Ask a researcher what she sees, and she probably would come up with the verdict: traditional and low-growth entrepreneurship, if innovative at all, rather incremental improvements and of course all low-tech plus displaying social responsibility. Nearby, a team of two young entrepreneurs have realized a new business idea: selling recipes for whole menus, which change from week to week and seasonally, together with all the ingredients needed to cook these meals for one, two or several persons. The assessment by our entrepreneurship researcher: very innovative, although not particularly technologically driven; as to their growth perspectives, that depends – there may be a franchising model in the idea in the longer run, provided they keep hold of and manage to exploit their first-mover advantage.

These examples and their ad hoc assessments from an entrepreneurship researcher's perspective illustrate which model of entrepreneurship still appears to dominate our thinking: much of our research has hyped a standard model of entrepreneurship that does not fit the entrepreneurial reality, by connecting entrepreneurship – sometimes exclusively so – to technology and research and development (R&D) driven innovation, to fast growth and job creation, to very large companies and to economic wealth. But why are we so hooked onto high-tech and highly innovative ventures as in the first example? Why do we tend to overlook the smaller ventures as in my other examples, implicitly even devaluing their ways of entrepreneurship by classifying them as low- or non-tech, low-growth, non-innovative or at most incremental innovators? Why do we focus on some – and not other – examples of entrepreneurship?

Recently, more and more researchers have started to argue for entrepreneurship to be seen differently and to be studied in a more realistic way, for entrepreneurship scholars to accept the variances and differences between ventures and their outcomes and for more realistic models of entrepreneurship (Aldrich and Ruef 2018; Gartner 2013; Sarasvathy et al. 2015; Welter et al. 2017). In this chapter, I will add to this call. Perhaps not surprising, given my long-standing research interest (Welter 2011, 2016), I am going to illustrate how contextualizing entrepreneurship and innovation can assist us in gaining a more realistic understanding, whilst at the same time offering scope for theory development and novel research questions. In particular, I want to draw attention to the power of words and images in how we construct, understand and interpret entrepreneurship and innovation, thus building on the recent contextual debate which emphasizes the construction of contexts (e.g., Baker and Welter 2018; Brännback and Carsrud 2016; Elfving et al. 2017; Steyaert 2016). In the next section, I introduce a few thoughts in relation to our constant obsession with defining entrepreneurship and innovation, arguing for a perspective of understanding, before I turn to discuss how we can use words and images to support a different understanding of entrepreneurship and innovation, in particular its diversity and heterogeneity.

2.   Getting out of the definition trap: towards understanding instead of defining

As researchers, we are hooked on definitions. Definitions are the first step, so I was taught, to understand a phenomenon. They reduce uncertainty, by framing something we are not – yet – familiar with. But, how to define entrepreneurship: is it restricted to those individuals who recognize and exploit opportunities? Is entrepreneurship only connected to new and young ventures, i.e., to the creation of new organizations? Is it something which small business owners also display – then, maybe, in the form of entrepreneurial management? Is it also possible in established and larger organizations, as a form of corporate entrepreneurship? Similar definitional issues arise when considering innovation.

As the field of entrepreneurship research has grown over the past decades, so have our – sometimes frantic – attempts to define the phenomenon, resulting in a somewhat scattered and fragmented landscape of what we see as entrepreneurship, innovation and how to delimit the domain of entrepreneurship research. Most researchers probably would agree that entrepreneurship has something to do with the creation of organizations, and many would restrict this to business-oriented organizations. Every now and then, the definitional debate flares up again, as scholars continue to question the legitimacy and boundaries of the research field. Each time I read yet another one of those – to me, as a policy-oriented researcher, very theoretical – debates, I keep asking myself whether we need those discussions. Wouldn't it be more appropriate for us to search for better ways to capture the real world of entrepreneurs to be able to be relevant for entrepreneurship practice, be that teaching, consultancy or policy-making? Do definitional debates help us to further the research agenda in our field? Each definition includes some aspects of entrepreneurship and innovation and excludes others. It is not surprising, then, that the entrepreneurship field has branched out into many separate subfields – women's entrepreneurship, rural entrepreneurship, family businesses, migrant entrepreneurship, refugee entrepreneurship, to name but a few – each with its own definition of a small part of the phenomenon.

Definitions are, of course, a requirement as soon as we start fieldwork, set up empirical studies and collect data – we need to decide what and how to measure as entrepreneurship and innovation. Such empirical studies help us to gain a deeper understanding of the phenomenon, each adding another piece to the puzzle that constitutes entrepreneurship and innovation. Nevertheless, many definitions we use are much too narrow, not allowing us to capture the nuances and heterogeneity of the phenomenon we are interested in – we are caught in a definition trap.

This is best illustrated by taking a closer look at some of the public debates research has initiated and contributed to, such as, for example, the recent discussion around innovation and entrepreneurship in Germany. For a few years now, public debate has lamented an ever-decreasing share of innovators and innovative small businesses in the German economy (e.g., Zimmermann 2017), whilst other studies show Germany's Mittelstand firms by no means to be less innovative (see the discussion outlined in Pahnke and Welter, 2019). Differing measurements and understandings of what constitutes innovation are the main reason for the ambiguous picture painted by empirical research. For the purposes of empirically studying innovation, most studies have operationalized – and thereby defined – innovation as R&D activities, measured by R&D input (expenses, personnel) or output (share of R&D-driven products or services). However, official R&D statistics do not include many SMEs because they are either too small, do not use R&D, at least not in-house, or do not incur any other R&D expenses. Studies have shown that many SMEs in Germany, particularly those in service industries, generate innovation without formal R&D; formally they belong to the category of "non-research-based" companies (Brink et al. 2018). Additionally, where innovation is restricted to technologically-driven results, this underestimates the substantial proportion of SMEs that rely on so-called non-technology innovations (Maaß and May-Strobl 2016). Both wordings, by the way, give us a first hint of how important words are in framing and conceptualizing innovation. Research on gender and innovation adds yet another facet, suggesting that male-dominated industries are automatically associated with technology-driven innovation (Alsos et al. 2016). Given the persistent gender gap in entrepreneurship and the female dominance in less innovative sectors – at least in those that are perceived as less innovative because they are not technology and R&D based (Bijedic et al. 2016) – this also may have contributed to our restricted understanding of innovative entrepreneurship.

With a single definition, be it of innovation or of entrepreneurship, we restrict ourselves to seeing and understanding entrepreneurship in one particular way, setting aside the variety and heterogeneity of the phenomenon. However, we may be able to gain a much better understanding of what constitutes entrepreneurship, and at the same time acknowledge its variety and heterogeneity, by looking at "ideas" of entrepreneurship. I owe this suggestion to one of the reviewers of Welter et al. (2017), who critiqued us mildly for not providing a definition but then went on to suggest that we could provide "ideas" of what entrepreneurship is. Such ideas of what constitutes a diverse view on entrepreneurship would include entrepreneurship to be understood as a broad and inclusive phenomenon and acknowledging that entrepreneurs set up businesses and other organizations for a multitude of reasons and with very different personal, business and social goals (e.g., Baker and Welter 2017), and that entrepreneurship also contributes to society and not solely to economic (individual) wealth (e.g., Zahra and Wright 2016). Similarly, innovation would be considered in the broad sense introduced by Joseph Schumpeter in the 1930s as one function of entrepreneurs, namely "the doing of new things or the doing of things that are already done, in a new way (innovation)" (Schumpeter 1947, p. 151). In fact, this understanding of innovation has been operationalized in the Oslo Manual as a new or significantly improved good, service or process, a new marketing method, or a new organizational practice (OECD 2005, p. 46). In bringing those two perspectives together, we can draw on Kao's understanding of entrepreneurship as the "process of doing something new and something different for the purpose of creating wealth for the individual and adding value to society" (Kao 1993, p. 69). Inherent in that is a diverse understanding of innovative entrepreneurship which is not restricted to the creation of new organizations and high-tech or R&D-based innovations.

But *how* can we incorporate such a different understanding of what constitutes entrepreneurship and innovation into our research models and theories? More than 20 years ago, Gartner (1990, p. 95) drew attention to the fact that much of the debate over the missing definition of entrepreneurship was fuelled by the worry "that entrepreneurship has become a label of convenience with little inherent meaning". In his study, he explored the meanings researchers and practitioners attached to entrepreneurship. He distilled eight themes which respondents connected to entrepreneurship and showed that participants fell into two broad groups: they either emphasized the characteristics of entrepreneurs (nearly 80%) or focused on outcomes of entrepreneurship such as value creation, for profit or owner-manager.

Gartner suggested that we do not need one definition, but instead that we clearly say what we mean and talk about when referring to entrepreneurship and also acknowledge that entrepreneurship is attached to very many different meanings. He concluded that language and ways of talking matter because we bring our own beliefs to these conversations: "Only by making explicit what we believe can we begin to understand how all of these different parts make up a whole" (Gartner 1990, p. 28).

3.   The linguistic turn: talking about entrepreneurship and innovation differently

Words are powerful – in that they impact on and frame the ways we construct and understand our world through talking about it: they are "windows for seeing what was earlier hidden or missing" (Gartner 1993, p. 238). Recently, more research follows Gartner's suggestions of paying more attention to words, also looking at images and metaphors. In the following section, I will review some of this research, pointing to a few ideas as to how entrepreneurship scholars could study the ways we talk about entrepreneurship and innovation to generate a more realistic picture of it.

3.1   Simplifying the entrepreneurial reality: the role of stereotypes

When I started teaching small business management and new venture creation, I searched for images of entrepreneurship – compiling, over time, a substantial body of caricatures. Caricatures pinpoint current discussions showing us how society perceives a phenomenon. Entrepreneurs have been shown as working too much, caricatures included wordplays with the German word *selbstständig* (deconstructing the word into its two parts: *selbst* means that entrepreneurs work on their own, thus offering a positive view of entrepreneurship, whilst *ständig* refers to the fact that entrepreneurs work all the time, thus offering a more negative assessment of entrepreneurship) or society's critique of entrepreneurs as exploitative – male – capitalists. Many of those caricatures nowadays are dated and can only be understood by someone familiar with the – then – political debates. That implies that images themselves are bounded in contexts.

To illustrate this, let's go back to the examples I presented in the introductory section of this chapter. Which images came to your mind when you read through the descriptions? The successful automotive supplier: did he appear to you as someone who is very proprietary towards his business, with success demonstrated in his behaviour, probably his dress, and in the way he showed me around? The honey producer: did you picture her as a green-party member, in ecological footwear and with little attention to her clothes otherwise? The team of young entrepreneurs, just out of school or fresh from university – an eager and young team with lots of ideas? Some or most of you may not understand the picture I just painted of the honey producer whilst I believe that scholars of my generation most likely would be able to decode this reference. In the early 1980s, with the emergence of the green party, so-called "alternative entrepreneurship" flourished across Germany, where collectives searched for different ways of operating small businesses, aiming at fair working conditions, and offering ecologically produced and – preferably – locally sourced products and paying more attention to community welfare and their own well-being than business profit. When describing the honey producer to you, the reader, I stereotyped her based on the then-typical dress code for many of that group, and in a way that would have been immediately recognizable to some (those who grew up during those years and in that culture) but not to others (those socialized in different cultures and times).

We tend to perceive stereotyping as something negative – because it portrays individuals or groups in particularly restricted ways and oftentimes comes with a derogatory connotation. Stereotyping as such, however, is helpful, because it allows us to cope with the unfamiliar in drawing on something that we perceive as familiar and known. We use known images, symbols and stories to familiarize ourselves with the unknown, which process Luhmann (2000) described as familiarity breeding unfamiliarity. In that sense, stereotypes initially are value-free means of simplifying our world and ensuring that we come up with a picture of entrepreneurship and innovation we recognize and can identify with – at least to a certain extent.

3.2   Constraining the entrepreneurial reality through words?

However, what can happen over time is that stereotypes gain a life of their own as they are perpetuated and used in the sense of "I know what entrepreneurship looks like and how innovation is supposed to be." They become loaded with either positive or negative connotations. Language may contribute to reinforcing stereotypes in such ways that it restricts access to entrepreneurship respectively to transport a more negative image of what constitutes entrepreneurship and innovation. In this regard, a recent stream of studies more directly analyses the role language plays in terms of the nature and extent of entrepreneurship. For example, research has looked at language and access to funding for women and men entrepreneurs (Gorbatai and Nelson 2015; Kanze et al. 2018; Malmström et al. 2017), at whether and how language contributes to the gender gap in entrepreneurship in general (Hechavarría et al. 2018), and at how it influences the reputation of entrepreneurship in different places and communities (Parkinson et al. 2017).

For example, Parhankangas and Renko (2017) studied video pitches on crowdfunding platforms, looking into how the linguistic styles of venture pitches influenced the access to funding. They found that social and commercial entrepreneurs differed widely in the styles they respectively were expected to use to pitch for crowdfunding. Their study draws attention to the fact that language expectations differ according to whether a group is established (commercial entrepreneurs) or new and not yet legitimized (social entrepreneurs). Their findings illustrate – once more – the ways in which words create and reinforce differences within the entrepreneurship community.

Hechavarría et al. (2018) analyse the impact of language on the gender gap in entrepreneurship. They distinguish between sex-based language systems where a language is linked to biological sex, and gender-based systems where a language ascribes semantic and formal genders to nouns or not. They find that gendered linguistic structures can explain around 4% of the previously unexplained gender gap in early stage entrepreneurship (Hechavarría et al. 2018, p. 10). It is not simply the words as such but also the ways in which they are used in conversations that separate out entrepreneurs, that contribute to promoting a wanted image of entrepreneurship and innovation, and that reinforce differences – in this case gender differences. For example, Kanze et al. (2018) illustrate that investors tend to favour men by asking them questions that are focused on promotion (i.e., positively framed) and disfavour women by asking them questions that are focused on prevention (i.e., negatively framed) whilst entrepreneurs react with matching responses. Their findings also illustrate how it is not words as such that are gendered but the fact that they reflect prejudgements in our behaviour – in this case the gendered questioning also may be a consequence of stereotypes regarding women.

In some of my own research we looked at entrepreneurship, and women's entrepreneurship more indirectly, through its representation in media such as newspapers. Our studies show how media construct a typical picture of entrepreneurship, entrepreneurial culture and women's entrepreneurship, through metaphors and images and through the context within which specific words are used, that in turn influences those wanting to start a business. In Achtenhagen and Welter (2006), we illustrated the – indirect – assessment of the concept "entrepreneurial spirit", that media through the words they use transmit to either comparing its level positively or negatively to other countries or to describe it as passive (e.g., it can be destroyed) or active (e.g., it slumbers). In Achtenhagen and Welter (2011) and in Ettl et al. (2016), we took a close look at the media representation of women's entrepreneurship in German newspapers, over the time period 1995–2005. Our conclusion: the overall share of reports on women entrepreneurs has increased over time, and they are also increasingly depicted as professional women (and the media reports are published in the economy section of the newspapers) instead of as mothers whose entrepreneurial activity is a burden or side activity (with the media reports published under the society rubric of the newspapers). They are no longer invisible, as shown in an early study on this subject by Baker et al. (1997), but the prevailing image of entrepreneurship may still be androcentric. Implicitly that is reflected in the language, metaphors and words used in German newspapers which too frequently still transmit a different reality of women's entrepreneurship, one where women are reduced to their gender instead of being seen as entrepreneurs in the first instance.

Researchers also have studied whether practitioners and scholars talk about the same thing when referring to entrepreneurship and innovation. Their results point to contextualized understandings that differ between groups and communities. For example, Achtenhagen et al. (2010) find that practitioners understand growth as complex and focus on internal developments, whilst scholars – not surprisingly – tend to use a simplified conceptualization, based on the need to study this empirically.

The disconnect between explicit messages and the implicit – wanted – reality transported through the language and images used, and visible in the studies I report on here, can deter any group of potential entrepreneurs from entering entrepreneurship and reduce their intentions. Language, both in its written form and as it is communicated through interactions, shapes entrepreneurial cognitions (Clarke and Cornelissen 2016), acting either as an enabler or as a constraint. But non-verbal images also shape how we perceive the world. For example, Hentschel et al. (2017) explore advertisements for entrepreneurship programmes and the impact on applications by women, given potentially gendered images and linguistic forms. Their findings show that women were less interested and perceived themselves as less suitable in those cases where the programmes were advertised using typically masculine images and/or a solely masculine form for an entrepreneur. Their findings illustrate in which ways non-verbal images can influence and contribute to a gendered identification with entrepreneurship – a theme I will explore further in the next section.

3.3   Imagining entrepreneurship and innovation: the role of metaphors

In this section, I turn to research that has studied the images we use to talk about entrepreneurship and innovation. Metaphors (or analogies) influence our understanding of entrepreneurship and innovation, for example when talking about entrepreneurship and characterizing successful entrepreneurs as heroes. Like stereotypes, they are a trope of speech, allowing us to familiarize the unfamiliar by offering us a means to compare something new to something we are familiar with. They help us to make sense of our world. In that, they are helpful in illustrating the complexity of a phenomenon and in theory building (Weick 1989); and they have been widely used in the management discipline (e.g., Cornelissen 2005, 2006; Ketokivi et al. 2017). Metaphor-based entrepreneurship research falls into three broad groups: studies look at the metaphors that entrepreneurs use; or they analyse the metaphors that are generally used to characterize entrepreneurship and innovation by various groups; or, in an emerging stream of research, they have turned to study the role and importance of root metaphors.

The first group of metaphor-related studies in entrepreneurship research generally has confirmed their central role for entrepreneurial sense-making. For example, Clarke and Holt (2010), in a study on entrepreneurial goal-making, illustrate that entrepreneurs drew on metaphors to articulate both their personal goals such as independence and goals that evoked public, social and moral concerns. Entrepreneurs also use images and metaphors to create legitimacy for their idea for a venture or new business. Studying the process of venture creation, Cornelissen et al. (2012) conclude that novel entrepreneurs employ sense-giving (reflected in metaphorical speech and gestures), communicating what is a meaningful course for their venture (idea) and as a means to ensure the support of investors and employees for their venture. In another study, Bruni et al. (2017) investigate how entrepreneurs talk about innovation, based on interviews with companies in Northern Italy. Entrepreneurs were much more likely to draw on metaphors when talking about organizational innovations (48%) compared to, for example, product innovations (18%) or others – entrepreneurs either used more metaphors in – to them – complex innovation processes, or they are more attuned to what they thought their audience would not understand without metaphors.

The second group of studies has looked at the metaphors used to describe entrepreneurship and innovation in general. The findings of these studies illustrate how, at least to some extent, our current understanding of entrepreneurship and innovation may have emerged and how entrepreneurship is socially constructed. For example, De Koning and Drakopoulou-Dodd (2002) show commonalities in the use of metaphors across the media in six countries but also a few localized stories such as the Wild West metaphor for entrepreneurship in the US. They highlight how the use of metaphors is grounded in national cultures (and, I add, in time as their data collection took place after the dotcom bubble had burst in 2001). As a dominant narrative in four out of their six countries, they identified "the fight is on" as a category which includes aggressive, competitive metaphors from team sports and the military. The underlying implicit connotation here is of entrepreneurship as an activity which is characterized by typically masculine qualities. Dodd (2002) further illustrates how metaphors used to describe entrepreneurship as a journey, a race or a building are deeply grounded in US images of (successful) entrepreneurship.

Research also suggests that the culturally-grounded meaning of entrepreneurship (i.e., how it is understood) influences whether it is seen as an attractive employment option (Dodd et al. 2013). Gathering data on the meanings of entrepreneurship from schools across seven European countries, Dodd et al. (2013) show how entrepreneurs and entrepreneurship are "value-laden social constructions which have substantial differences across Europe" (p. 80) and which diverge from the "Americanized hero" (p. 84). Hyrsky (1999), one of the pioneers of metaphor-related studies in entrepreneurship research, demonstrated that differences in metaphor use, and consequently interpretation of what constituted entrepreneurship, depended on the population group, on nation and on sex. His study was based on a large-scale comparison of respondents from Finland, Sweden, Norway, Ireland, Canada and Australia. Entrepreneurs, Scandinavians and men in general perceived entrepreneurship as more positive compared to non-entrepreneurs, non-Scandinavians and women. These findings support both the use of metaphor analysis in detecting and illustrating the variety of entrepreneurship as well as the stance taken against the dominant (US-based) model of entrepreneurship.

Other studies which analyse the use of metaphors reveal the underlying myth-making inherent in entrepreneurship (research) which in turn influences and forms the assumptions we bring to our research (Rehn et al. 2013). Although research started to question the notion of the entrepreneur as a heroic figure more than two decades ago (e.g., Gartner 1988; Ogbor 2000; Warren 2005), these studies seem not to have had a large impact in the field, suggesting that their reception may have been restricted to small communities of like-minded (primarily European?) researchers. Some research shows how the entrepreneur (exclusively a male person, in this case in a reputable British newspaper – *The Independent*) is portrayed through mythical "aggressive, magical, giant, and religious imagery" in contrast to a more rational undercurrent, representing him as "human, fallible, creating problems and misfortune" (Nicholson and Anderson 2005, pp. 163–164) – a bit of all or nothing, at least not a realistic picture drawn of the entrepreneur in this case. All these images are representative of the "hero" myth-making which, at least implicitly, continues to underpin the standard entrepreneurship model.

This myth-making is also visible in research that looks at place-based discourses in relation to entrepreneurship or the place-based construction of entrepreneurial identities. For example, Gregory (2012) deconstructs the journalistic discussion around entrepreneurship in the city of Detroit, showing that entrepreneurs are perceived as "salvationists" of a "victimized place". Gill and Larson (2014) have studied the links between high-tech entrepreneurial identities and place-specific discourses. They argue that high-tech entrepreneurs use discourses that both transcend places (in their study, entrepreneurs draw on discourses that are linked to the Silicon Valley model of entrepreneurship) *and* that are localized. Their findings explain how entrepreneurs simultaneously construct similar and different "ideal identities", depending on their perception of what best fits the places they operate in and how they want to be perceived by others.

Some research has turned to analyse root metaphors used to explain new firm formation or innovation processes. For example, Cardon et al. (2005) have compared the process of new firm formation to the birth, and upbringing, of a child, whilst venture failure before firm birth is referred to as miscarriage. The authors suggest that applying such root metaphors links entrepreneurship to everyday life experiences and at the same time highlights the passion involved in pursuing entrepreneurial activities. With regard to innovation, Bruni et al. (2017) confirmed that entrepreneurs used different root metaphors depending on the type of innovation they talked about: innovation generally was framed as a journey; strategic innovation was connected to the war metaphor; organizational innovation to sports and risk; and product innovation to the life cycle from birth to death.

An emerging stream of metaphor analysis in the entrepreneurship field draws our attention to the overarching importance of root metaphors. Gaddefors (2007) points out the contextualized nature of metaphors, and suggests that entrepreneurship scholars analysing metaphors should pay more attention to their role in the construction "of an environment to act on" (p. 180) as a precondition for opportunity creation than to any linguistic characteristics. Nielsen and Lassen (2012) categorize entrepreneurship process research through five images, based on a systematic literature review: the image of machines, the image of evolution, the image of contingencies, the image of mind, and the image of social becoming. Furthermore, in a review of highly-cited entrepreneurship articles, covering seven entrepreneurship journals during the years 2011–2015, Lundmark et al. (2017) identify eight root metaphors for the entrepreneurship field: parenthood, mutagen, conduit of knowledge, method, mindset, networking, exploration, and politics. The authors claim that these root metaphors "capture central thought patterns in the mainstream entrepreneurship literature", although by no means do they claim to have identified all of them (Lundmark et al. 2017, p. 22). They conclude that root metaphors also can be used to change prevailing discourses – something which obviously is required for us to fully acknowledge the diversity of entrepreneurship and innovation.

4.   The visual turn: seeing entrepreneurship and innovation differently

In my free time, I like to go for long walks, taking my camera along and photographing whatever takes my interest out there: cloudscapes, trees and the shadow play in woods, the ways the light changes throughout the day and how that creates new and different patterns. Sometimes, I snap the everyday life I encounter in the small villages I pass through alongside the Rhine, for example. Over the past few years, I have become increasingly interested in whether I could combine my interest in photography with my interest in contextualizing entrepreneurship. Discussions with a couple of friends, both professional art photographers, revealed that they do (want to) contextualize their photography and they also contextualize their photography respectively to create individualized world views, because each viewer puts their own individual interpretation to their photography.

But how can we capture these ideas and thoughts for entrepreneurship research? A quick search on research that visualizes in social sciences surfaced the field of visual studies in anthropology and in sociology – going back to the photographic sequence analysis Bateson and Mead (1942) used for exploring the "Balinese Character".[1] The dividing line between images transported through metaphors and visual studies focusing on pictures and photography is thin. For visual sociology, Grady (1996) suggests a distinction between three distinct areas of investigations: seeing; iconic communication (similar to the metaphor analysis reviewed in the preceding section); and doing sociology visually. In this section, I am more interested in "seeing" as the "study of the role of sight and vision in the construction of social organization and meaning" (Grady 1996, p. 14), and in the techniques for visual studies. Additionally, visual props (films, photography, etc.) also can be used to transfer research results. Thus, visual studies also emphasize the subjectivity of contextualization, pointing to the fact that, for example, photography is not

---

1 My search on visual studies, driven by my interest in photography, has produced a few interesting reviews and introductions. Howard S. Becker (1974) has written an early paper on photography and sociology, also pointing to the challenges of marrying both disciplines; similarly Douglas Harper (1988). Harper also published a – personal – reflection on the value of photographic ethnography (Harper 2003), based on his own ethnographic work on, for example, the changing face of agriculture, and he published, more specifically, on photo elicitation as one possible technique (Harper 2002).

objective evidence and passively received by the spectator, but, rather, the spectator makes sense out of what he or she sees in the photography (Schwartz 1989) – and, obviously, this sense-making and construction of reality also can change over time.

A focus on seeing would imply – for entrepreneurship research – a study of how entrepreneurs construct and enact their contexts through visual imagery, including, for example, visual design, the use of photos, videos, or any other visual means, and of how researchers contextualize through seeing and interpreting these visual means. Rereading Gartner et al.'s (2003) study on the language of opportunity, I realized that many of the verbs that entrepreneurs used to talk about opportunity discovery (Table 7.1, pp. 117–18), are connected to visualizing opportunities: seeing, looking, and, more implicitly, also noticing. However, few studies so far appear to have studied this aspect of "seeing" and/or applied visual techniques in entrepreneurship research. Based on a visual ethnographic study, Clarke (2011) analysed the visual symbols entrepreneurs employ to achieve support for their ventures. She identified setting, props, dress and expressiveness as visual symbols – or signals – that entrepreneurs used in various ways: to present an appropriate scene to stakeholders, to construct their professional identity, to emphasize control, and to regulate their emotions. Her results also demonstrated that entrepreneurial experiences go hand in hand with a wider range of visual symbols entrepreneurs could use during their interactions with stakeholders. Her findings resonate those of Davison's study on the business elite (Davison 2010). The author analyses visual portraits of successful managers and entrepreneurs in annual reports and on websites, distilling the (in)tangible messages sent through four rhetorical codes in those photos (physical, dress, spatial and interpersonal).

Robert Smith has been a pioneer regarding the incorporation of visual analysis and techniques into entrepreneurship research. I still remember discussions we had a long time ago, about how we would go about comparing the caricatures of entrepreneurship both of us apparently collected. Together with Alistair Anderson, he has argued for semiotics to be a potential qualitative method in the field (Smith and Anderson 2007). In some research, he more implicitly looked at visual elements and images. For example, in Smith (2010) he studied alternative social constructions of entrepreneurship, in particular the influence of masculinity on entrepreneurial identities, triangulating his biographical analysis of a novel that depicted a typical "bad boy entrepreneur" with photos downloaded from the internet. In Smith (2013) he illustrated typical "crimino-entrepreneurial identities" in the UK, such as the "Essex-Boy" (p. 190), through textual and semiotic analysis, including TV serials and other pictorial elements. In yet another study (Smith 2014), he used semiotic analysis together with a photomontage technique[2] on 100 images of women entrepreneurs. He discovered a few archetypical, gendered stereotypes: the Business Woman, the Matriarch, the Diva, and the Pink-Ghetto Girl.

---

2 John Berger and Jean Mohr introduced this technique in their photo essays on, for example, migrant workers in Europe (Berger and Mohr 2010, first published in 1975) and the story of a country doctor (Berger and Mohr 2015, first published in 1967).

Smith (2015a, 2015b) reviews methodological approaches for visual analysis in entrepreneurship research. In Smith (2015a), he con'text'ualizes images, in this case the jacket cover photography of entrepreneurship textbooks. He identified several overarching visual metaphors – ranging, for example, from biological and scientific/ technological ones to craft-based metaphors, metaphors representing masculinity (such as the picture of a gentleman smoking a cigar) or surrealist ones which appear to be action related but without a clear visual meaning. Interestingly, the visual images do not present much evidence of the entrepreneur as hero – thus demonstrating how a visual analysis can add to a broader and more realistic picture of entrepreneurship.

In Smith (2015b), the author suggests that family business researchers use visual ethnography (e.g., films, photos) as a means to analyse the contexts in which family businesses operate and family relations occur: "Visual ethnography (. . .) captures so much more, for example, feelings, emotions and values . . ." (p. 78). He draws on visual content analysis (see Bell and Davison 2013, p. 173) to identify additional aspects of the family business he studied, concluding that visual analysis can be theory generating.

There is certainly scope for more entrepreneurship research that explicitly looks at how photos and pictures can enrich our understanding of the real world of entrepreneurs and their innovative behaviour, thus contextualizing entrepreneurial diversity. For the management field in general, Bell and Davison (2013) present a review and critique of visual management studies, categorizing existing research based on whether the methods used were theory driven or empirically driven. Several of the studies I have reviewed in this section are more empirically driven, which is understandable in terms of making sense of a new method and testing its applicability to entrepreneurship research. Importantly, visual analysis can also generate new and respectively challenge existing theory through exposing us to different narratives. This has been shown by Smith (2015a) whose findings highlight the disconnect between the cover pictures of textbooks and the understanding of entrepreneurs as "heroes". Also, Berglund and Wigren-Kristoferson (2012) illustrate how a visual analysis can bring silenced stories to the forefront. These and similar studies emphasize the visual side of the social construction of what constitutes entrepreneurship and innovation – introducing wider and different narratives and thus challenging existing theories. In short, I believe that visual entrepreneurship studies open an interesting research opportunity for entrepreneurship scholars, in particular for further developing our theorizing.

5.   Outlook: towards a different understanding of entrepreneurial reality

By now, hopefully I have persuaded some of you that the reality of entrepreneurship and innovation needs to be analysed in different ways, and that looking, seeing and talking can help us remodel and broaden our understanding of entrepreneurship and innovation. Entrepreneurship is neither exclusively connected to high-growth and high-tech ventures nor to the business world – if it ever has been seen as such, beyond the scholarly community. The technological developments of the past decade also have increasingly blurred the boundaries between work and private lives. This also impacts on the nature of entrepreneurship. We see an upsurge of solo entrepreneurs around the world – not all of them necessity driven because of job loss or similar reasons, but many of them exploiting opportunities to work on their own, which originate from technological changes and the increasing digitization of our daily life. This, once more, questions the fascination of our research field with high-growth firms (Kiviluoto 2013). Enterprise development has never been a linear process in the sense of "start small, grow big" but it has always displayed widely diverse patterns: business growth, for example, can happen as rapid growth, it can be discontinuous (growth followed by sharp retrenchment), or it can stop altogether at one point in time (Brush et al. 2009). In today's digital and technology-driven world, enterprise growth has become even more of a temporary phenomenon, as solo entrepreneurs can use technology to form temporary and project-based networks, if needed, around the world. Even in Germany – where enterprise creation and development implicitly has been understood and propagated as a task for life – increasing numbers of business founders develop into serial entrepreneurs, realizing one business idea today, selling it the next month or year, and setting up their next venture or taking up employment somewhere else. Exit – and not necessarily generational continuation of the business – is one option, particularly with younger entrepreneurs.

The Swiss writer and publicist Robert Nef, in a private communication to the author, coined the term "*Lebensunternehmertum*" (life entrepreneurship) for these developments. For him, entrepreneurship has been, and increasingly is, part of everyday life and an attitude towards life, not solely related to business activities. He plays around with a concept that many entrepreneurship researchers tend to see – more or less – exclusively connected to business life, putting forward a broad understanding of the phenomenon. In this chapter, I have introduced selected research studies that, by focusing on language, metaphors and images, capture these nuances and much more of entrepreneurial heterogeneity.

In this chapter, I have reviewed research that draws on linguistic and visual methods and concepts, to distil a few ideas as to how entrepreneurship and innovation can be contextualized differently. Seeing and talking differently will help us to develop a more realistic understanding of entrepreneurship and innovation. Words direct the way we think and act as researchers and, consequently, which questions we ask and which we do not ask: "The words we use to talk about entrepreneurship influence our ability to think about this phenomenon, and subsequent to these thoughts, direct our actions towards research that might be conducted on this topic" (Gartner 1993, p. 231). Gartner (1993, p. 238) also states that "we cannot behave in ways we cannot imagine" – thus implicitly pointing to the importance of not only words but also pictures and images. If we expand on the language, images and pictures we use to describe and visualize innovative entrepreneurs, we will be able to study and see the greater variety and heterogeneity of the phenomenon, adding to more realistic entrepreneurship research.

References

Achtenhagen, Leona and Friederike Welter (2006), '(Re-)Constructing The Entrepreneurial Spirit', *Frontiers of Entrepreneurship Research*, **2005**, 104–17.

Achtenhagen, Leona and Friederike Welter (2011), '"Surfing on the Ironing Board" – The Representation of Women's Entrepreneurship in German Newspapers', *Entrepreneurship & Regional Development*, **23** (9–10), 763–86.

Achtenhagen, Leona, Lucia Naldi and Leif Melin (2010), '"Business Growth"—Do Practitioners and Scholars Really Talk About the Same Thing?', *Entrepreneurship Theory and Practice*, **34** (2), 289–316.

Aldrich, Howard E. and Martin Ruef (2018), 'Unicorns, Gazelles, and Other Distractions on the Way to Understanding Real Entrepreneurship in America', *Academy of Management Perspectives*. Doi: 10.5465/amp.2017.0123.

Alsos, Gry Agnete, Ulla Hytti and Elisabet Ljunggren (2016), 'Gender and Innovation – An Introduction', in Gry Agnete Alsos, Ulla Hytti and Elisabet Ljunggren (eds), *Research Handbook on Gender and Innovation*, Cheltenham, UK and Northampton, MA, USA: Edward Elgar, pp. 3–16.

Baker, Ted and Friederike Welter (2017), 'Come On Out of the Ghetto, Please! – Building the Future of Entrepreneurship Research', *International Journal of Entrepreneurial Behavior & Research*, **23** (2), 170–84.

Baker, Ted and Friederike Welter (2018), 'Contextual Entrepreneurship: An Interdisciplinary Perspective', *Foundations and Trends® in Entrepreneurship*, **14** (4), 357–426.

Baker, Ted, Howard E. Aldrich and Nina Liou (1997), 'Invisible Entrepreneurs: The Neglect of Women Business Owners by Mass Media and Scholarly Journals in the USA', *Entrepreneurship & Regional Development*, **9** (3), 221–38.

Bateson, Gregory and Margaret Mead (1942), 'Balinese Character: A Photographic Analysis', in Wilbur G. Valentine (ed.), *Special Publication of the New York Academy of Sciences* (Vol. II), New York: New York Academy of Sciences, pp. 17–92.

Becker, Howard S. (1974), 'Photography and Sociology', *Studies in Visual Communication*, **1** (1), 3–26.

Bell, Emma and Jane Davison (2013), 'Visual Management Studies: Empirical and Theoretical Approaches', *International Journal of Management Reviews*, **15** (2), 167–84.

Berger, John and Jean Mohr (2010), *A Seventh Man: A Book of Images and Words about the Experience of Migrant Workers in Europe*, London and New York: Verso.

Berger, John and Jean Mohr (2015), *A Fortunate Man: The Story of a Country Doctor*, Edinburgh and London: Canongate.

Berglund, Karin Anna Elisabeth and Caroline Wigren-Kristoferson (2012), 'Using Pictures and Artefacts in a PAR Process to Disclose New Wor(l)ds of Entrepreneurship', *Action Research*, **10** (3), 276–92.

Bijedic, Teita, Siegrun Brink, Silke Kriwoluzky, Kerstin Ettl and Friederike Welter (2016), 'Women's Innovation in Germany – Empirical Facts and Conceptual Explanations', in Gry Agnete Alsos, Ulla Hytti and Elisabet Ljunggren (eds), *Research Handbook on Gender and Innovation*, Cheltenham, UK and Northampton, MA, USA: Edward Elgar, pp. 51–71.

Brännback, Malin and Alan Carsrud (2016), 'Understanding Entrepreneurial Cognitions Through the Lenses of Context', in Friederike Welter and William B. Gartner (eds), *A Research Agenda on Entrepreneurship and Context*, Cheltenham, UK and Northampton, MA, USA: Edward Elgar, pp. 16–27.

Brink, Siegrun, Sebastian Nielen and Eva May-Strobl (2018), *Innovationstätigkeit des nicht-forschenden Mittelstands*, IfM-Materialien 266, Bonn: IfM Bonn.

Bruni, Elena, Sara Bonesso and Fabrizio Gerli (2017), 'Metaphors for Innovation: How Entrepreneurs Narrate Different Types of Innovation', *Academy of Management Proceedings*, **2017** (1), 13415.

Brush, Candida G., Dennis J. Ceru and Robert Blackburn (2009), 'Pathways to Entrepreneurial Growth: The Influence of Management, Marketing, and Money', *Business Horizons*, **52** (5), 481–91.

Cardon, Melissa S., Charlene Zietsma, Patrick Saparito, Brett P. Matherne and Carolyn Davis (2005),

'A Tale of Passion: New Insights into Entrepreneurship from a Parenthood Metaphor', *Journal of Business Venturing*, **20** (1), 23–45.

Clarke, Jean S. (2011), 'Revitalizing Entrepreneurship: How Visual Symbols are Used in Entrepreneurial Performances', *Journal of Management Studies*, **48** (6), 1365–91.

Clarke, Jean S. and Joep P. Cornelissen (2016), 'How Language Shapes Thoughts: New Vistas for Entrepreneurship Research', in J. Robert Mitchell, Ronald K. Mitchell and Brandon Randolph-Seng (eds), *Handbook of Entrepreneurial Cognition* (paperback edition), Cheltenham, UK and Northampton, MA, USA: Edward Elgar, pp. 383–97.

Clarke, Jean and Robin Holt (2010), 'The Mature Entrepreneur: A Narrative Approach to Entrepreneurial Goals', *Journal of Management Inquiry*, **19** (1), 69–83.

Cornelissen, Joep P. (2005), 'Beyond Compare: Metaphor In Organization Theory', *Academy of Management Review*, **30** (4), 751–64.

Cornelissen, Joep P. (2006), 'Metaphor in Organization Theory: Progress and the Past', *Academy of Management Review*, **31** (2), 485–8.

Cornelissen, Joep P., Jean S. Clarke and Alan Cienki (2012), 'Sensegiving in Entrepreneurial Contexts: The Use of Metaphors in Speech and Gesture to Gain and Sustain Support for Novel Business Ventures', *International Small Business Journal*, **30** (3), 213–41.

Davison, Jane (2010), '[In]Visible [in]Tangibles: Visual Portraits of the Business Élite', *Accounting, Organizations and Society*, **35** (2), 165–83.

De Koning, Alice and Sarah Drakopoulou-Dodd (2002), 'Raising Babies, Fighting Battles, Winning Races: Entrepreneurial Metaphors in the Media of 6 English Speaking Nations'. Paper presented at the Babson-Kauffman Research Conference, Boulder, Colorado.

Dodd, Sarah Drakopoulou (2002), 'Metaphors and Meaning: A Grounded Cultural Model of US Entrepreneurship', *Journal of Business Venturing*, **17** (5), 519–35.

Dodd, Sarah Drakopoulou, Sarah Jack and Alistair R. Anderson (2013), 'From Admiration to Abhorrence: The Contentious Appeal of Entrepreneurship Across Europe', *Entrepreneurship & Regional Development*, **25** (1–2), 69–89.

Elfving, Jennie, Malin Brännback and Alan Carsrud (2017), 'Revisiting a Contextual Model of Entrepreneurial Intentions', in Malin Brännback and Alan L. Carsrud (eds), *Revisiting the Entrepreneurial Mind: Inside the Black Box: An Expanded Edition*, Cham, Switzerland: Springer International Publishing, pp. 83–90.

Ettl, Kerstin, Friederike Welter and Leona Achtenhagen. (2016), *"Das 21. Jahrhundert ist weiblich": Unternehmerinnen in der Presse*, IfM-Materialien 249, Bonn: IfM Bonn.

Gaddefors, Johan (2007), 'Metaphor Use in the Entrepreneurial Process', *International Journal of Entrepreneurial Behavior & Research*, **13** (3), 173–93.

Gartner, W. B., N. M. Carter and G. E. Hills (2003), 'The Language of Opportunity', in Chris Steyaert and Daniel Hjorth (eds), *New Movements in Entrepreneurship*, Cheltenham, UK and Northampton, MA, USA: Edward Elgar, pp. 103–24.

Gartner, William B. (1988), '"Who is an Entrepreneur?" is the Wrong Question', *American Journal of Small Businesses*, **12** (4), 11–32.

Gartner, William B. (1990), 'What Are We Talking About When We Talk About Entrepreneurship?', *Journal of Business Venturing*, **5** (1), 15–28.

Gartner, William B. (1993), 'Words Lead to Deeds – Towards an Organizational Emergence Vocabulary', *Journal of Business Venturing*, **8** (3), 231–9.

Gartner, William B. (2013), 'Creating a Community of Difference in Entrepreneurship Scholarship', *Entrepreneurship & Regional Development*, **25** (1–2), 5–15.

Gill, Rebecca and Gregory S. Larson (2014), 'Making the Ideal (Local) Entrepreneur: Place and the Regional Development of High-Tech Entrepreneurial Identity', *Human Relations*, **67** (5), 519–42.

Gorbatai, Andreea Daniela and Laura Nelson (2015), 'Gender and the Language of Crowdfunding'. Paper presented at the Academy of Management Proceedings.

Grady, John (1996), 'The scope of visual sociology', *Visual Studies*, **11** (2), 10–24.

Gregory, Siobhan (2012), Detroit is a Blank Slate: Metaphors in the Journalistic Discourse of Art and Entrepreneurship in the City of Detroit, *EPIC*, **12** (1), 217–33.

Harper, Douglas (1988), 'Visual Sociology: Expanding Sociological Vision', *The American Sociologist*, **19** (1), 54–70.

Harper, Douglas (2002), 'Talking about Pictures: A Case for Photo Elicitation', *Visual Studies*, **17** (1), 13–26.

Harper, Douglas (2003), 'Framing Photographic Ethnography: A Case Study', *Ethnography*, **4** (2), 241–66.

Hechavarría, Diana M., Siri A. Terjesen, Pekka Stenholm, Malin Brännback and Stefan Lång (2018), 'More than Words: Do Gendered Linguistic Structures Widen the Gender Gap in Entrepreneurial Activity?', *Entrepreneurship Theory and Practice*, published online early. Doi: 10.1111/etap.12278.

Hentschel, Tanja, Lisa Horvath, Claudia Peus and Sabine Sczesny (2017), 'Raising Women's Interest in Entrepreneurship – Effects of Images and Language in Advertisements', *Academy of Management Proceedings*, **2017** (1), 16894.

Hyrsky, Kimmo (1999), 'Entrepreneurial Metaphors and Concepts: An Exploratory Study', *International Small Business Journal*, **18** (1), 13–34.

Kanze, Dana, Laura Huang, Mark A. Conley and E. Tory Higgins (2018), 'We Ask Men to Win and Women Not to Lose: Closing the Gender Gap in Startup Funding', *Academy of Management Journal*, **61** (2), 586–614.

Kao, Raymond W. Y. (1993), 'Defining Entrepreneurship: Past, Present And?', *Creativity and Innovation Management*, **2** (1), 69–70.

Ketokivi, Mikko, Saku Mantere and Joep Cornelissen (2017), 'Reasoning by Analogy and the Progress of Theory', *Academy of Management Review*, **42** (4), 637–58.

Kiviluoto, Niklas (2013), 'Growth as Evidence of Firm Success: Myth or Reality?', *Entrepreneurship & Regional Development*, **25** (7–8), 569–86.

Luhmann, Niklas (2000), 'Familiarity, Confidence, Trust: Problems and Alternatives', in Diego Gambetta (ed.), *Trust Making and Breaking Cooperative Relations*, New York: Basil Blackwell, pp. 94–107.

Lundmark, Erik, Anna Krzeminska and Dean A. Shepherd (2017), 'Images of Entrepreneurship: Exploring Root Metaphors and Expanding Upon Them', *Entrepreneurship Theory and Practice*, published online early. Doi: 10.1177/1042258717734369.

Maaß, Frank and Eva May-Strobl (2016), *Der Stellenwert nicht-technologischer neuerungen im Innovationsgeschehen der mittelständischen Wirtschaft*, IfM-Materialien 250, Bonn: IfM Bonn.

Malmström, Malin, Jeaneth Johansson and Joakim Wincent (2017), 'Gender Stereotypes and Venture Support Decisions: How Governmental Venture Capitalists Socially Construct Entrepreneurs' Potential', *Entrepreneurship Theory and Practice*, **41** (5), 833–60.

Nicholson, Louise and Alistair R. Anderson (2005), 'News and Nuances of the Entrepreneurial Myth and Metaphor: Linguistic Games in Entrepreneurial Sense-Making and Sense-Giving', *Entrepreneurship Theory and Practice*, **29** (2), 153–72.

Nielsen, Suna and Astrid Lassen (2012), 'Images of Entrepreneurship: Towards a New Categorization of Entrepreneurship', *International Entrepreneurship and Management Journal*, **8** (1), 35–53.

OECD (2005), *Oslo Manual: Guidelines for Collecting and Interpreting Innovation Data*, Paris: OECD Publications.

Ogbor, John O. (2000), 'Mythicizing and Reification in Entrepreneurial Discourse: Ideology-Critique of Entrepreneurial Studies', *Journal of Management Studies*, **37** (5), 605–36.

Pahnke, André and Friederike Welter (2019), 'The German Mittelstand: Antithesis to the Silicon Valley Entrepreneurship Model?', *Small Business Economics*, **52** (2), 345–58. DOI: https://doi.org/10.1007/s11187-018-0095-4.

Parhankangas, Annaleena and Maija Renko (2017), 'Linguistic Style and Crowdfunding Success Among Social and Commercial Entrepreneurs', *Journal of Business Venturing*, **32** (2), 215–36.

Parkinson, Caroline, Carole Howorth and Alan Southern (2017), 'The Crafting of an (un)Enterprising

Community: Context and the Social Practice of Talk', *International Small Business Journal*, **35** (4), 385–404.

Rehn, Alf, Malin Brännback, Alan Carsrud and Marcus Lindahl (2013), 'Challenging the Myths of eEntrepreneurship?', *Entrepreneurship & Regional Development*, **25** (7–8), 543–51.

Sarasvathy, Saras D., Anusha Ramesh and William Forster (2015), 'The Ordinary Entrepreneur', in Ted Baker and Friederike Welter (eds), *The Routledge Companion to Entrepreneurship*, London: Routledge, pp. 227–44.

Schumpeter, Joseph A. (1947), 'The Creative Response in Economic History', *The Journal of Economic History*, **7** (2), 149–59.

Schwartz, Dona (1989), 'Visual Ethnography: Using Photography in Qualitative Research', *Qualitative Sociology*, **12** (2), 119–54.

Simon, Hermann (1992), 'Lessons from Germany's Midsize Giants: An Inside Look at How Smaller German Companies Have Come to Dominate their Markets Worldwide', *Harward Business Review*, **70** (2), 115–22.

Smith, Robert (2010), 'Masculinity, Doxa and the Institutionalisation of Entrepreneurial Identity in the Novel Cityboy', *International Journal of Gender and Entrepreneurship*, **2** (1), 27–48.

Smith, Robert (2013), 'Documenting Essex-Boy as a Local Gendered Regime', *International Journal of Gender and Entrepreneurship*, **5** (2), 174–97.

Smith, Robert (2014), 'Images, Forms and Presence Outside and Beyond the Pink Ghetto', *Gender in Management*, **29** (8), 466–86.

Smith, Robert (2015a), 'Con"text"ualizing Images of Enterprise: An Examination of "Visual Metaphors" Used to Represent Entrepreneurship in Textbooks', in Helle Neergaard and Claire Leitch (eds), *Qualitative Research Techniques and Analysis in Entrepreneurship*, Cheltenham, UK and Northampton, MA, USA: Edward Elgar, pp. 139–69.

Smith, Robert (2015b), 'Seeing the Light: Using Visual Ethnography in Family Business Settings', *Family Business Review*, **28** (1), 76–82.

Smith, Robert and Alistair R. Anderson (2007), 'Recognizing Meaning: Semiotics in Entrepreneurial Research', in Helle Neergaard and John Parm Ulhoi (eds), *Handbook of Qualitative Research Methods in Entrepreneurship*, Cheltenham, UK and Northampton, MA, USA: Edward Elgar, pp. 169–92.

Steyaert, Chris (2016), '"After" context', in Friederike Welter and William B. Gartner (eds), *A Research Agenda for Entrepreneurship and Context*, Cheltenham, UK and Northampton, MA, USA: Edward Elgar, pp. 28–53.

Warren, Lorraine (2005), 'Images of Entrepreneurship: Still Searching for the Hero?', *The International Journal of Entrepreneurship and Innovation*, **6** (4), 221–9.

Weick, Karl E. (1989), 'Theory Construction as Disciplined Imagination', *Academy of Management Review*, **14** (4), 516–31.

Welter, Friederike (2011), 'Contextualizing Entrepreneurship – Conceptual Challenges and Ways Forward', *Entrepreneurship Theory and Practice*, **35** (1), 165–84.

Welter, Friederike (2016), 'Wandering between Contexts', in David Audretsch and Erik Lehmann (eds), *The Routledge Companion to Makers of Modern Entrepreneurship*, London: Routledge, pp. 213–32.

Welter, Friederike, Ted Baker, David B. Audretsch and William B. Gartner (2017), 'Everyday Entrepreneurship – A Call for Entrepreneurship Research to Embrace Entrepreneurial Diversity', *Entrepreneurship Theory and Practice*, **41** (3), 311–21.

Zahra, Shaker A. and Mike Wright (2016), 'Understanding the Social Role of Entrepreneurship', *Journal of Management Studies*, **53** (4), 610–29.

Zimmermann, Volker (2017), KfW-Innovationsbericht Mittelstand 2016. Innovationen konzentrieren sich auf immer weniger Unternehmen. Frankfurt am Main: Kreditanstalt für Wiederaufbau.

13 Artificial intelligence and entrepreneurship: some thoughts for entrepreneurship researchers

Sameeksha Desai

Introduction

Artificial intelligence (AI) is the current big transformation facing scholars, practitioners, and policymakers interested in entrepreneurship. The "AI revolution" is met with excitement about the potential – and concern about the risks – for future economic productivity, employment, and policy.

In 1950, Alan Turing asked several questions that are relevant now, as the use of AI proliferates throughout economic and social life, including entrepreneurship. Turing's problematic question, "can machines think?" (1950: 433), can be broken down into several questions of direct interest to an entrepreneurship research and practice audience. Turing pointed out that asking if machines can think necessitates asking what happens when AI takes the place of a person (Fazi, 2018). Interestingly, the inquiries laid out by Turing in 1950 centered on digital computers but apply similarly in 2018 to AI. The use of AI raises a large set of complex and intertwined research questions related to entrepreneurship, ranging from relatively straightforward questions such as how and what will unfold, the extent of viability in decision-making, and questions about ethics, governance frameworks and structure, and potential bias.

This chapter offers a set of research agendas that are especially timely and pressing, and that can help lay foundations for wider knowledge generation on AI in the entrepreneurship context. I refer to AI broadly, as the goal of this chapter is to identify key questions relevant to the entrepreneurship literature.[1] The entire range of research questions and stakeholders in this space is simply not possible to lay out, so the research agendas described in this chapter by no means represent the entirety of worthwhile questions on AI and entrepreneurship. This chapter is an attempt to scratch the surface by laying out some key research directions

---

1 However, it is important to point out that the concept of AI creates ambiguity for researchers because applications cut across many domains (Taddy, 2018) including machine learning, neural networks, natural language processing, robotics, vision, and so on. As research interest in AI and entrepreneurship grows, it will be important to consider the heterogeneity of different applications and their unique roles.

that are important as building blocks for insights on entrepreneurship, such as how AI affects firms and industries, as well as key context questions which are urgent, such as priorities for a governance framework. It is outside the scope of this chapter to discuss the use of AI in research methods and scholarship, but this is a worthwhile exploration as there is significant potential for methodological and data advancement in research.[2]

In the remainder of this chapter, I lay out three themes to organize research agendas on AI and entrepreneurship (AI and decision-making in the firm, AI and industries, and AI and stakeholders relevant to entrepreneurship), followed by a brief conclusion.

How will AI affect firms?

An important foundational research trajectory is on the microeconomics of the firm in the AI context. AI can restructure firm internal organizing activities as well as how firms evolve (see Aghion et al., 2017). AI can reshape the cost structure in a firm by itself serving as a new form of input, as well as by intermediating or processing other inputs (like data). The nuances in how, when, and what types of firms are useful avenues for future research.

AI in firms is not, in many ways, a new story. Aghion et al. (2017) point out that AI can be thought of as the latest form of automation, as were previous major technological disruptions like electricity, internal combustion engines, and semiconductors. A useful way to conceptualize AI is to consider its effects on the cost of prediction, using data[3] needed for decision-making (Agrawal et al., 2017a). AI indeed can reshape information costs, i.e. by offering faster, cheaper, and more effective ways to identify, acquire, sort, and process information. It can lower the costs of experimentation by allowing firms to generate rapid and more feedback from customers, which can affect how they engage in product development. AI could enable firms to reduce their time to market by shortening steps in the process, but it is not clear how and when this happens, and how the characteristics of the product market could matter. For example, machine learning applications – where a machine processes data with only basic instructions, finds patterns on its own, and connects them to outcomes (O'Neill, 2016) – could affect processes at very early stages of ideation and product testing.

---

2 It is also worth pointing out that while the topics discussed here specifically concern entrepreneurship, the uptake of AI is occurring across sectors, actors, and economic functions – and rapidly. Many of the research agendas in this chapter are relevant to other activities and other scholarly traditions. For example, the question of how AI affects decision-making outcomes is relevant to government agencies as much as it is to entrepreneurship support actors, like incubators and funders.

3 This increases predictive power not only because it allows firms to use existing data resources better, but it also allows them to use existing data to generate new data that may not have even been thought of as data (Mullainathan and Spiess, 2017), e.g. breaking down data embedded within images (Agrawal et al., 2017a).

The nature of these types of effects in firms – both new firms and incumbent firms – is still unraveling. Is the effect of AI on firms fairly consistent, or are there conditions under which firms do – and do not – see cost advantages from AI? Of significant value to early-stage entrepreneurs is knowing if, how, and when AI could be advantageous to them. Is the potential of AI limited to firms in some key industries or related to some specific characteristics of industries, e.g. those which are more reliant on data?

In this context, two points raised by Agrawal et al. (2017a, 2017b) lead to fruitful directions for future research. As with a decline in the price of an input, two things can be expected to happen with AI: the functions enabled by AI (in this case, functions related to information and prediction) will start to be used in other ways, and, second, the value of associated complements will rise. The second point applies to decision-making because the human dimension cannot be separate from decision-making; in fact, humans are involved in controlling and supervising technology because elements like time pressure, uncertainty, and risk cannot be mastered by machines (Johannsen, 1986). Decision-making requires – at least – both prediction and *human* judgment (see Agrawal et al., 2017a, 2017b).

While prediction can be enabled by AI, human judgment plays an important role, i.e. to factor in emotional and ethical dimensions, prioritize outcomes for firms, and so on. This means that while there may be less need for human participation in some parts of the decision-making process that become more reliant on AI, the unique component of *human judgment* in decision-making could become much more valuable (Agrawal et al., 2017a). As AI allows more and earlier data sorting and prediction, this can also open up many new questions that need decisions; this, in turn, will need more human judgment. For example, if AI provides early-stage prediction capabilities to investors, this can expand the range of entrepreneurial firms they may consider as desirable targets for investment. This becomes especially interesting when investors can make judgments about combinations of activities, like conditioning or supplementing financing with managerial or technical support.

This also implies that there should necessarily be tradeoffs between AI and human activities within the decision-making context, as a pure automation approach cannot appropriately factor human interface at the right time (see Johannsen, 1986). In fact, "role and function allocation is as much art as science" (Cummings, 2014: 8). The interaction between AI and "traditional" means of decision-making – i.e. the part that relies on human judgment, context, emotions, and feelings – represents an important area for research. These tradeoffs are at the heart of Turing's original question in 1950. This raises not only the question of the extent to which AI can replace, substitute, or strengthen human judgment in decision-making in firms, but it also raises the question of how firms – and new firms, especially – can use AI most effectively in their decision-making processes.

An important line of inquiry is how AI handles uncertainty. A related set of questions addresses how AI performs in decision-making: are there contexts and firm level characteristics where AI is appropriate and others where it is not? What is the shared space for human-automation collaboration (Cummings et al., 2011)? While AI will radically change economic activity, if humans and AI become more collaborative as each becomes more responsive to each other (Wilson and Daugherty, 2018)? Will AI be more useful for certain functions with less inherent uncertainty? The cost of innovation in firms could be reshaped by AI as it becomes a general new "method of invention," which could allow firms to take advantage of the opportunity to replace labor-intensive research with passively generated datasets and enhanced prediction algorithms (Cockburn et al., 2017).

The complexity and uncertainty surrounding tasks could play a role in understanding the partnerships and tradeoffs between humans and AI, as automated planners can "be brittle and unable to respond to emergent events" (Cummings et al., 2011: 660). Answers to this cluster of questions could shed light on how employment and labor markets may evolve over time (see Autor, 2015), which is of interest to entrepreneurs and policymakers. Similarly, how should tasks be allocated between AI and between humans – and is there an optimal or superior division of these joint "labor" resources? Research in some domains, like unmanned vehicle control, suggests that human collaboration can improve machine results in some highly complex, "real-world" scenarios, compared against tasks that need precise and rapid calculations (see Cummings, 2014; Cummings et al., 2011). Entrepreneurship is inherently "real world" in that uncertainty originating in various sources is a constant, and ever-changing, consideration for the entrepreneur (Knight, 1921). Emergent events – like droughts, floods, political change, human-induced disasters, rapid migration flows, and so on – can create uncertainty for entrepreneurs at the firm level that may not be easily understood and managed by AI, even as predictive capabilities for these types of events improve.

Research on the above questions could inform many parts of the entrepreneurial process, such as if potential entrepreneurs can use AI to assist in making the decision to enter or not, and if and when early-stage entrepreneurs should use AI. Research could shed light on how, over the lifecycle of a firm, entrepreneurs and managers should consider the tradeoff between investing in judgment-related capabilities and AI (Agrawal et al., 2017b), as the needs of a firm will change as it evolves, e.g. through periods of growth and expansion, crises and obstacles, innovation, exports, and so on.

How will AI affect industries?

Relatedly, future research could be well served by investigating the differences in uptake and use of AI among new firms and incumbent firms, and the implications for industry dynamics. A cluster of research questions addresses what happens at the industry level – and, specifically, how AI can (re)shape competitive dynamics in an industry.

This brings up the classic questions of why people start firms, and who becomes an entrepreneur (Audretsch and Thurik, 2003). For example, what kind of capabilities do new firms need to have in order to take advantage of AI? The question of where entrepreneurial firms get the knowledge inputs they need (see Audretsch and Thurik (2003)) is also salient in the AI context. Any expectation of lower costs related to AI reasonably assumes that firms will be able to acquire or develop AI, which in turn assumes that a certain level of skill or resource is available. This could have implications for the kind of preparation and background that founders in an industry need to have, which may have been different even five years ago. The kind of knowledge prioritized and rewarded in an industry could also see a corresponding change.

Also, how does AI reshape entry and the early life of a firm? Future research should investigate if, and how, entrepreneurs use AI to experiment with product design, and if costly mistakes could be avoided. If this is the case, could supporters of new firms, like investors, incubators, accelerators, and so on, consider how AI relates to the mechanisms they use to strengthen the firms they support?

Industry dynamics in the AI context are also worth examining. AI is expected to radically transform industries. Though the effects may be similar as they have been in past technological shifts (see Aghion et al., 2017), future empirical investigation at the industry level can identify priorities to enhance or mitigate specific effects within an industry. Does greater use of AI in an industry favor incumbent firms, given that entrepreneurs tend to be more resource constrained? Or does AI lower barriers to entry by reducing costs of search and experimentation for new firms? Does this vary depending on the nature of the industry, its reliance on R&D, availability and quality of data, and so on?

How will AI affect important stakeholders for entrepreneurship?

Stakeholders related to entrepreneurship

AI's proliferation is not, of course, limited to entrepreneurial firms. AI also is positioned to change the way consumers interact with firms. For example, if AI applications allow consumers to search through more data rapidly, this could cut search costs to find the products and services they want. This also implies that it has taken less time for the firm to serve the customer, and this could be meaningful for small and new firms. Researchers could study if AI reduces search costs for consumers, and how this affects entrepreneurial firms – does it play a sort of equalizing role in industries dominated by large firms, or does the nature of the underlying data being searched reinforce incumbent firm dominance?

AI will also affect many other stakeholders in their interactions with entrepreneurs, such as investors, support organizations ranging from local economic development decision makers to incubators, and policymakers. Stakeholders that serve entrepreneurs struggle with at least two critical sets of decision contexts in the process of screening and selecting firms: *eligibility* and *selection* (see World Bank, 2018). This applies to many types of investors, incubators, economic development organizations and their intermediaries, industry associations, and so on. An investor or a support organization does not have access to all the potential entrepreneurs in the universe of possibilities: some may simply not exist, and the investor is constrained by finite time and search capabilities. Narrowing down the potential pool of desirable candidates is a determination about what firms (or individuals) can be eligible for consideration or competition.

The second important decision context is around selection. For example, if AI provides early-stage prediction capabilities to investors, this can expand the range of entrepreneurial firms they may consider as desirable targets for investment. This becomes especially interesting when investors can make judgments about conditioning or supplementing financing with other types of support, like managerial or technical support.

There is limited evidence on how eligibility criteria and selection processes (Fafchamps and Woodruff, 2016; McKenzie, 2015; Scott et al., 2016) influence entrepreneurship outcomes in the pre-AI context, and research integrating AI into these questions would be a productive pursuit. For example, are business plan competitions better than psychometric surveys of entrepreneurs? Despite their growth in popularity, previous research on business plan competitions is limited in extent of explanatory power (Fafchamps and Woodruff, 2016) or explaining part of but not all desirable outcomes (see Fafchamps and Woodruff, 2016; McKenzie, 2015). How does AI influence potential tools, like business plan competitions, for screening entrepreneurs? Early findings from a business plan competition in Nigeria compares three machine learning approaches with business plan scoring from judges (McKenzie and Sansone, 2017), and finds that overall predictive power of the approaches is low, and that machine learning does not offer noticeable improvements to judges. Future research on this question in different contexts and using different settings would provide valuable insight for the work of entrepreneurship support organizations.

Do surveys which collect data from entrepreneurs become more effective determinants of future outcomes when used by AI? The use of mentors in entrepreneurship support organizations is popular, and in some interventions they may be used in the startup evaluation process. There is still limited evidence on how a constellation of mentor factors (e.g. industry experience, educational background, interests, commitment) interact with firms (e.g. firm capabilities, established revenues, founding team characteristics) and industries to evaluate and select promising firms (see Scott et al., 2016). Can AI-powered insight complement human judgment gained from watching presentations, or peer feedback based on interviews? These questions could yield useful information for the design of these frameworks for a wide range of stakeholders. For example, if AI provides stronger early-stage prediction capabilities to investors, this can expand the range of entrepreneurial firms they may consider as desirable targets for investment. This becomes especially interesting when judgments fall along a spectrum, e.g. when financing can be conditioned or supplemented with other things, like managerial or technical support.

Policy and governance questions

The use of AI – in the entrepreneurship context and in many other contexts – presents a challenge and shift for existing governance frameworks and capacities. Existing governance frameworks will need to manage the nature and the magnitude of economic changes expected with AI, presenting an opportunity – and some time pressure – to catch up quickly.

A priority for research on entrepreneurship and economic development is to better understand the implications of AI for the basic characteristics of firms. For example, AI could boost firm productivity at the same as it could restructure a firm's need for workers who would have otherwise provided the same information and prediction functions. This could mean that as AI continues to proliferate, average firm size may get smaller while firm functions are more reliant on technology (see Agrawal et al., 2018), raising questions for future research on the role of entrepreneurship in driving job creation (Haltiwanger et al., 2013) and how the sources of new jobs may evolve in the future with AI (see Autor, 2015).

Stevenson (2018) describes two important questions for policy (Agrawal et al., 2018): the employment question, which asks what humans will do as jobs transform, and the income question, which asks what will happen to income distribution. These questions have important implications for entrepreneurs and managers, employees, as well as industry regulators and policymakers. Greater understanding of the effect of AI on employment structure, and on where and what kind of jobs exist, is relevant to a wide range of decisions about resources, including those in domains related to education policy and content, tax administration especially at the local level, industry regulation, labor market regulation, and employment-related economic interventions, e.g. unemployment programs, job training, and so on.

Another research agenda is around how AI will change what we know about the importance of local conditions for entrepreneurship – in other words, can (and will) AI play a sort of equalizing role for future entrepreneurs? The role of place is a consistent (unchanging) condition for entrepreneurs (Audretsch et al., 2018), as are advantages of knowledge spillovers, agglomeration economies, and so on (see Audretsch et al., 2006). If AI reduces reliance on local human capital engaged in information and prediction functions, could this affect entrepreneurs in otherwise less entrepreneurially active places? Will AI change opportunities and resources to the extent that what we know about the local dimensions of entrepreneurship (see Glaeser et al., 2014) will also change significantly? Does it mean that local employment and economic growth gains from entrepreneurship (Audretsch et al., 2015) start to become less local? These questions are especially relevant for regional and local stakeholders. For example, if AI enables prediction for entrepreneurs who otherwise do not have local access to human capital needed for prediction, this could mean greater opportunities. Economic development strategies, many of which are place based, can be better informed by answers to these questions in order to be responsive as the needs of potential entrepreneurs may change.

The discussion above highlights some governance and policy challenges for AI in the entrepreneurship context. In the policy context, even if the "right" answer can be predicted, other factors can still be important determinants of adoption and uptake (Mullainathan and Spiess, 2017). Governance practices face many questions brought about by AI, including questions of ethics, opportunity and access, and accountability. For example, what happens if machines cheat? Or what happens if machines overoptimize one metric but not a desired outcome for the firm (see Agrawal et al., 2017a)?

AI also brings risks associated with the nature of the underlying data, training methodologies, and assumptions (see Noble, 2018; O'Neill, 2016). This goes beyond simply the question of how to govern, regulate, and manage AI. This necessitates greater consideration of social justice and ethics (Cooke et al., 2016) in the entre-preneurship literature. Machines are taught by people. People can have biases (see Kahneman, 2011), and therefore machines can learn bias, introducing it into the algorithms they use to make predictions. These predictions could be used, for example, by investors to determine what founders will be expected to achieve strong firm performance (i.e. representing good targets for investment), leading to investment decisions being generated from an algorithm that was programmed by a human with bias. Even when bias is not explicitly introduced into an algorithm, gaps in target populations could create challenges for policy.[4]

AI and big data

An important consideration is that technologies and infrastructure enabling "big data" could make tools like AI more relevant to firms, because data is both more plentiful and more available. How the phenomenon of AI and big data are connected is an important consideration for entrepreneurship research. If entrepreneurial firms use machines because they offer advantages of greater predictive ability from big data, they also expose themselves to the possible underlying biases embedded in what machines learn. This could mean machines leave things out or could simply lead to them being inaccurate or wrong (see Turing, 1950) if the underlying data is inadequate or biased (Noble, 2018). For firms with limited resources, like small and new firms, recovering from mistakes could be more difficult than for incumbents. The nature of machine learning, for example, is such that the machine learns from ever-growing amounts of data. Learning from layers of data upon data upon data means that understanding the nature of the data itself is crucial (Noble, 2018), as

---

4 For example, Lambrecht and Tucker (2018) studied the delivery of STEM career ads and found that an algorithm designed to prioritize cost-effectiveness will deliver ads intended to be gender neutral in an apparently discrimina-tory way (due to crowding out).

is managing bias early (O'Neill, 2016). If the underlying data is biased, such as in construction or the method of acquisition, or if the human providing the training introduces bias, this will affect the predictions made by machines. This draws attention to the risk that AI could further embed existing biases in entrepreneurship, biases which are evident in the differences in the attempts and outcomes among men and women founders, for example. At the same time, AI could enable firms to spot mistakes sooner, so an important question is on the nature and magnitude of these types of risk associated with predictions from AI.

The intersection of big data with AI comes with opportunity and perhaps not yet fully appreciated risks. Concerns about a race for data among firms seeking control over high-value, large datasets and algorithms (see Cockburn et al., 2017) may not be misplaced, and such behavior could affect entry barriers and the competitive dynamics in industries. Entrepreneurs can be concerned with many outcomes, including things like personal satisfaction and future family succession, that cannot easily be captured by machine functions. Another question is what happens if AI leads to a discriminatory decision based on the data? These questions filter into the entrepreneurship literature because investors and entrepreneurship support organizations make selection decisions based on prediction.

Conclusion

AI carries tremendous promise for entrepreneurship, the full potential of which represents a large research agenda. This relationship is ripe for study and comprises many dimensions related to individuals, firms, industries, and a wide range of users and consumers. In addition to some early studies on this relationship (e.g. McKenzie and Sansone, 2017; see Agrawal et al., 2018), a growing body of work from other fields can inform studies in entrepreneurship. It is productive for future research agendas to consider a strong user orientation. Future research could also be well served by paying attention to the heterogeneity of AI domains (see Taddy, 2018) as they proliferate more into the entrepreneurship context. Finally, future research could strongly consider the tradeoffs and settings for human-machine interaction, as well as the advantages and potential risks associated with AI.

References

Agrawal, A., Gans, J. and Goldfarb, A. (2017a) "How AI will change the way we make decisions," *Harvard Business Review*.

Agrawal, A., Gans, J. and Goldfarb, A. (2017b) "The simple economics of machine intelligence," *Harvard Business Review*.

Agrawal, A., Gans, J. and Goldfarb, A. (2018) (eds) *The Economics of Artificial Intelligence: An Agenda*, Chicago, IL: University of Chicago Press.

Aghion, P., Jones, B. and Jones, C. (2017) "Artificial intelligence and economic growth," NBER Working Paper 23928.

Audretsch, D. and Thurik, R. (2003) "Entrepreneurship, industry evolution and economic growth," in Koppl, R., Birner, J. and Kurrild-Klitgaard, P. (eds.), *Austrian Economics and Entrepreneurial Studies*, Volume 6, pp. 39–56, Bingley, UK: Emerald Group Publishing.

Audretsch, D., Keilbach, M. and Lehmann, E. (2006) *Entrepreneurship and Economic Growth*, Oxford: Oxford University Press.

Audretsch, D., Belitski, M. and Desai, S. (2015) "Entrepreneurship and economic development in cities," *The Annals of Regional Science*, **55** (1): 33–60.

Audretsch, D., Belitski, M. and Desai, S. (2018) "National business regulations and city entrepreneurship: A nested multilevel analysis," *Entrepreneurship Theory and Practice*. doi.org/10.1177/1042258718774916

Autor, D. (2015) "Why are there still so many jobs? The history and future of workplace automation," *Journal of Economic Perspectives*, **29** (3): 3–30.

Cockburn, I., Henderson, R. and Stern, S. (2017) "The impact of artificial intelligence on innovation," NBER Working Paper 24449.

Cooke, N., Sweeney, N. and Noble, S. (2016) "Social justice as topic and tool: An attempt to transform an LIS curriculum and culture," *The Library Quarterly*, 86(1): 107–24.

Cummings, M. (2014) "Man versus machine or man + machine," *IEEE Intelligent Systems*, **29** (5): 62–9.

Cummings, M., How, J., Whitten, A. and Troupet, O. (2011) "The impact of human-automation collaboration in decentralized multiple unmanned vehicle control," *Proceedings of the IEEE*, **100** (3): 6606–71.

Fafchamps, M. and Woodruff, C. (2016) "Identifying gazelles: Expert panels vs. surveys as a means to identify firms with rapid growth potential," World Bank Policy Research Working Paper 7647.

Fazi, B. (2018) "Can a machine think (anything new)? Automation beyond simulation," *AI and Society*. doi.org/10.10007/s00146-018-0821-0

Glaeser, E., Ponzetto, G. and Tobio, K. (2014) "Cities, skills and regional change," *Regional Studies*, **48** (1): 7–43.

Haltiwanger, J., Jarmin, R. and Miranda, J. (2013) "Who creates jobs? Small versus large versus young," *Review of Economics and Statistics*, **95** (2): 347–61.

Johannsen, G. (1986) "Architecture of man – machine decision making systems," in Hollnagel, E. et al. (eds.), *Intelligent Decision Support in Process Environments*, Berlin Heidelberg: Springer-Verlag.

Kahneman, D. (2011) *Thinking, Fast and Slow*, New York: Farrar, Straus and Giroux.

Knight, F. (1921) *Risk, Uncertainty, and Profit*, Boston and New York: Houghton Mifflin.

Lambrecht, A. and Tucker, C. (2018) "Algorithmic bias? An empirical study into apparent gender-based discrimination in the display of STEM career ads," Working Paper, March.

McKenzie, D. (2015) "Identifying and spurring high-growth entrepreneurship: Experimental evidence from a business plan competition," World Bank Policy Research Working Paper 7391.

McKenzie, D. and Sansone, D. (2017) "Man vs. machine in predicting successful entrepreneurs: Evidence from a business plan competition in Nigeria," World Bank Policy Research Working Paper 8271.

Mullainathan, S. and Spiess, J. (2017) "Machine learning: An applied econometric approach," *Journal of Economic Perspectives*, **31** (2): 87–106.

Noble, S. (2018) *Algorithms of Oppression: How Search Engines Reinforce Racism*, New York: New York University Press.

O'Neill, C. (2016) *Weapons of Math Destruction: How Big Data Increases Inequality and Threatens Democracy*, New York: Crown Publishers.

Scott, E., Shu, P. and Lubynsky, R. (2016) "Are "better" ideas more likely to succeed? An empirical analysis of startup evaluation," Harvard Business School Working Paper 16-013.

Stevenson, B. (2018) "AI, income, employment, and meaning," in Agarwal, A., Gans, J. and Goldfarb, A. (eds.), *The Economics of Artificial Intelligence: An Agenda*, Chicago, IL: University of Chicago Press.

Taddy, M. (2018) "The technological elements of artificial intelligence," NBER Working Paper No. 24301.

Turing, A. (1950) "Computing machinery and intelligence," *Mind*, **49**: 433–60.

Wilson, J. and Daugherty, P. (2018) "Collaborative intelligence: Humans and AI are joining forces," *Harvard Business Review*, July–August.

World Bank (2018) "The search for unicorns: Facts and fiction of high-growth entrepreneurship in developing countries," World Bank Report.

14 Entrepreneurship studies: the case for radical change

Mark Casson

Introduction

This chapter advances a challenging and potentially unpopular proposition: namely that entrepreneurship studies needs to re-engage with classic social science disciplines such as economics, history, statistics, geography and sociology if it is to progress. It may be a branch of business and management studies, but it cannot thrive solely in that environment. The classic social science disciplines provide essential techniques of analysis and, in their traditional form, share a methodology that helps to guarantee the quality of published research. In many areas of entrepreneurship studies, the techniques employed are too simple, and the methodologies employed too varied, to guarantee the quality of research.

Journal editors maintain that new research must build on the foundations of the old. This would be fine if those foundations were sound. But certain parts of entrepreneurship studies are, arguably, like houses built upon sand, to use a Biblical analogy; they do not provide a secure basis for future research. Compared to early work in the field, many recent papers appear to be based on weak technique and poor methodology. It is necessary to dig down further, and, like an archaeologist, go back in time, until secure foundations for future research are reached. That time was 50 years ago or more, it is suggested here.

This proposition is a special case of a more general proposition, namely that business and management studies as a whole faces a crisis of academic credibility. Within this field, international business studies, organisational studies and leadership studies face similar problems (Casson, 2018). Each has an enormous literature, comprising many papers, each of which contains an extensive literature review. Each researcher cites other researchers, who quickly amass an impressive list of citations. Most citations are to papers in the same field, rather than to relevant papers in other fields. Each field becomes a silo; each silo reinvents the same set of concepts that are used in other silos, but gives those concepts a different name (Goldsmith, Komlos and Gold, 2001). If a researcher in one field consults the literature in another field, he or she may learn very little because what they will discover is the same ideas repackaged under different names. Anyone who is new to the field simply gets confused.

Unified social science: a missed opportunity?

Fifty years ago, by contrast, there was greater interaction between social science disciplines. It was believed that it was possible to construct a unified social science that would command the same respect as the natural sciences. It would not be the same as a natural science because it would focus not on atoms and atomic structure but on people and their social structures. Politics would study how people governed themselves, economics how they made a living, psychology how people made decisions, linguistics how people communicated, and sociology how people interacted within the family and other social groups. The post-war business schools were seen as a useful laboratory for piloting the development of this unified social science. Bringing together people from different social sciences to study business would demonstrate how different disciplines could work together to develop a better understanding of business, and to promote improved business performance. The lessons learned from interdisciplinary research on business could then be rolled out to other subject areas.

A promising start was made. Most of the scholars recruited to business schools had been trained in one of the traditional disciplines. With the exception of the Marxists, there was general agreement on the kind of methodology that would guarantee the reliability of research results. Compliance with this methodology was believed to guarantee the reliability of research results. The methodology had general consent and was perceived as a "gold standard" for the quality of published research.

Traditional research methodology

The methodology which guided research at this time may be summarised as follows (Rescher, 1977). It had four main elements.

Results should be *meaningful*.

- A *small number of key concepts* should be employed. Each concept should be *carefully defined*, to avoid misleading connotations (e.g. "capital" has many possible meanings and using it in different ways within the same discussion can create confusion).
- The scope of the study should be set out and *the context described in detail* (e.g. the population of firms from which a sample has been taken). This avoids spurious generalisations from specific results.
- The results should be written up *precisely and grammatically* to make their meaning clear (e.g. excessive use of jargon can mislead).

Evidence should be *reliable*.

- A research study may offer new evidence or rework existing evidence.

- New sources *widen the evidence base* and lead to more robust results. But they need to be carefully validated (e.g. is the sample biased? Has data entry been checked for accuracy?).
- Research should be *replicable*. Replication is a valuable check on previous work.

Interpretation should be *rigorous*.

- Evidence does not speak for itself; it needs to be interpreted. This requires a *theory*. A theory consists of one or more *hypotheses*. Hypotheses should be deduced from a common set of *assumptions*.
- Assumptions should be made *explicit*. This facilitates discussion and debate.
- A theory should be *simple*. For this reason, *the assumptions should exclude those aspects of the problem that do not relate directly to what the theory seeks to explain.*
- A theory should have a clear *logical structure*. A good theory is a *general theory*; it effects economy of thought. Because it needs to apply to different situations it must include *contingent* factors (e.g. a general theory of entrepreneurship should take account of different forms of entrepreneurship).
- A theory should *predict* specific *patterns* in the evidence. Otherwise it cannot *explain* anything, and so the validity of the theory cannot be *tested*.

Results should be *relevant*.

- Research may satisfy personal curiosity (e.g. explaining anomalies or paradoxes). A *culture of curiosity* stimulates research. Research results should therefore be presented in an *engaging and entertaining way* to reach as wide an audience as possible.
- Researchers should *engage with policy and practice* by developing the practical implications of their results. But the *ethical implications* should be considered too.

Although this methodology is still pursued by some "traditionalists" in the social sciences, its influence has declined, especially in businesses studies. It has lost ground to a range of "modernist" methodologies.

Modernist methodologies

Modernist methodologies are characterised by concerns for pluralism (e.g. toleration of minority opinions) and political correctness (e.g. avoiding demeaning descriptions of vulnerable social groups). They tend to favour research methods derived from the arts (e.g. literary criticism) rather than the sciences (e.g. neoclassical economics). Three of the most common modernist methodologists are examined below.

Free-thinking

According to free-thinkers, traditional methodology is an instrument of social power by which researchers are coerced into following a pseudo-scientific approach. Methodology should be a matter of personal choice, they affirm. Those who make similar personal choices should be free to associate together, creating special interest groups that publish their own journals and organise their own conferences. Members who gain faculty positions should seek to influence recruitment in their institution in order to create a cell with a critical mass of like-minded researchers.

Free-thinkers position themselves in opposition to the traditionalist elite, as they perceive it. Traditionalist publications are simply advocacy packaged in pseudo-scientific jargon, they claim. Economists produce forecasts that serve the interests of right-wing governments, while traditional business historians write business biographies that uncritically glorify the founders of the firm. Everything is advocacy, and the role of the scholar is to expose it. This has two unfortunate implications. First, free-thinkers tend to the use the literature as a source of evidence rather than looking behind the literature to re-examine the evidence on which it is based. "Well, they would say that, wouldn't they?" is a common theme in free-thinking critiques of the literature. Second, if everything is advocacy then the best papers are the most compelling pieces of advocacy. Thus, much of the free-thinking literature seems to exemplify the very thing it sets out to criticise; namely, advocacy masquerading as research.

Inspirational thinking

Inspirational thinking is popular among entrepreneurship researchers. It is a form of intellectual innovation that can be made by people who lack the resources to make a practical innovation. Typically, a problem with conventional theory is identified. This may arise from the discovery of some new phenomenon which, it is alleged, conventional theory cannot explain. The answer is a new concept, which appears to the researcher in a "Eureka moment". The concept is labelled by a buzz-word, and the word is linked to the name of the researcher who thought of it first. "Strategy" is the oldest, and still the most popular, business buzz-word, it would seem, although "vision", "charisma", "competence" and "capability" are popular too. All of them apply, it seems, to the successful entrepreneur (Casson and della Giusta, 2013).

Ethical thinking

Ethical thinking combines elements of inspiration and free-thinking. While free-thinkers operate mainly through organised groups, and inspirational thinkers by individual initiative, ethical thinkers combine the two. Ethical thinkers prefer to test theories by the perceived morality of their policy implications rather than by the weight of evidence in their favour. They are particularly active in gender studies and the emerging field of "history of capitalism". Traditional methodology, some argue, serves to legitimate the immoral. It normalises assumptions that property is private, action is rational, and profit is a reward. For ethical thinkers, the role of evidence is mainly as a source of supporting anecdotes for a chosen policy stance, rather than a valuable resource to be quarried for the information it contains. Contemporary ethical thinking is particularly important in gender studies and industrial relations, where traditionalists often seem to have little to say on high-profile policy issues.

The switch to modernism

Why have modernist methodologies become so popular? Three main factors may be identified.

Modernist methodologies make less use of formal models, mathematical methods and advanced statistical techniques. They make a research career accessible to a wider range of people. The first generation of scholars recruited to post-war business schools mostly came from traditional disciplines. Business economists developed theories of competitive strategy, sociologists developed theories of managerial bureaucracy, statisticians developed theories of inventory management and process control, while business historians researched the "managerial revolution" and the apparent decline of family firms. They all had specialist research techniques at their disposal (Beissel-Durrant, 2004).

However, the rapid expansion of business schools in the 1970s and 1980s led to growing recruitment of scholars who had no training in a traditional discipline but had simply studied business from the outset. They were often teaching business practitioners from a variety backgrounds, and so lack of technique was no hindrance to a teaching career. As these new recruits rose to prominence in their profession, they changed the rules to reward themselves. They gained control of leading journals, and banished techniques derived from traditional disciplines. Journals began to publish papers that cited "gurus" and "thought leaders" rather than traditional researchers. The new generation marginalised the "technocratic elite" that they replaced.

Modernist methodologies make less use of primary evidence. The first generation of business researchers compiled their own databases from business accounts, censuses of production, VAT registrations, and so on. They carried out in-depth, face-to-face interviews with entrepreneurs. Today, databases are downloaded off the internet, but the evidence, it seems, is rarely checked because there is so much of it. Meanwhile comprehensive interview programmes have been abandoned because many entrepreneurs can no longer spare the time. Research time is scarce for the academic too. Methods that rely on low-cost evidence produced by third parties are therefore preferable to traditional methods dependent on high-cost evidence. Research continues to be published, but much of the evidence is of lower quality than before.

Finally, modernist methodologies generate results that are better adapted to mass dissemination. If the final stage of research is to write an executive summary or a press release, or give a radio interview then why bother with all the intervening complications? Why not devise a simple buzz-word, find a couple of anecdotes and announce the result? You can then add a literature review and publish a paper that anyone can understand, and that may get lots of cites.

This cavalier approach to evidence and authenticity has serious implications for the profession, however. In law and medicine evidence is crucial because a person's life may depend on it being right. Law and medicine are both traditional in their methodology. Both involve "trials" which test alternative views in a highly structured manner. Legal trials, for example, are preceded by detective work, regulated by strict rules governing the admissibility of evidence, involve the testimony of witnesses who are cross-examined before an independent third party, namely a judge. Trials between alternative views in business studies are, by comparison, relatively rare. By contrast, conference debates on fundamental issues are uncommon, and speakers are rarely forced to engage with their opponents in a meaningful way.

Economic dynamics of entrepreneurship: a traditionalist view

Modernists, of course, do not explain their popularity in these terms. They focus on the alleged shortcomings of the traditional approach. They allege, for example, that traditional disciplines like economics are based on static equilibrium thinking and therefore ignore the dynamics of entrepreneurship. They claim that assumptions are absurd, being based on a form of perfect rationality that is incompatible with entrepreneurial decision-making. Above all, they claim to study "process", which they say is fundamentally different to studying an equilibrium state. By emphasising the shortcomings of the traditional approach, they divert attention from the shortcomings of their own approach, as outlined above.

These criticisms of the traditional approach represent "outsider" criticism. They are criticisms of how a methodology appears to those who do not use it. They are not "insider" criticism, expressed by those who understand traditional methodology and who are aware of its weaknesses in certain areas. Consider, for example, the assumption of perfect rationality mentioned above. If a research question concerns the personal psychology of the entrepreneur, then the assumption is unhelpful because it assumes the answer before the question has been investigated. But if the question is "How do businesses grow?" then it is less objectionable: it is likely that growing businesses are managed in a reasonably rational way because otherwise they would fail to grow. Managers of growing businesses may not be perfectly rational, but they are probably more rational than the managers of businesses that fail to grow. Thus, the relevance of an assumption depends on the research question being asked: as noted earlier, the role of assumptions is to focus attention on factors that really matter in the context of the problem and to abstract from factors that do not.

Traditional methods do not ignore dynamics. Dynamics are critical to analysing the stability of a system. The stability of general equilibrium in a multi-market system, for example, is analysed in terms of changes in price that are driven, in speed and direction, by the magnitude of excess demand (Arrow and Hahn, 1971). In other words, the speed of market adjustment is governed by the deviation of prices from their equilibrium levels.

The difference between traditionalists and modernists is not that traditionalists ignore dynamics but that traditionalists believe that economic and social systems are mostly stable. Whenever the environment changes, the system changes, but it changes in a way that restores equilibrium. The system adapts, in other words. This process may take some time, but although the system is often out of equilibrium it is always tending towards one. Modernists, on the other hand, tend to argue that the system just evolves. One thing follows from another but there is little direction or purpose to it; anything can happen because evolution is blind.

But even biological evolution – a favourite source of modernist metaphors – has direction to it. Darwin's theory of natural selection is based, in part, on the Malthusian economic theory of competition (Vorzimmer, 1969). Natural selection weeds out inefficient species, so that in the long run only efficient species survive. Thus, in the long run equilibrium prevails. As the environment changes, so the forces of natural selection change direction too.

The business system is just another system, from this perspective. Profit seeking and competition are the economic drivers of the business system. Genuine opportunities make profits and fake opportunities make losses. Entrepreneurs with good judgement succeed and those with poor judgement fail. Good judgement tends to drive out bad judgement, and equilibrium prevails once the process is complete (Casson, 2003; Foss and Klein, 2012). Even "disruptive" technological change is part of this process because it eliminates inefficiencies in technology and so helps good judgement to prevail.

In the context of entrepreneurship studies, Markov chains provide a useful tool of dynamic analysis. They are ideal for analysing the growth and decline of firms in an industry. They were first applied in this context by the Nobel Laureate Herbert Simon some 50 years ago, and are still used today, but remain underutilised in modern entrepreneurship studies (Ijiri and Simon, 1964).

Some simple examples of Markov chain analysis are described below (for a review see Stroock, 2014). The technical details have been omitted, but the methods are so well known that good accounts appear in Wikipedia and various mathematics teaching websites. Only the first of these examples has been extensively applied elsewhere. The other examples have a distinctive "entrepreneurship" twist and are therefore novel to some extent. Consider, therefore, a group of 100 potential entrepreneurs who are looking for opportunities in an emerging industry. Suppose that in each period on average 30 per cent of entrepreneurs who have not yet entered the industry believe that they have discovered an opportunity and decide to establish a firm. Entrepreneurs who have established a firm experience a failure rate of 10 per cent over the same period. In steady-state industry equilibrium the 30 per cent who enter must match the 10 per cent who fail, for otherwise the average number of firms will change. Thus, the population of entrepreneurs who manage firms must be three times the size of the population that do not. Thus, in the steady state there are 75 firms and 25 entrepreneurs still searching for an opportunity (as either employees or unemployed). The industry is stable: whatever the initial number of firms, the industry will always converge on this steady state. The speed with which the industry converges is greater, the greater the volatility in the system. The speed of convergence is greater, the greater the sum of the firm formation rate and the firm failure rate. The speed of convergence is also greater, the greater the divergence between the initial state and the steady state. In an emerging industry the initial state is one with no firms, and so the greater the number of steady-state firms, the faster the industry will grow. All of this is easy to prove by elementary calculation. Furthermore, the basic technique can be extended to far more complex, and therefore more realistic, cases.

The second example presents an extension of this analysis that involves both large and small firms (see Figure 14.1). Small firms can grow large through innovation, but they run a risk of failure if the market changes or they lack organisational capability. Decision-making is rational but myopic: small firms decide to innovate on the basis of information available to them while they are small, and they need to reconsider their decision in the light of experience. If they do not innovate, they do not discover, but they do not consider every possible thing that they might discover before they innovate. This means that managers are rational in the way that they use the information they possess but they are not far-sighted and not perfectly informed. This may sound complicated, but in practice it is easy to analyse.

To vary the numbers, suppose that the birth rate of firms, driven by opportunity discovery, is lower at 20 per cent, and the failure rate for small firms is higher at 30 per cent. Only 10 per cent of small firms innovate to grow large, but these firms perform relatively well; their failure rate is only 10 per cent. These numbers have been chosen to generate a simple result: in the steady state half of the firms are small and half are large. The total number of firms is the same as before, however; three-quarters of the entrepreneurs are managing a firm and the other quarter are still looking for opportunities. Analysing the dynamics shows that the number of large firms is slow to grow to its steady-state level because the innovation rate is relatively modest, and so convergence on the steady state is slower than before. By contrast, if the innovation rate were higher then the steady-state number of large firms would be higher, the number of small firms would be lower, and convergence to the steady state would be faster.

The third example involves entrepreneurial learning. Learning can be analysed using the same technique, and so can serial entrepreneurship. All that is necessary is to postulate two kinds of firm founder: the novice entrepreneur who has

Entrepreneur: They are seeking an opportunity. They are not managing a firm; they are an employee or are unemployed (state 0).

Entrepreneur: They may believe that they have identified an opportunity. If so, they decide to establish firm (enter state 1).

Reality: Entrepreneur in state 1 gains experience which they feed back into their next decision.

Entrepreneur: In the light of feedback the entrepreneur decides whether to scale up through innovation (to state 2), remain small (in state 1) or close down (re-enter state 0).

Entrepreneur: They innovate and become the owner and manager of a large firm (enter state 2).

Reality: The entrepreneur gains experience to feed back into their next decision.

Entrepreneur: In the light of feedback the entrepreneur decides whether to continue with a large firm (remain in state 2) or close down (enter state 0).

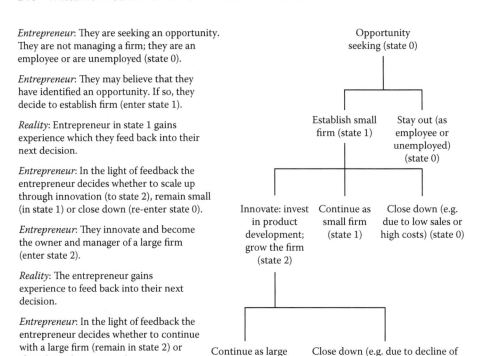

Note: These options relate to a given individual and the growth of a single firm. There are other options too, but their inclusion would complicate the figure. An entrepreneur may replicate a successful small firm start-up (perhaps with minor variations) and become a portfolio entrepreneur. An entrepreneur whose firm fails might not exit entrepreneurship but instead might learn from their mistake and re-enter as a serial entrepreneur. An individual can, in principle, sell out at any stage, although in practice it is easier to sell a large successful firm (e.g. through a share issue) than sell a small firm as a going concern.

Figure 14.1   Decision tree analysis of firm foundation and survival

either never founded a firm or has learned nothing from a previous failure, and the experienced entrepreneur who has learned something from a previous failure. The two groups have different propensities to start a business and different propensities to fail. A new equilibrium condition requires that the number of experienced entrepreneurs setting up new firms is equal to the number of firm failures with learning. Once again, the system is stable, and volatility (a high propensity to start new businesses and a high propensity to fail) leads to rapid convergence, as before. The solution of the equations determines both the numbers of novice and experienced entrepreneurs who are seeking an opportunity and also the numbers who are managing firms.

Anyone could have published these examples at any time in the last 50 years, but no one did so. In the light of the previous discussion, the most probable explanation is that no one was willing to publish them, and that this was so obvious that no one even bothered to try. Had such a paper been submitted for publication the response may have been: "There is nothing original; everyone knows this already." While the first part of this criticism would be true, the second half is almost certainly false; many entrepreneurship scholars would not have known it already. Another response could have been classic outsider criticism: "The approach is oversim-plified and mechanistic; furthermore, it assumes that the propensities are stable over time, whereas we all know that they change." Here the second part is true but the first is false; the approach is probabilistic rather than mechanistic, and therefore does justice to the notion that only statistical averages can be predicted where entrepreneurship is concerned. Simple techniques are always vulnerable to criticism because of the strong assumptions that they make. The solution is not less technique, but more sophisticated technique. But sophisticated technique is more difficult to understand and requires the professional specialism of the traditional researcher.

Conclusion

The case for traditionalism has two main pillars. The first is the weaknesses of the modernist critique, and the second is the numerous positive advantages that it provides. Traditionalism is fundamentally progressive because it lays secure foundations on which future research can build. Traditional knowledge therefore accumulates over time, as knowledge should. It gives a field of study reputation with scholars working in related fields. Standardisation on methodology facilitates the movement of ideas across fields, while the reputation of each field gives scholars in other fields the confidence to import ideas.

Traditional methodology does not need to be modified to address the criticisms of modernists, because these criticisms are largely misplaced. The criticisms derive mainly from the fact that many modernists do not fully understand the techniques that they are criticising. There are many valid criticisms of traditional methods, but they are specific criticisms of the way that specific techniques are applied to specific issues; they are well-informed insider criticism and they provide a dynamic for self-improvement within traditional methodology. Entrepreneurship studies needs to address this methodological problem by recruiting more scholars with a command of traditional disciplines, and by facing up to the serious limitation of modernist methodologies.

References

Arrow, Kenneth J. and Frank Hahn (1971) *General Competitive Analysis*, San Francisco, CA: Holden-Day.

Beissel-Durrant, Gabriele (2004) *A Typology of Research Methods within the Social Sciences*, London: Economic and Social Research Council, National Centre for Research Methods.

Casson, Mark (2003) *The Entrepreneur: An Economic Theory*, 2nd ed., Cheltenham, UK and Northampton, MA, USA: Edward Elgar.

Casson, Mark (2018) The theory of international business: the role of economic models, *Management International Review*, **58** (3), 363–87.

Casson, Mark and Marina della Giusta (2013) Buzz words in international management education, in D. Tsang, H.H. Kazeroony and G. Ellis (eds), *Routledge Companion to International Business Education*, Abingdon: Routledge, pp. 344–57.

Foss, Nicolai and Peter G. Klein (2012) *Organizing Entrepreneurial Judgment: A New Approach to the Firm*, Cambridge: Cambridge University Press.

Goldsmith, John A., John Komlos and Penny Shine Gold (2001) *The Chicago Guide to Your Academic Career*, Chicago, IL: University of Chicago Press.

Ijiri, Yuji and Herbert A. Simon (1964) Business firm growth and size, *American Economic Review*, **54** (2), 77–89.

Rescher, Nicholas (1977) *Methodological Pragmatism: A Systems-theoretic Approach to the Theory of Knowledge*, New York: New York University Press.

Stroock, Daniel W. (2014) *An Introduction to Markov Processes*, 2nd ed., Berlin: Springer.

Vorzimmer, Peter (1969) Darwin, Malthus and the theory of natural selection, *Journal of the History of Ideas*, **30** (4), 527–42.

Index

Aamoucke, R. 79
academic entrepreneurship 40–50, 109, 122
    leadership in the academic community 168–77
    role of entrepreneurial universities 107–24
    student entrepreneurship in university
        ecosystems 155–65
accelerators 41, 45, 49–50, 156–7, 159, 201
Accumulation Regimes approach 5, 7–9, 11
Achtenhagen, L. 185–6
Agarwal, A. 199
Aghion, P. 198
Aglietta, M. 7
alumni impact surveys 30–38
Ambos, T. 56
Ambrosini, V. 159
analogies see metaphors
Anderson, A. 190
Anderson, D.W. 140
angel funding 155
Antonelli, C. 2
Ardichvili, A. 61
artificial intelligence 197–205
Astebro, T. 82
Audretsch, D.B. 91, 112, 115
Autio, E. 109, 157
Avram, G. 163, 165

Baglieri, D. 59
Baker, T. 185
Balgieri, D. 60
banks 16
barriers to entry 18, 74, 205
barriers to growth 37
Bateson, G. 189
Baumol, W.J. 108
Bayh-Dole Act 115, 168
Behfar, K.J. 141
Bell, E. 191
Berglund, K.A.E. 191
bias 13, 18, 80, 84, 197, 204–5
big data 204–5
Big Five approach 82

boards of directors 134–5, 137–44
Boehm, D. 59–60
Bonardo, D. 43
boundary spanning 55–70
Bowman, C. 159
Boyer, R. 7–8
Brexit 45, 107
Breznitz, S. 2
British Household Panel 85
Brown, R. 122
Bruni, E. 187–8
Brush, C.G. 171
business models 81, 119
business plan competition 46
business schools 33, 35, 45–6, 156–7, 165, 209,
    212

Cabrera, A.F. 30–32
Cardon, M.S. 188
Cardozo, R.N. 61
Carter, C. 163, 165
Casati, A. 59–62
Casson, M. 3
Castellacci, F. 5
Castro, C.B. 137, 140
CEOs 135–6, 139, 143, 150–54
Chandler, A. 1
Chandler, G.N. 68
Chiesa, V. 56
Chubin, D.E. 58
Civera, A. 2, 42–4
Clark, B.R. 107
Clarke, J. 186, 190
Cockburn, I.M. 55
Cognitive Capitalism approach 9
commercialization 2, 40–41, 45–6, 48–9, 55, 57,
    59, 63–6, 68, 75, 81, 86, 107, 109, 115–18,
    122, 169
competitiveness 1, 6–8, 57, 107–8, 115, 118,
    123–4, 214
    monopolistic competition 12, 16, 20
Cornelissen, J.P. 186

corporate governance 134–44
corporate growth regimes 15, 17–19
crowdfunding 157, 184
Crunchbase 164
Cunningham, J. 2, 56–7, 59–60, 62–4, 68

Dalziel, T. 139
Darwin, C. 214
Davison, J. 190–91
De Koning, A. 187
Dean, H. 168, 170, 174, 176
Desai, S. 3
DeTienne, D.R. 68
digital technology 20, 47, 107, 121–3, 192
    see also artificial intelligence
disability 117
division of labour 6, 14, 19
Djokovic, D. 40
Dodd, S.D. 187

École de la régulation 7–8
economies of scale and scope 18
ecosystems, entrepreneurial and innovative 41,
    47, 49, 63, 65, 67, 107, 119, 121–3, 155–65
Eesley, C. 34, 36–7
Elfenbein, D.W. 82
entrepreneurial ecosystems 41, 47, 49, 63, 65, 67,
    107, 109, 119, 121–3, 155–65
entrepreneurs in residence 155, 161–2
entrepreneurship 1–2
    academic *see* academic entrepreneurship
    and artificial intelligence 197–205
    case for radical change 208–17
    corporate governance 134–44
    different perspective on 179–92
    entrepreneurial growth regimes 14–17, 22,
        24–5
    heroic entrepreneurs 173–4, 176, 186–8, 191
    leadership in the academic community 168–77
    measuring impact through alumni impact
        surveys 30–38
    principal investigators and recognition 55–70
    public and policy entrepreneurship 91–105
    regional emergence of innovative start-ups
        74–86
    role of entrepreneurial universities 107–24
    and Schumpeterian growth regimes 14–17,
        20–21
    scientific 20–22, 25, 46–7, 56–7, 62–3, 65–70,
        109, 169
    see also principal investigators
    spillover 21–2

see also knowledge spillovers
    student entrepreneurship in university
        ecosystems 155–65
entry barriers 18, 74, 205
ethics and social responsibility 49–50, 116, 197,
    199, 204, 211–12
Ettl, K. 185
Etzkowitz, H. 112
European Commission 40
Ewell, P. 31

family firms 151, 179, 181, 191, 205, 212
Feeney, M.K. 59
Fini, R. 158
Finkelstein, S. 137, 140
firm size 6, 10, 15, 25
first-mover advantage 179
Florida, R. 81–2
Ford, J. 168, 170, 174, 176
Fordism 7–8, 23
Freeman, C. 5
free-thinking 211
Fritsch, M. 2, 79–80, 158

Gaddefors, J. 188
Gaebler, T. 94–5
Galloway, L. 171
Gartner, W.B. 182–3, 190, 192
Gates, B. 81
gender 60, 68, 117, 159, 161, 164, 168, 170–74,
    176–7, 181–2, 184–7, 190
Genet, C. 59–62
George, G. 163
germinators 155
Gill, R. 188
Gingerich, D.W. 9–10
globalization 18–19, 23, 95
Goel, R. 3, 169, 171, 175
Göktepe-Hultén, D. 3, 169
Google 36
Grady, J. 189
Greene, P.G. 171
Gregory, S. 188
Grimm, H. 2
gross domestic product 10
growth regimes *see* Schumpeterian growth
    regimes
Guerrero, M. 3, 109

hackathons 155
Hackett, E.J. 58
Hall, P.A. 9–10

Hambrick, D.C. 137, 140
Hamilton, B.H. 82
Hamilton, E. 171
Harrison, R. 168, 170, 172–6
Hechavarría, D.M. 185
Henderson, R.M. 55
Henry, C. 170–71, 176
Hentschel, T. 186
"heroic" entrepreneurs 173–4, 176, 186–8, 191
Hewitt-Dundas, N. 158
higher education institutions *see* universities
Hilbert, D. 163
Hillman, A.J. 139
Hills, B. 2
Hogan, T. 59–60
Holt, R. 186
Horta, H. 42
Hoyte, C. 161
Hsu, D.H. 37
human capital 2, 17, 23, 67, 117–18, 136, 204
human resources 49–50, 59, 67, 135
Hyrsky, K. 187

income inequality 23
incubators 41, 44–6, 50, 75, 81, 119, 122, 155–7,
    159, 162, 201–2
industrial relations 6, 9–10, 14, 17, 21, 212
initial public offerings 41, 43, 48
innovation 1–2
    and academic entrepreneurship 40, 46, 158,
        161, 168–9
    and artificial intelligence 200
    and corporate governance 135–6
    different perspective on 179–92
    entrepreneurial and innovative ecosystems 41,
        47, 49, 63, 65, 67, 107, 109, 119, 121–3,
        155–65
    and principal investigators 55–8, 61, 63–4, 69
    and public and policy entrepreneurship 91–6
    role of entrepreneurial universities 107–24
    and Schumpeterian growth regimes 5–8,
        10–13, 16–18, 21–2, 24–5
    and startups 75–86
    see also startups
intellectual property rights 18, 26, 40, 78, 115,
    120, 122, 156, 158
    see also patents
internationalization 135

Jain, K.K. 40
Jobs, S. 81
joint ventures 119

Kanze, D. 185
Kao, R.W.Y. 182
Katz, J.A. 156
Kenworthy, L. 9–10
Kidwell, D. 59–60, 67–8
King, P.J. 96
Kirkham, P. 3
knowledge creation 55
knowledge economy 1, 9, 11–12, 20, 26, 95
knowledge filter 2
knowledge generation 5–6, 9, 11–13, 19, 21,
    23–5, 116, 197
knowledge growth regimes 15, 19–26
knowledge intensive industries 15, 19, 22–4,
    77–9, 108
knowledge spillovers 2, 6, 21–2, 48, 55, 74–5, 80,
    112, 115, 118, 203
knowledge transfer 40, 44, 48, 57, 109, 116, 118,
    158
knowledge-intensive business services (KIBS)
    19–21
Konon, A. 80
Kor, Y.Y. 141
Kritikos, A. 80

Lacetera, N. 168
Larson, G.S. 188
Lassen, A. 188
Lee, Y.S. 37
Lehmann, E.E. 112, 115
Lewis, K.V. 170
Li, H. 3, 134
licensing 40, 49, 66
Link, A.N. 96
Link, J.R. 96
LinkedIn 34
loans 16
Lorenzoni, G. 59–60
Louçã, F. 5
Luhmann, N. 184
Lundmark, E. 189
Lundvall, B. 6

Malerba, F. 5
Mangematin, V. 56–7, 60
manufacturing industry 23, 77
marketing 19–20, 22, 33–5, 61, 76, 83–4, 135,
    151–2, 182
Mars, M.M. 40
Marxism 209
Mason, C. 122
mass production 1, 17

massive online open courses 121
Mead, M. 189
mentors 45–7, 49, 60, 117, 135, 153, 202
Meoli, M. 2, 42–3
mergers and acquisitions 41, 43
metaphors 183, 185–9, 191–2
mind maps 159–61
minority groups 117
Mintrom, M. 98
Minztberg, H. 158
Miranda, F.J. 40, 50
mobility 18, 44–5, 50, 80–82, 85
modernist methodologies 210–17
monopolistic competition 12, 16, 20
monopolistic rents 18, 24
Mosey, S. 3, 158
Munoz, C. 159
Mustar, P. 40

Nabi, G. 159, 161
National Institutes of Health 169
National Science Foundation 169
National Systems of Innovation approach 5–7, 11
natural selection 214
Nef, R. 192
Nelson, R.R. 5
new public management 94
Nielsen, S. 188
Norman, P. 98

OECD 77
O'Kane, C. 59, 62, 64
O'Reilly, P. 63
organizational behaviour 49–50
organizational theory 49–50
Orsenigo, L. 5
Osborne, D. 94–5
O'Shea, R. 40, 109, 112
Oslo Manual 182

Panel Studies of Entrepreneurial Dynamics 85
Parhankangas, A. 184
patents 25–6, 40, 49, 78, 169, 172, 175
Pearce, J.A. 141
photography 189–91
Piccaluga, A. 56
prime-mover advantages 18
principal investigators 34, 55–70
profitability 16, 77, 153
Project 985 37
public and policy entrepreneurship 91–105

public research institutes 6, 21–2, 55–6, 68, 74–5, 83, 171
publicly funded research 55–69, 96

Quadruple Helix concept 108

Ram, R. 3
Ratzinger, D. 164
Renko, M. 170, 172, 176, 184
research and development 2, 5, 17–18, 20, 22, 46, 55, 62, 67, 76–8, 84, 123, 141–2, 180–82, 201
research autonomy 65–6
Rich, D.P. 169
Rico, R. 141
Rios-Aguilar, C. 40
risks 10, 25, 47, 84, 91, 188, 197, 199, 204–5
Roberts, E. 33
Roberts, N. 96
role models 122
Romano, M. 61
Rothaermel, F.T. 40, 93
Roux, V. 156

Sapienza, H.J. 135
Say, J-B. 156
Schumpeter, J. 4, 14, 17, 95, 108, 182
Schumpeterian growth regimes 4–5, 23–6
    the antecedents 5–10
    corporate growth regimes 15, 17–19
    entrepreneurial growth regimes 14–17, 22, 24–5
    knowledge growth regimes 15, 19–26
    at work 10–23
scientific entrepreneurship 20–22, 25, 46–7, 56–7, 62–3, 65–70, 109, 169
    see also principal investigators
seed capital 120, 155
Shane, S. 109, 115, 168
Siegel, D.S. 49, 115
Silander, C. 96
Silander, D. 92, 96
Simon, H. 179, 214
Singh, R.P. 61
size of firms 6, 10, 15, 25
small and medium-sized enterprises 63, 181
Small Business Innovation Research 40, 96
Small Business Technology Transfer 40
Smith, E. 137, 139, 141
Smith, R. 190–91
Snow, C.P. 165
social capital 94, 136, 150
social networks 134, 136

Social Science Citation Index 93, 100
social sciences 1, 41, 66, 79, 109, 189, 208–10
socialization 83, 115
Socio-Economic Panel 85
Solow, R. 1
Souitaris, V. 40
spillover entrepreneurship 21–2
  see also knowledge spillovers
spin-offs 40–50, 66, 75–6, 78, 81–2, 84, 112, 169,
    172, 175
  see also startups
stakeholders 134, 201–3
startups 20–22, 36, 40, 45–6, 49, 61, 109, 116, 134
  regional emergence of 74–86
stereotypes 183, 185–6, 190
Stevenson, B. 203
strategic decision making 134, 136, 140–41, 144
student entrepreneurship 155–65
sustainable development 104–5, 163
sustainable development goals 163

Technological Regimes approach 5–7, 11
technology transfer 55, 63–4, 67, 107, 109, 112,
    169, 175
technology transfer offices 45–6, 48, 50, 55, 64,
    67, 119, 122
Terjesen, S. 3, 134
Thursby, J.G. 112
Thursby, M.C. 112
top management teams 134, 137–44
total factor productivity 11, 13
trademarks 25
Triple Helix concept 108
Trump, D. 45
Turing, A. 197, 199

Umans, T. 3, 134, 137, 139, 141
unions 10
United Nations 163
universities 6, 21, 55, 69, 79–83, 85
  see also academic entrepreneurship

alumni impact surveys 30–38
leadership in the academic community 168–77
principal investigators 34, 55–70
role of entrepreneurial universities 107–24
student entrepreneurship in university
    ecosystems 155–65
Urbano, D. 3, 109

value added 22
value chains 19, 22
value creation 57–8, 60–63, 66, 116, 119, 142, 182
Varieties of Capitalism approach 5, 7, 9–11
Vassiliki, B. 171
venture capitalism 19–22, 24–5, 77–8, 85, 115,
    120, 134–6
Vismara, S. 2, 42
Vohora, A. 112

Walrasian approach 4
Wang, Y.L. 62
wealth 22–3
Web of Science 91, 93, 96–8, 100–101, 109–14
Welch, E.W. 59
Welter, F. 3, 182, 185
Wigren-Kristoferson, C. 191
Wikipedia 214
Winter, S.G. 5
women's entrepreneurial leadership 170, 176–7
  see also gender
Wright, M. 49, 108, 115, 156, 158–9, 161
Wyrwich, M. 79

Yousafzai, S.Y. 170, 172
Yusof, M. 40

Zahra, S.A. 108, 141
Zenger, T.R. 82
Zhang, Q. 2
Zheng, J. 5
Zuboff, S. 159
Zuckerberg, M. 81